Helping Children and Adolescen

Robert Henley Woody, PhD, ScD, JD, Professor of Psychology, University of Nebraska at Omaha, has provided, throughout his career, professional services to children, families, and community agencies. In addition, he has written thirty-four books and several hundred articles, which reflect his academic training in psychology and education (PhD, Michigan State University), health services (ScD, University of Pittsburgh), and law (JD, Creighton University). He is a Fellow of the American Psychological Association and a Diplomate in Clinical and Forensic Psychology, ABPP. He is a Licensed Psychologist in Florida and Michigan and a member of the Florida, Michigan, and Nebraska Bars. He has held and currently holds numerous leadership positions in national and state professional associations, especially the American Psychological Association and the Florida Psychological Association.

Helping Children and Adolescents

Evidence-Based Strategies from Developmental
and Social Psychology

Robert Henley Woody

HOGREFE

Library of Congress Cataloging in Publication

is available via the Library of Congress Marc Database under the
LC Control Number 2010941620

Library and Archives Canada Cataloguing in Publication

Woody, Robert Henley
      Helping children and adolescents : evidence-based strategies from developmental
and social psychology / Robert Henley Woody.

Includes bibliographical references.
ISBN 978-0-88937-397-6

    1. Child psychology. 2. Adolescent psychology. I. Title.

BF721.W65 2011   155.4   C2010-907693-1

© 2011 by Hogrefe Publishing

PUBLISHING OFFICES
USA: Hogrefe Publishing, 875 Massachusetts Avenue, 7th Floor,
                      Cambridge, MA 02139
                      Phone (866) 823-4726, Fax (617) 354-6875;
                      E-mail customerservice@hogrefe-publishing.com
EUROPE: Hogrefe Publishing, Rohnsweg 25, 37085 Göttingen, Germany
                      Phone +49 551 49609-0, Fax +49 551 49609-88,
                      E-mail publishing@hogrefe.com

SALES & DISTRIBUTION
USA: Hogrefe Publishing, Customer Services Department,
                      30 Amberwood Parkway, Ashland, OH 44805
                      Phone (800) 228-3749, Fax (419) 281-6883,
                      E-mail customerservice@hogrefe.com
EUROPE: Hogrefe Publishing, Rohnsweg 25, 37085 Göttingen, Germany
                      Phone +49 551 49609-0, Fax +49 551 49609-88,
                      E-mail publishing@hogrefe.com

OTHER OFFICES
CANADA: Hogrefe Publishing, 660 Eglinton Ave. East, Suite 119-514, Toronto,
                      Ontario, M4G 2K2
SWITZERLAND: Hogrefe Publishing, Länggass-Strasse 76, CH-3000 Bern 9

Hogrefe Publishing
Incorporated and registered in the Commonwealth of Massachusetts, USA, and in Göttingen,
Lower Saxony, Germany

Printed and bound in the USA
ISBN: 978-0-88937-397-6

Table of Contents

Preface

At some level and at some time, every adult senses a wish to help children become healthy, have enjoyable lives, and be constructive members of society. In turn, due to their immaturity, youngsters present challenges that understandably lead some adults to shy away or flounder around in their commitments to and relationships with children.

Certainly parents face decisions every day that require them to make decisions about how to respond to their offspring, and they commonly benefit from professionals trained to understand and help youngsters. The career choice of mental health practitioners (e.g., psychologists, social workers, mental health counselors, psychiatrists, marriage, and family therapists) and other responsible adults (e.g., educators and health care and law enforcement personnel) creates a social responsibility, perhaps even a legal duty, to be of assistance; and they grapple with how they can best make short- and long-term contributions to children and adolescents.

Despite good intentions, even the most skilled professional may end up in a quandary. Decision-making about how to deal with and help youths requires knowledge of child development and human behavior. In other words, there are certain times that a child's needs, emotions, and actions are products of the stage of development, and social factors wield powerful influence. The professional helper needs to use knowledge about how kids mature, to gain understanding that is unique to the particular child, always being cognizant of the fact that social influence are continuous. Understanding child development is acquired in many ways, such as reflecting on one's own childhood, observing how other adults and children interact, and reading and studying the subject.

This book is intended for the various types of professionals cited earlier, referred to herein as *mental health professionals* (since all of the disciplines mentioned focus on, among other things, the mental health of the child or adolescent) and *professional helpers* (which is potentially even more inclusive than *mental health professionals*). The primary purpose of this book is to offer information from developmental and social psychology that is empirically and evidence-based and offer pragmatic suggestions for putting the ideas into practice.

In addition to knowledge, a professional helper must build skills for helping youngsters. This requires being able to talk to them in a manner that is meaningful and helpful, governing one's own behavior to provide a positive model, defining and maintaining expectations (e.g., family rules), and offering specific ideas or information that will help children and adolescents get and stay on the straight and narrow into health and constructive adulthood.

It is no shortcoming for a mental health professional to encounter a child-related scenario in which there seems to be no assured solution. Because of the complexity of human behavior, which immaturity makes especially ambiguous, a helper may find children and adolescents to be bewildering. However, those dedicated to professional helping, as well as parents and other responsible adults, do not have an escape route – they must face up to the issues and set about gaining the knowledge and skills that will allow them to offer the child guidance.

Having worked professionally with kids for many years (and raised three of my own), I have dutifully studied authoritative information and research. I have found that scholarly works in the specialties of developmental and social psychology are particularly helpful for gaining understanding of childhood and adolescence and identifying and acquiring the skills that can be useful to efforts to guide youngsters.

For clarification, I use the terms *child, children, youths, youngsters,* and *kids* generically (and they are always said with respect), with no age distinction. If a point has relevance to a given age, so that it is appropriate to use terms such as *infants* (generally from birth to 2 years), *young children* (generally 2–9), *middle childhood* (generally 10–12), *adolescents* (generally 13–18), or *teenagers,* I will use those to specify the age level. (I am aware that a recent trend, due to societal changes, is for youths from about 18 to 22 to be considered late adolescents, but I will not deal with that issue per se.)

I believe that every adult, and certainly every mental health professional, should be dedicated to nurturing, protecting, and guiding children and adolescents to healthy and productive lives. Although the parents have the primary duty of child guidance, there are often others who provide psychological parenting, such as extended family members. Mental health professionals must work with the social system in which a child or adolescent lives, which means dealing with, for example, extended family members and educators. Of course, as I mentioned, those adults who are professional helpers have both a responsibility and often a legal duty to promote the welfare of the child. Therefore, the substance of this book is that it is intended to help the mental health professional deal with more than, say, the biological parents. Rather, the goal is to be competent to help every adult become a contributing member to the "village" in which a child develops and lives.

For a personal framework: I began working with children as a classroom teacher and school psychologist. In those days, the *child guidance concept* was popular. That is, instead of emphasizing mental or conduct problems, child guidance clinics assisted parents in coping with childhood difficulties to ward off the occurrence of major problems, often involving other community resources to support the family. I seek to offer evidence-based information that will prepare professional helpers to reintroduce child guidance into family life and further connections between families and, say, the schools and community service agencies.

As my career track progressed, I moved from education to clinical/ counseling psychology, on to public health services, and then into law. These other disciplines have allowed me to reexamine certain ideas that were formed initially during my early days as an educator, and to integrate these various perspectives. Hopefully this results in unique information for child and adolescent guidance.

In my role as a professor, I have often heard students say, "Theory is fine, but how do I use the information in real life?" To fulfill such a request, I adhere to a modern framework for psychology, which uses an approach that is "represented in a structured format composed of concepts and their interrelationships," "composed of general classes of concepts that can be populated with specific subclasses and instances," and "a coherent means of integrating and/or analyzing a wide range of ideas, findings or theories" (Milton, 2010, p. 1). Such a framework is compatible with the contemporary quest for empirically supported treatments and evidenced-based practices (e.g., see Koocher & Keith-Spiegel, 2008, pp. 104–108).

Although this book is intended for training professionals to be more effective in helping children and adolescents, as well as their families and others (e.g., educators), I purposefully avoid heavy reliance on citations of publications. This does not mean that I am not fulfilling the requirements for empirical and evidence-based standards. There are, of course, numerous scholarly citations herein, but every idea presented in this book has been distilled and developed from research and authoritative statements. For example, when considering an idea about developmental or social psychology, checking the index of any major textbook on the subject will yield a plethora of scholarly sources.

It should be acknowledged that most of the research relied upon and the ideas set forth are derived from a framework for the United States and

Canada. That said, there is reason to believe that the majority of the ideas are common to child development and social behavior in many other countries, as long as the information is passed through the relevant cultural filter. In other words, this information has international usefulness.

To maximize knowledge acquisition, I use simple clear language, appropriate for most adults, including (but not limited to) mental health professionals. To illustrate, I will describe actual cases involving people with whom I have worked as a mental health professional (or educator or attorney), and there will be concrete suggestions about how the problem being considered could have been avoided or how it should be handled.

Robert Henley Woody, PhD, ScD, JD
Omaha, Nebraska

1 Adult Responsibility

All life is precious, but children merit special honor. Both philosophically and practically, children have the potential to enrich life for others. Beyond the joys of parenthood, all adults can gain personally from contacts with kids, whose youthful spirit and energy can counterbalance the weight of the world which adults must shoulder.

One objective for mental health professionals who wish to help youngsters is to construct adult–child relationships that will promote flourishing (Keyes, 2007). Fredrickson and Losado (2005) say:

> To *flourish* means to live within an optimal range of human functioning, one that connotes four components: (a) *goodness,* indexed by happiness, satisfaction, and superior functioning; (b) *generativity,* indexed by broadened thought-action repertoires and behavioral flexibility; (c) *growth,* indexed by gains in enduring personal and social resources; and (d) *resilience,* indexed by survival and growth in the aftermath of adversity. (p. 685)

A mature adult knows that life should not be impaired or limited by languishing or adverse emotions. Rather, one's lifestyle, at any age, should seek to enhance mental abilities, broaden behavioral repertoires, increase intuition and creativity, and maintain healthful bodily conditions. A premise underlying this book is that mental health professionals should be devoted to and competent for building adult–child relationships that will produce flourishing.

In addition to the benefits that adults experience personally from contacts with children, there is the obvious cliché "Children are society's resources of tomorrow." Indeed, the fact that children will eventually be generating income and fulfilling civic duties and responsibilities is what has led our society to establish formal laws and informal expectations that children will be nurtured and safeguarded. It is essential for society to have children develop into productive, healthy, and law-abiding citizens. Therefore, mental health professionals should reinforce social responsibility with everyone with whom they deal.

There is nothing that has the potential to make life as fulfilling and positive as parenthood. Conversely, there is nothing that can result in life being as disappointing and negative as parenthood. The route to positive parenting leads to children who are mentally and physically healthy and able to grow into adults who achieve acceptance and rewards in their lives, as opposed to stumbling and faltering in ways that result in penalties (e.g., poor academic achievement, behavior problems, juvenile delinquency). Because of the challenges, it is common for parents to turn to mental health professionals for help. Consequently, mental health professionals should be competent in effective parenting and family relations.

This book is devoted to providing information to mental health professionals about how adults can help children flourish, learn, mature, think, feel, and behave in positive ways. Although my parenting of two sons and a daughter has given me considerable firsthand experience with what helping kids develop is all about, my career as a psychologist, educator, and attorney has allowed me to study the authoritative sources and research that have relevance to the onerous task of helping children in general and of parenting in particular. This information will be useful to professionals in mental health, education, health care, social service, and law enforcement.

The ideas that I present in this book are empirically and evidence-based. That is, underlying every comment is behavioral science research. Moreover, every idea has passed a reality test. In my work with children and families, each of the ideas has been tested with people facing real-life problems or issues. Moreover, I have observed countless professional helpers make positive use of ideas of this nature.

To avoid unnecessarily weighty language, I have decided to avoid a batch of research citations. Instead, I stick to everyday language, much like a mental health professional, educator or other professional, or a parent would use when discussing a particular child.

There are three underlying premises for my ideas.

First, I believe that every child needs and can benefit from interactions with adults who understand the developmental aspects of childhood.

By *developmental,* I mean that helping a child can best be accomplished by knowing how the age and characteristics of the child influence emotions, thinking, and behavior. Indeed, professional ethics places strong emphasis on maintaining knowledge competency relevant to developmental and social factors (Campbell, Vasquez, Behnke, & Kinscherff, 2010).

Second, I believe that heredity is important but does not necessarily dominate a child's development.

I do not doubt that genetic and biological endowments give the child a hereditary potential, which can create definite limitations. Nonetheless, research supports the idea that experiences and interventions, such as learning and social interactions, can reinforce a child toward qualities or characteristics that are not subjected to, or restricted (or constricted) by, heredity. For example, Preves and Mortimer (2011) frame contemporary social psychology as follows: "An individual's beliefs shape interpersonal behavior, relationships, and ultimately social institutions. This occurs even if those beliefs are not factually correct" (p. 3).

Third, I believe that every adult has a raison d'être of helping children develop into productive, healthy, and law-abiding citizens.

It goes without saying that this is the commitment of professionals in education, mental health, health care, social service, and law enforcement (and, of course, of parents). This objective can be achieved by an adult's trying to assure that any contact with a child will embrace five essential conditions: caring, nurturance, reinforcement, respect, and protection. Of course, this notion is the backbone of professional mental health services.

When thinking about helping children develop into adulthood, the first thought is "that's what the biological parents should do." Granted, the biological parents do have life-long duties and responsibilities for helping their offspring, but there are two other considerations.

All over the world, and most certainly in the United States and other Western countries, the structure of the family has changed from the "nuclear" stereotype. In some societies, a child is raised by an extended family more often than by the two biological parents. In many countries today, there is a plethora of alternative family structures.

In American society, cultural changes, such as the high incidence of divorce, have led to all sorts of unique family structures. A partial list would include: one-parent homes, step parents, adoptive parents, same-sex parents, situations in which a series of romantic partners live in the household with the one-parent and children, blending of several families, blood relatives (aunts, uncles, grandparents, etc.) having important and significant roles in raising a child, foster placements – and the list goes on and on.

The restructured concept of family is supplemented by the notion, which I mentioned earlier, that every adult should help children develop into productive, healthy, and law-abiding citizens. Mental health professionals and virtually any other adult who accepts social responsibility should constantly and consistently strive to help children, which means offering positive influence to families and communities as well.

In this book, it may seem that professional helping is intended primarily for the biological or custodial parents. But of equal importance are all of the other adults who are willing and able, either through their chosen careers (e.g., being a teacher, health care provider, law enforcement officer) or personal values (e.g., being nurturant and altruistic), to interact with a child in a way that will help the child and society. Recall the five essential conditions that the adult should bring to contacts with a child: caring, nurturance, reinforcement, respect, and protection. The professional helper should strive to activate all adults to help children and adolescents.

The Parenting Village

If asked the question, "Who is responsible for that kid's behavior?" the most common and correct answer would be the parents. As discussed previously, there is a more modern and proper answer, namely "potentially every adult who has contact with a child has a social responsibility, maybe even a legal liability, for a child's behavior."

Back in about 1970, professionals who worked with children and families recognized that the evolution of society had resulted in a viewpoint that the biological parents are not the only possible caregivers for children and youths. The term that became popular was *psychological parents*. That is – perhaps because of death, divorce, or abandonment – some children were raised by other than their biological parents. Instead, members of the child's extended family, such as grandparents, or foster or adoptive parents, assumed "parenting" for the child's well-being. Indeed, those adjudicating child custody disputes and abuse-neglect cases often replaced biological parents who jeopardized their children, with psychological parents, even though there was no blood connection. This legal option continues today.

It is logical nowadays to assume that some parenting functions should extend to professional helpers who provide services to children and families. Immediately teachers and other educators come to mind – they routinely offer extensive care for a child's health, safety, well-being, learning, and development. But there are other adults who can and should step forward to "parent" children. Certainly children with problems can benefit from the help of physicians, nurses, mental health and social service personnel, law enforcement officers, religious leaders, and a host of other sources within the community.

The term *community* deserves special consideration. Clinton (1996) says:

> Children exist in the world as well as in the family. From the moment they are born, they depend on a host of other "grown-ups" – grandparents, neighbors, teachers, ministers, employers, political leaders, and untold others who touch their lives directly and indirectly. Adults police their streets, monitor the quality of their food, air, and water, produce the programs that appear on their televisions, run the businesses that employ their parents, and write the laws that protect them. Each of us plays a part in every child's life: It takes a village to raise a child. (p. 11)

This viewpoint is strongly supported by social and behavioral science.

In everyday life, immature judgments and a lack of behavioral controls by children and youths readily result in troublesome actions. Some of these miscreant behaviors may even be potentially criminal.

For example, let's assume that some teenagers foolishly resort to putting graffiti on public property. Who is to blame? Of course, the youths did the act, and should be held accountable. However, it would also be easy to say, "Parents are responsible." But wait a minute. Who are the parents? Are there not other adults who are potentially responsible for monitoring the youngsters' conduct? It is a given that the youths should be subject to possible discipline, such as by the juvenile court. But should not other responsible adults in the community contribute to guiding the children and cultivating improved judgments and behavior? With support from responsible adults (beyond the parents per se), it may be possible to prevent some youthful destructive or criminal behaviors. It seems that Clinton's assertion is valid for all adults who reside in the child's "village."

The Ideal Helper

Responsible adults are the mainstay of society for promoting the healthy development of children and youths. To strengthen this quest, society has established and funds education and other professional services that support parents in helping their kids. In addition, society has laws that impose penalties on parents who fail to fulfill their responsibilities, such as statutes for punishing child neglect and abuse, and on adults who criminally victimize children and youth (as well as vulnerable adults).

The responsibility for helping children goes beyond the parents to potentially every adult in the community. Although the rights and needs of the child must always be primary and honored, an adult can personally benefit from taking care of children. The payoff for non-parents is gaining self-satisfaction from helping children and promoting a new generation that will strengthen the quality of life in the community.

The foregoing focus on responsible adults ushers in consideration of the role and functions of mental health professionals. In discussing what it takes to be an effective helper, Corey and Corey (2007) draw from research and experience to encourage adoption of certain characteristics. The following reflects their views in a nutshell as to what constitutes an ideal professional helper.

The ideal professional helper has an honest assessment of his or her own personal strengths and weaknesses. It is a reality that each of us has some things that we can achieve, some things that we would never be able to accomplish. This *awareness of self* prevents missteps in a professional helping relationship. Through being realistic about personal capabilities and resources, professional helpers are more likely to see positive results from their efforts.

There should be a curiosity about and openness to learning. No one knows all the answers. Being open-minded to new information, such as about child-rearing, is important.

Whether a mental health professional is or is not involved, any helping relationship requires empathy, respect, and honesty, along with expressing genuine caring for others. These qualities are necessary for dealing effectively with another person's thoughts, feelings, and behaviors. These are the research-based ideas that led me to posit the five essential conditions that were discussed earlier, namely that the professional helper or other responsible adult provides the child with caring, nurturance, reinforcement, respect, and protection.

The mental health professional should expect to encounter barriers to helping, and major changes will not occur overnight. With some children, it may be disappointing when a child behaves in an unacceptable way or does not respond immediately to the mental health professional's effort to help, but these sorts of things are common to the human condition in general and to development of children and youths in particular.

The professional helper should not hesitate to call in the cavalry. When additional firepower is needed to help a child or teenager, support from family and educational, health care, social, and law enforcement service providers should be sought.

Understanding the unique cultural characteristics of children and families is essential to the professional helping process. Informal and professional helpers alike must be fair-minded and respect the many ethnic and cultural backgrounds within society.

To be at one's best, the mental health professional should value being physically, mentally, psychologically, socially, and spiritually healthy. This means having a realistic self-evaluation and plans for becoming a better person. It does not, in the least, mean being self-absorbed. Rather, the professional helper will reap personal benefits from placing a premium on helping others, particularly children and youths, as well as their families and the community.

Being a Team Player for Children and Adolescents

Whether professionals or laypersons, responsible adults have one thing in common: they want to help kids to have lives that are healthy, productive, and law-abiding. In turn, the adults sense personal rewards for their caring, nurturance, reinforcement, respect, and protection, as well as getting to live in a better society.

A healthy child makes the most of schooling, and has wholesome, rewarding relationships with others people of all ages. As youths mature, they seek to contribute to the betterment of society through a career and lawful behavior, and look forward to enjoying a healthy and constructive life.

Given the shared commitment to cultivating healthy youngsters, parents, educators, and professional helpers of every ilk should all be unified in their efforts. Regrettably, all too often they pursue their respective roles with kids, without knowing or communicating adequately with others who share the same goals.

In urban areas, it is somewhat understandable that the size of the population and the complexity of the children's service system would make it difficult for personal contacts to occur easily between professional helpers working on behalf of youths. However, the lack of coordinated efforts is not unique to urban areas.

In rural (sparsely populated) and urban (heavily populated) areas alike, I have talked to, for example, teachers who had no idea about who the mental health personnel were in the same locale. And in the same town, therapists in a community clinic were not collaborating with the teachers of the children to whom they were providing treatment.

With parents being the key players, it is obvious that they need to be team members, if not leaders. The effectiveness of their parenting can improve with support from the other responsible adults who are in their children's lives, notably teachers. Strong links between home and school can yield useful information to all of the adults who are intent on helping the same child. Later in this chapter, I shall discuss how to create effective collaboration between the home and school.

I believe that the collaboration should go well beyond the parents and educators. There should be teamwork involving all sorts of professionals. It should be considered part of the job to know the other child-service workers in the same community.

In my first job as a school psychologist, my office was in a courthouse in a rural Michigan county. Every day, my coffee break allowed me to converse with employees of the health department, social service agencies, the courts, and law enforcement. We knew each other's capabilities. When one of us was uncertain about how to handle a problem, we were all quick to ask for or offer help. It is, of course, impossible, to house every professional or responsible adult in a child's life under the same roof, as I benefited from in the courthouse. But we can at least strive to create that kind of team spirit with those who are committed to helping kids.

If teamwork by professional helpers and responsible adults can be achieved, resources will be more efficiently used. There will be better decisions about service options. And of most importance, children and youths, as well as their families and the community, will have the best chance of attaining healthy, productive, and law-abiding lives.

Health Risk Behaviors

Helping children develop into healthy and constructive adulthood requires constant emphasis on learning how to think, feel, and behave. The school classroom may seem like, and often is, the primary source of this effort, but the family provides as great, or greater, an influence as well.

It goes without saying that health in general is a major objective for everyone throughout life. Essentially every learning activity has implications for the concept of health. For example, a child who reads a novel (like a Harry Potter book) can gain insight into certain positive and negative effects from the characters' behavior. Playing a musical instrument brings about perseverance, fine motor control, and concentration, all of which can be relevant to health. Engaging in a sport, cheerleading, marching band, or any of numerous other activities will add to physical fitness.

When considering the health risk behaviors for adolescents and young adults, the US Centers for Disease Control and Prevention (Eaton et al., 2008) monitors the following six factors: "behaviors that contribute to unintended injuries and violence; tobacco use; alcohol and other drug use; sexual behaviors that contribute to unintended pregnancy and sexually transmitted diseases (STDs), including human immunodeficiency virus (HIV) infection; unhealthy dietary behaviors; and physical inactivity" (p. 1). Other health consequences are also monitored. With these six health risk behaviors as a developmental roadmap, responsible adults should consider eight steps in their contacts with kids.

Step one requires all mental health professional to learn about each health-risk behavior, and communicate this information to others. Popular magazines, television programs, and so on recognize the importance of health information and provide frequent and easily obtained access. Talking to teachers and other educators, health care and social service professionals, friends and neighbors, and family members can also lead to helpful information about health.

Step two, the mental health professional should think about what children in general need to know. This informal assessment of childhood and adolescence helps the adult decide what information to communicate to youngsters and to periodically evaluate whether some addition or change to that information is needed.

Step three goes beyond children in general to considering a particular child's unique needs. At the different stages of childhood and adolescence, these needs will change. For example, information about sexuality for a child in, say, the fourth grade would be different from what a youngster reaching puberty needs.

Step four calls on the mental health professional to continually and purposefully seek useful health-related information and recognize that personal values and beliefs will be a filter that can have a positive or a negative effect. Open-mindedness to new information is essential. Search engines (e.g., Google.com) for Internet resources are potentially valuable, but information on websites must be scrutinized carefully to be sure of accuracy and appropriateness. Public libraries are still important sources of information, as are health care professionals, such as primary care physicians. Often forgotten, public health agencies commonly have a wealth of information available for anyone who needs it.

Step five specifies that, as with any communication between an adult and a youth of any age, the information conveyed by the mental health professional must fit the youngster's ability and willingness to comprehend. Certain topics may trigger defensiveness, perhaps within both the adult and the child, which could reduce the effectiveness of the guidance effort.

Step six supports the idea that the professional helper who offers health-related information should follow a consistent schedule or plan. That is, making a statement about heath should not be an isolated event; both the professional and youngster should expect that healthy behavior will be a topic of discussion over and over.

Step seven calls for evaluation. What has the youth learned about health, and does his or her behavior reflect the learning? Just as the classroom uses testing to determine learning, child and adolescent guidance needs to double-check whether the young person has learned health information and uses it in everyday conduct.

Step eight requires use of the evaluation results. With guidance from the mental health professional, the parents and other responsible adults can see how well they are doing in their efforts – and make changes in their information-giving strategies as needed. Incidentally, as with many aspects of development, once a step has been taken, it is not forever finished. Learning about health-risk behaviors should continue throughout life, and helpful information should be communicated to anyone who needs health-related guidance.

Helping Kids in the Community

As said several times and in several contexts, there is a universal belief that children and youths are vulnerable and all adults should protect them and support their healthy development. That is, professional helpers should reinforce parents and responsible adults accepting responsibility for safeguarding all kids from the many sources of potential harm that they will face and preparing them to care for themselves as they mature.

Society considers parents and other family members to be the primary caregivers for children. As I have already said, the modern definition of the term parents has taken on several meanings other than that of "biological" parents. Today stepparents, adoptive *parents*, extended family members (such as grandparents, aunts, and uncles), and those who are either legal or self-appointed guardians are deemed parents.

In modern societies when parents and family members are not able to cope successfully with the trials and tribulations of raising children, public policies and laws assign legal duties for protecting children to mental health professionals, educators, social service workers, other health care professionals, and law enforcement and the courts.

Due to political and cultural factors, one contemporary problem is that society is not consistent in its commitment of resources for education and the other professional services intended to benefit young people. This inconsistency leaves many children and youths and their families in need.

As citizens and as part of their professionalism, mental health professionals should promote obtaining a remedy for the inconsistent commitment of resources. If society ceases to provide adequate funding for services, professional helpers throughout the community should increase their efforts to cultivate and protect its children.

Being a mental health professional means being aware of the needs of all kids in the community and taking on the role of helping to "grow" healthy children. Everyone benefits when children and people of all ages can have a decent life and be contributing members of the community.

Extensive research has studied the psychological needs of humans. Going beyond survival needs such as food and shelter, humans gain much from nurturing others (more will be said about *prosocial* behavior later). Through helping another person achieve goals, the mental health professional gets a payoff of self-satisfaction.

For a nurturing relationship, such as that between the professional helper and a child, there should be an effort to understand or be empathic with what the child is experiencing mentally, and offer useful information in a caring and sharing manner that will strengthen the child. The child needs acceptance, approval, support, and recognition of his or her unique qualities and talents. Again, whether professionals or laypersons are involved, all adult–child relationships must be genuine and sincere, not based on acting or pretense.

Although it is quite respectable and indeed necessary for the professional helper to gain a sense of personal gratification from helping or working with children and youths, the primary purpose must always be the cultivation and protection of the youngster. Every child can benefit from positive, supportive relationships with adults other than his or her parents and family members: for example, teachers, coaches, church leaders, and mentors. But such relationships must be geared toward fostering a good life and future for the child.

For emphasis, once again I say that mental health professionals and other responsible adults should provide five essential conditions – caring, nurturance, reinforcement, respect, and protection – in their contacts with children and youths. The outcome will be productive, healthy, and law-abiding young people and a stronger society in the future.

Avoiding Throwaway Kids

There is well-justified concern about children who develop conduct disorders involving antisocial, aggression, destructive, or violent behavior. Unless turned around, the child who shows this sort of negativity is apt to be on a destructive path.

I remember a discussion with a school principal about an overly aggressive 10-year-old boy. To my dismay, the principal said, "Given his background, there is nothing the school can do – he is a throwaway kid." No child should be labeled a "throwaway."

Beyond the parents, the school is the first line of defense against destructive aggression. Throughout the years of growing up, a child spends more time in school than in any other place, except (we hope) at home.

With professionals trained in education and child development, the school is a critical setting for recognizing and dealing with problem behaviors. Moreover, research tells us that often the behavior problem child will have significant impairment in the social, academic, or occupational activities that occur at school. Without a change toward positive school experiences, a vicious cycle keeps a child stuck in the problem behaviors.

As for the causes of behavior problems involving destructive aggression, the first thought is usually whether there are biological factors or environmental causes, such as bad influence from friends or ineffective parenting. In most cases, several factors often interact to cause or maintain the problem. That is, inappropriate conduct can potentially be linked to biological factors, adverse influences from others with whom the child associates, and parenting that fails to nurture healthy and wholesome development. The professional helper should be prepared to counteract these negative forces.

Whatever the cause(s) of inappropriate conduct such as aggression toward others, schools must help children learn to manage their own behavior. A disruptive student can impede the learning of all of the other students in the class. Nonetheless, the mental health professional should reinforce the school's not giving up on a problem child.

Since it is extremely difficult to remedy conduct problems in the teenage or adult years, schools should focus detection and prevention efforts on young children. It has been amply documented that conduct disorders that start early in childhood may lead to criminal conduct later on.

With the primary responsibility on their shoulders, parents and family members who are concerned about their child's conduct should approach mental health professionals, teachers, and other school personnel with a request for assistance. Chances are that what the parents and family members have noticed, the professionals have also detected.

Of course, in the event that the parents have not been responsive to the early stages of a problem, professional helpers, teachers, and other responsible adults should approach the parents. There is no honor in waiting for someone else to pick up the ball and run with it.

A unified team approach is best in planning for how to help the child. Parents can offer examples of the child's behavior at home and in the neighborhood, and teachers can apply academic ideas about strategies to change. It is important to remember that aggressive behavior may impact negatively on learning objectives.

Later in this book, I will talk about night and day differences in the behavior of a child or adolescent. Consequently, collecting information from divergent sources about behavior in different contexts is the best approach (Dishion & Stormshak, 2007).

If the parents and teachers do not accomplish change in a youngster's problem behavior, they should turn to mental health professionals and other health care and social service professionals within the community. Since modern training in law enforcement emphasizes crime prevention, the involvement of a law enforcement officer may add an important component to the interventions being applied by the parents and teachers.

All possible resources should be called into service to remedy conduct problems. The goal is to keep all children healthy and constructive in their behavior. None should be "thrown away."

Enriching Education

When citizens are asked to "tell me about your community," typically the local school system is one of the first things mentioned. For most people, the schools, social and health services, and governmental efforts define the community.

It has long been true that education is viewed as a cornerstone of the community. Discussing the history of American education, Urban and Wagoner (1996) point out that "the education of children proceeded down through the centuries along the same lines and involved the same learnings as had long been the pattern" and observe that education serves "to unite the generations and define one's place among 'the people'" (p. 11).

Uniting and defining the community explains why citizens have strong interest in their schools. Having a strong interest is one thing, but it is not enough – there must also be actions to enrich the education.

From my long-time awareness of a number of school systems, I believe that today there are more similarities with the past than there are differences. Although the content of textbooks for use in the classrooms has changed, over time there has been surprisingly little change in the general topics covered, the dynamics between teachers and students, and the organizational structure.

Major differences have, however, occurred because of increased governmental regulations (e.g., pertaining to funding), the advent of technology (e.g., computerized learning), and the social influences on schooling (e.g., the mass media). Also, the surge of cultural diversity among students has created an important new objective for public education. This leads Urban and Wagoner (1996) to opine that, as an institution, the public school must be responsive to all sorts of people and "be an institution in which the principle of serving the public at large is rewarded as well as the principle of serving various interest groups" (p. 350).

With concern about developing children for healthy and productive lives, professional helpers have a special mandate to be involved with the schools. The relationship between family, school, and community is more than citizen awareness of how tax dollars are spent. All citizens should strive to introduce healthy energy for change and development into the educational system. Citizen involvement can come in the form of participating in school activities in a supportive way or communicating ideas and concerns to educators. Such involvement need not be viewed as cynical, intrusive, or negative; it is a matter of contributing an important resource: parental or community reinforcement for enhanced education.

Obviously the public schools belong to the citizens. This means that everyone, not just parents, has the responsibility to try to maximize educational opportunities for youngsters. By promoting quality education, the community should see benefits flow to the child, the family, and our society.

Leading Education

Being elected to the local board of education is a major accomplishment and honor. Each candidate has to convince the electorate that he or she has the competencies and vision to improve the school system.

In this day and age, few citizens, particularly if they have children in the schools, are content for a board of education to maintain the status quo. Regardless of the culture or society, it is part of the social fabric to want improvements, especially in its educational system.

Too often, governmental sources, such as public schools, equate progress to gaining increased tax dollars. It is a false assumption to believe that the size of the budget determines the quality of education. Certainly great wealth for the school budget might allow hiring of personnel and purchase of resources and facilities that would upgrade the school. Such a financial windfall is a fantasy, and it has been well documented that money alone does not accomplish the ultimate objective. Rather, school leaders, such as those who serve on the board of education and all of the educators employed, must face the reality that spending alone is no solution. Ingenuity is necessary.

I recently visited two rural school systems, located in similar-sized towns less than an hour's drive apart. One was clearly struggling, whereas the other seemed endowed with all sorts of benefits. In interviewing the chief administrator in each of the districts, I learned that the one with the thriving school system had cultivated strong support from the parents and community leaders, sought out special funding sources (e.g., grants and donations), and created a verve that extended to all ages throughout the community (e.g., a unique after-school program for working parents, an abundance of donated top-notch computers). These positives were lacking in the lackluster community.

Being a leader in education does not rest just on the shoulders of the members of board of education or the educators. As mentioned earlier, all citizens (which includes, of course, mental health professionals) have a social responsibility to promote educational opportunities for every youngster that can benefit the child, the family, the community, and our society.

Any would-be leader of education should seek to be committed to constructive actions, to create a unity with all elements of the educational system, to be focused on what will help all student learners, and to emphasize empowerment of everyone who is working to develop and enrich the school. A leader is not a boss who dictates – rather, a leader wants everyone in the school system and community to sense his or her unique role in contributing to the school and to bring independent thinking to the table. Overall, there must be an allegiance to participatory decision-making, which leads everyone to believe that his or her competencies and vision to improve the school system are appreciated, valued, and a valid part of the educational enterprise. With this process, people become team players, build consensus, and endorse group decision-making.

Home–School Collaboration

What the last two sections have been leading up to is that children benefit from their parents and other responsible adults being involved with the educational system. Mental health professionals are no exception – involvement in education is essential. The modern concept is *home–school collaboration,* meaning that the family and school personnel are unified in the educational effort. Incidentally, although this section focuses on parents, the implicit notion continues to be that all citizens should interface with the school; professional helpers should be active in the educational system and, of course, encourage parents and other citizens to collaborate with the school.

Most parents place a premium on educational programs. Wanting to encourage their child's learning and development, they expect and demand the best possible experiences at school.

Some parents may see a childhood or adolescent problem as being the fault of the teachers. This is, however, seldom the case. From the classroom teacher to each member of the board of education, we typically see impressive commitment to high-quality education.

To ward off problems for kids, the parents need to be involved in the educational process. In part, this means that the parents should stay in touch with teachers so they can assist their child's learning efforts and cooperate to motivate better achievement and conduct. Parents should also contribute ideas, by whatever means, to bettering the schools. Among educators, this is, as I said earlier, referred to as home–school collaboration. Mental health professionals should reinforce the foregoing linkage between the parents and the school.

Research supports the belief that the relationship between the parents and the school is critical to preventing school failure for children. That is, the family–school relationship is a protection against failure and an incentive for success. Christenson and Sheridan (2001) say,

> The goal of family involvement with education is not merely to get families involved, but rather to connect important contexts for strengthening children's learning and development. Family-school relationships have been described as a safety net to promote children's learning and school experiences. (p. 7)

In its *Position Statement on Home-School Collaboration*, the National Association of School Psychologists (2005) states:

Potential avenues for family participation may include, but are not limited to:

- Active involvement in school decisions and governance
- Participation at school as volunteers and committee members
- Participation in leisure reading with their children
- Participation in school functions, athletics, and other extra-curricular activities
- Monitoring homework completion
- Regular communication with school personnel about their child's progress
- Frequent communication with their children about academic and behavioral expectations and progress
- Participation as fully informed, decision-making members of problem-solving teams (e.g., Individualized Education Program [IEP] teams)
- Participation in adult educational opportunities offered by the school

- Active support of the school through communication, sharing resources and seeking partnership with educators. (http://www.na-
sponline.org/)

In other words, parents are clearly not limited to conferences with teachers about their child's progress.

Obviously home–school collaboration requires both commitment by
the parents to support and work with the school AND a willingness by
the school system to embrace parental involvement. Regrettably, some
educators, thinking there may be negative criticism, may be reluctant to
open the doors of the school house to parents. Thus, it is important for
the parents and all other citizens or responsible adults to always communicate and act in a way that proves they are not critics, that they are allies
of education and partners of the educators. Mental health professionals
should facilitate these collaborative ideas.

Reforming Education

Taxpayers want the biggest bang for the buck, and parents particularly
want the best education possible for their children. These views lead to
public support for reforming education. It is human nature to believe that
there are better ways to do things. This can be a constructive point of
view, but it can also be counterproductive.

Modern schools have certainly had their fair share of educational reform efforts, such as demands for school vouchers, charter schools, home
schooling, consolidation of districts, etc. Urban and Wagoner (1996) are
critical about the educational reforms that have occurred over the past 25
years, saying: "Whether coming from the conservative Christians, free
marketers seeking school choice, or advocates of multicultural education, reformers exhibited an ideological certainty that made compromise
almost impossible" (p. 350). They warn: "If this type of thinking were to
gain more of a foothold in educational affairs, the prospects of a strong
public school system are *diminished"* (p. 350).

Throughout the history of American education, the public schools
have been a political football, bouncing from one public policy view
to another. (This is likely true in many other countries as well.) Again,
it can be healthy to want well-reasoned change, but at some point it
should be acknowledged that just like tradition for tradition sake has
little value, so change for the sake of change is not always logical. The

old adage "Don't throw the baby out with the bathwater" offers a useful reminder.

From working in public education, I have concluded that too often the wish for reform must be questioned. There seem to be four guidelines that should be promulgated and advocated by mental health professionals.

First, all adults should accept that the public schools are critical to the overall welfare of society. The quality of education impacts on everyone. Therefore, everyone connected to the schools must reflect concern, and constructive analysis and input are needed.

Second, any call for change cannot be justified merely by pointing to current shortcomings. Any proposed change must offer alternatives that have a solid empirical basis. In education, this means scholarly and objective analysis, as well as research on proposed ways of doing things differently.

Third, adults should view a public figure's dogmatic allegiance to any approach to education as unacceptable. Improving education requires open-mindedness.

Fourth, whenever change in education is contemplated, there should be no accommodation of ulterior motives. The political football analogy is a stark warning that proselytizing does not serve a constructive purpose and is not in the best interests of society.

For professionals in mental health, education, health care, social service, and law enforcement, there should be efforts to promote all adults (not just parents) to be interested in and supportive of education. As a citizen, every adult needs to communicate about educational issues and, if possible, engage in constructive collaboration with relevant educational and community sources.

2 Becoming a Parent

To assist others with children and adolescents, professional helpers must understand the nature of parenting. For example, many of my trainees in school psychology have told me how, as they consult with parents or teachers, they are commonly asked at the outset: "Do you have any children?" It is not that having birthed children is a mandatory professional credential, but to someone who will rely on the professional's expertise, the underlying concern is how well the professional understands the unique aspects of the parent–child or family relations.

In the preceding chapter, I explained why helping children goes beyond the biological parents, and how youngsters and society benefit from all adults being responsible for helping children develop to be healthy, constructive, and law-abiding young people. In adult–child contacts, the adults should provide five essential conditions: caring, nurturance, reinforcement, respect, and protection. Considerable emphasis was placed there on all adults being supportive of children, and on developing effective collaboration among the family, school, and community.

This chapter deals with the sort of knowledge and attitudes necessary for mental health professionals to set the stage for parenthood. The information has, of course, relevance for non-parents, including all sorts of professionals providing services, who choose to work with or help children and adolescents. By having a scholarly understanding of parenthood, the professional helper will acquire respected credibility for the helping processes.

Having an Effective Parenting Style

There is no one absolute answer to the question: What does it take to be a good parent? If there were a single and simple solution, everyone's life would be easier.

Research on parenting reveals a number of family conditions that can influence the success of parenting. The conditions to consider include family structure (who is acting as the caregiver), cultural background (the richness of language and other experiences), family livelihood (the pluses and minuses of the parents' work), disruptive influences (illnesses, traumas, and problems, such as alcoholism), maltreatment (injuries, abuse, and harmful encounters), and parenting styles (supportive relations).

Some of the conditions within the family are beyond the control of the parents. Certainly misfortunes, such as a natural disaster or an accident, are inflicted, not chosen. Also, everyone has limitations imposed by their lot in life, such as having grown up with parents and family members (referred to as the *family of origin*) who were not mentally or physically healthy, well educated, or blessed financially. Regardless, with persistent effort, people can improve negative conditions created and imposed by the family of origin.

Parents who wish to make the effort can change the parenting style they learned in growing up. The cornerstone for improvement is elevating the importance of the child's best interests.

The so-called best-interests-of-the-child approach is exemplified by child custody legal proceedings (Woody, 2000). When deciding on residential and visitation arrangements for the children of divorce, the court places a premium on how each parent can contribute to fulfilling the best interests of the child. Statutory law provides that the judge should consider such things as the capacity of a parent to give the child love, affection, and guidance, to continue the child's education and observance of a religion or creed, and to generally maintain a stable, satisfactory environment. In other words, how well a parent meets the best interests of the child is a major part of parenting style.

A positive parental style means the parent shows warmth and love, concern for the child's needs, and willingness to discuss problems and negotiate solutions with the child. Parents also should check to be sure that their expectations for the child's behavior and performance are healthy and realistic – that is, that they conform to the child's age and stage of development. Finally, the individual child's temperament needs to influence the parents' form of discipline. Professional helpers are important support sources for the foregoing parental efforts.

Many, perhaps most, parents adopt a parenting style that matches what they experienced as children. In some cases, the parent's childhood will be instructive and helpful, but all too often a parent retains negative ideas from childhood. For example, the parent who dwells on how he or she was ignored, disciplined harshly, or had cold, hostile parents needs to move past these memories and focus on the child in the present day. Parenting style needs to be caring, empathic, and supportive, not uncaring, harsh, or rejecting. Professional helpers should cultivate positive parenting qualities.

With insight into the importance of the best interests of the child, parents can choose ways to improve how they talk to and deal with the child. Solutions to problems are possible, but require a loving commitment to changing a hurtful parenting style. Research tells us that the youths who make the best decisions and experience good mental health are those who have a warm relationship and good communication with their parents.

Moody Adults

Moods are important to the parenting relationship. Moods differ from emotions in that a mood occurs without a good reason, with the person often not knowing why he or she reacted in a given way.

Vacillation in moods, such as from happy to sad, is a red flag of a possible mood disorder. Concern is merited when there are changes or swings in moods and in the intensity of reactions in similar circumstances.

Although growing up commonly involves children struggling to understand the ways of the world and themselves, developmental stage alone does not justify moodiness. In Chapter 8, I will say more about emotions and moods in childhood and adolescence.

Letting a predisposition for moodiness persist from childhood and adolescence into adulthood increases the likelihood that the person's response to events will be inappropriate; ever-changing and intense, inappropriate moods may require medical or mental health services. Regardless of age, the goal for any person is to be able to react realistically to the particular communication or event, rather than acting in a restricted or preordained manner – and moodiness can hamper the achievement of this goal. By nature of their training, mental health professionals are well prepared to deal with moodiness and emotions, and should do so routinely.

All adults must be concerned about any tendencies toward moodiness in themselves, because their moodiness will adversely affect their lives and relationships. In the quest to benefit children and adolescents, adults (including professional helpers) need to monitor whether their own moodiness is having an adverse impact on kids.

Children need stable and predictable responses from the adults in their lives. For example, whether in a classroom or the home, the child will gain healthful characteristics when he or she can depend on the adults communicating clearly, imposing expectations and rules fairly, and providing emotional support. In other words, moodiness can create uncertainty or ambiguity that adversely affects the relationship between the child and the adult.

Not surprisingly, some adults fail to recognize the unjustified moods they adopt and maintain. They are burdened, incapable of logical decisions, and inept in relationships with others are prone to deny that they possess qualities that cause problems for themselves and for those with whom they interact. Therefore, if a child has a problem, some parents believe that the kid is the problem, when, in point of fact, the emotions and moods possessed by other members of the family could be causing and perpetuating the child's difficulty. Also, with all due respect to teachers, there are times when the negatives in a teacher–student relationship are created by the teacher's emotional characteristics.

To help children, the challenge is for the mental health professional to attempt a reality check about how emotions and moods affect his or her dealings with the youngster. This effort at self-awareness requires seeking honest objective feedback from others.

To get constructive feedback from others often requires openly talking with an outsider, such as another professional helper (e.g., a teacher). Why an outsider? Because it is best to talk to someone who is not entangled in the emotional web in which parents and other family members are entrapped.

With teachers who might be vulnerable to emotions or moods, turning to an in-house supervisor, such as a principal, may not produce adequate objectivity. That is, a supervisor or evaluator of a teacher's performance for employment will have a role conflict that precludes total honesty. Thus, teachers too need to go "outside," perhaps setting up an appointment with a professor where the teacher received training in the past – or with a mental health professional. Thus, professional helpers should let others, such as teachers and other responsible adults, know of their availability and competency for providing guidance.

The bottom line is straightforward: effective nurturing of a child goes best when the adults in the child's life are free from negative moodiness. A positive and appropriate approach to life is best for everyone. As already mentioned, moods and emotions should routinely be addressed by the mental health professional working with a child or adolescent and the family.

Family Management

At one time or another, all parents experience difficulties with their child. Most often, the problem is relatively small and may reflect a child's passing fancy, or be part of the normal problems of growing up.

When parents find that the problem is difficult to solve, they may, out of frustration, resort to demands or discipline to forcefully shape up the youngster. In some instances, it is effective for the mental health professional to simply enforce expectations that both parents and child are aware of. But there are times when the parents will not be able to fashion a remedy with just a firm stance.

Instead of immediately thinking that "it is hopeless" or "my kid needs therapy," parents should be helped to take a closer look at the kind of parenting that has preceded the problem. Although well intentioned, parents often are not themselves very effective in family management.

There has been extensive research about family management that identifies five areas or principles that adults need to adopt and maintain in their dealings with children and adolescents (Dishion & Bullock, 2002; Dishion, Burraston, & Li, 2002; Dishion & Stormshak, 2007). In addition, they must always be aware of the youngster's development, since an adult's responses must be connected to the maturity of the child.

The first area for effective family management involves the *quality of the relationship* that each parent has with the child. Actually, the relationship between the two parents, as well as with and among the other members of the family, is also influential. Parents should consider whether there is adequate and consistent love, support, and trust being communicated.

Positive reinforcement is an important principle for effective family management. As distinct from bribery, which is when something is given to the child to induce a behavior, reinforcement occurs after the child has behaved in an acceptable manner to encourage it to occur again in the future. Whatever is used as rewards, such as opportunities to do preferred activities (e.g., go bowling or hanging out at a shopping mall with friends) or certain objects (e.g., a new download of music), the payoff should be provided only after the youngster has performed in an appropriate way. The professional helper should instruct the parents about how to use praise, attention, and time spent with the child in enjoyable activities to provide powerful reinforcement.

Family management benefits from *monitoring.* It is not "spying" to keep track of a child. Indeed, good parents (and other responsible adults) keep a watchful eye out for both good behavior and potential problems. For example, it is clear that a youth who hangs out with an antisocial crowd is on a dangerous path. The mental health professional should teach the parents and other adults in the youngster's life about how to best to explain their disapproval, take steps to put an end to the risky association, and help the child get into positives activities and relationships. (Chapter 10 will discuss vigilance in detail.)

It is critical that adults unapologetically, clearly, consistently, and logically set limits for how a youngster of any age can and must behave. Here again, the mental health professional can assist parents and other responsible adults with setting and enforcing limits with compassion, explanation, and guidance and providing a firm foundation for nurturing children and adolescents, all of which are essential for effective family management.

Finally, effective family management requires that parents and child engage in *collaborative problem-solving.* In other words, mutual respect and shared decision-making can result in meaningful solutions to any problem being experienced by the offspring. Nonetheless, in the end, it is the parents (and other responsible adults) who are in charge and must direct the course of action that will be taken by the child and the family. Through providing information, role-playing, and instructional readings and homework, the mental health professional can help facilitate collaborative problem solving.

There is no one formula for effective family management. Every family has its own values, standards, and aspirations that will figure in the parenting style. Certainly cultural considerations, such as from the family's religious or ethnic backgrounds, are important. However, the five foregoing areas or principles have relevance for all families.

Avoiding Coercion

Being an effective parent or a responsible adult requires supervising and monitoring the kid's activities. The professional helper should guide the parents and other responsible adults to consideration of what the child is doing and how the activity will influence the child's thinking, emotions, and behavior.

When it comes to child-rearing, it is incorrect to believe that the adult can act like a marching band director who controls the instrumentalists' performance. In everyday life, most youngsters do not readily march through life according to a dictated arrangement and cadence.

Responsible supervision and monitoring are not dictating. Parents and other adults need to provide structure that promotes success in a given activity. Children and adolescents appreciate and need guidance about organizing the accomplishment of a task or project.

The responsible adult, such as a parent or teacher, can provide instructions about how to do something, including how to behave in a certain situation. This kind of message does not dictate but should contain comments about clear expectations, limits, and positive consequences.

Perhaps one of the most important tasks for children is to complete homework that is required for school. Unfortunately, many parents find themselves and the child in conflict over this task and the parent may be prone to coercion and threats. (Chapter 5 will deal with homework in detail.)

In one family, the child was expected, understandably, to do the homework and to not rely on the parents to provide the answers. However, the child would dillydally, which frustrated everyone, and child and the parents exchanged negative comments. After talking with a teacher, the parents realized that the child was stymied by how to get under way. They began to spend time helping the child learn how to analyze the problem, plan what was needed to solve it, and initiate an effort – but the parents did not do the homework for the child.

In this example, consider how the parents must provide structure, which could include a quiet place for doing the homework (e.g., away from the sounds of a television), an agreed upon timeframe, suggestions for proceeding, and checking to see if the child has all the necessary materials and instructions. The youth can be allowed some choice in what the structure will be; but once agreed upon, the parent is responsible for monitoring, encouraging, and praising the child's accomplishment.

Note how the foregoing approach differs from coercion. A coercive relationship between an adult and child will be shrouded in unpleasantness. The child will resort to aversive or avoidance behaviors, and there will be no positive gain in development. Also, the adult will become increasing frustrated with the child's whining and complaining.

Since everyone has a breaking point, the frustrated adult may quit being helpful and become angry. When anger occurs, any chance of health and happiness for all concerned goes spiraling down the drain. From research, it is known that coercive interactions are connected to children adopting oppositional and antisocial behavior.

Coercion may occur in a parent–child relationship that is marred by overdependence. That is, if there is an unhealthy feeding off of each other in a way that creates problems, coercion becomes common. Coercive interactions are a call for a shift toward mutual respect and individuation – the adult and the child must each sense a personal identity and offer the other acceptance and support.

On the positive side, the adult who maintains acceptance of and respect for the child's need for individuality will begin structuring the adult–child relationship in a way that will be helpful. That is, the youngster will come to value the adult's wisdom and social reinforcement, and adopt values, ideas, and behaviors that will foster skills for dealing effectively with the challenges of life.

Helping parents develop and refine skills for avoiding coercion and favoring positivism merits the attention of the mental health professional. In many instances, this may be the primary objective for working with parents and other responsible adults.

What Is Childhood?

Professional helpers must realize that becoming a parent is a life-changing event. Upon the arrival of the first child, the new parents suddenly face many adjustments. Now there is a member of the family who is not an adult, who has profound expectations and needs that only the parents can satisfy. The parents must set aside their preferences and focus primarily on the child. When the mental health professional works with parents and other responsible adults, an underlying challenge is to develop an understanding of childhood.

Parents tend to act toward their first child, at least in part, according to their beliefs. From each parent's childhood and, to a lesser extent, observations of other children, the parents attempt to form and blend their ideas about what to expect from their newborn. Both parents need to agree on how to raise a child. The mental health professional should help resolve conflicts about child-rearing.

Sometimes the parents may differ greatly about how to treat a child. Because of personal experiences over many years, the parents may have difficulty resolving their differences about child-rearing and adopting new viewpoints. Effective parenting necessitates being open-minded about child development. An intervention goal for the professional helper may well be helping the parents achieve open-mindedness, which is often difficult to attain.

Parents need to talk freely and openly about their ideas and the immediate goals. This sharing of ideas will help them move toward a unified stance, which provides the child with a valuable sense of stability and consistency. The professional helper may facilitate the sharing of ideas.

The first parental task is to take care of the child's need for care, nurturing, and attention that fits the child's age and developmental stage. After this, parents can focus on the goal of bringing the child up to be responsible, polite, neat, and committed to learning and accomplishing tasks. These goals become easier to accomplish once the child has a consistent sense of security, love, and thrust in his or her relationships with the parents and the world.

The arrival of a second child is, logically, influenced significantly by what occurred in the parenting of the first child. And so it goes, with each additional child in the family being the beneficiary (or victim) of what the preceding siblings experienced. Parents must be ready to accept that each child is unique, and they should adapt their parenting to the particular child's characteristics and temperament. For example, the first baby may have a quiet, pleasant temperament, while the second one is highly active or not easily comforted.

In understanding childhood, great patience is needed. At any stage of development, from infancy through adolescence, the child cannot be expected to be as logical, intelligent, or consistent as an adult.

Logic develops from learning, whether it is by trial and error in everyday life or formal study to increase knowledge. Intelligence is complex, but includes heredity, memory, language, and all sorts of abilities that lead to practical wisdom. Consistency is a function of both behavioral skills and personal qualities.

As a parent, a hard lesson for me to learn was that my kids were not always perfect. Overall, each of them was, thankfully, reasonably well behaved, enjoyed learning, and was pleasant to be around (well, most of the time). Even so, I had to adjust my expectations. Countless times, they seemed to be unreasonable, make a dumb decision, or engage in an unanticipated action. I had to learn that these acts are part of childhood and that I, as a parent, needed to cope with them in ways that helped the kids grow in a healthy way.

What is childhood? By its nature, some aspects of childhood will always defy an adult's explanation or expectation. In a positive framework, however, the mystery of childhood can be the ultimate reward from being a parent. From a moment of dismay over a child's behavior, there will be a flood of joy due to the child's response. Having the opportunity of sharing the child's development, through the good and the bad, makes parenting priceless. The professional helper should convey this message to parents.

Who Needs Help?

Ideas about how to help children and adolescents are often based on what is useful to adults. That is, they tend to emphasize a specific problem and do not think about the child's level of maturity and development.

In contrast to adults who are presumably entrenched in stable maturity, young people are passing through a series of developmental stages. Their degree of maturing influences virtually all aspects of their mental processes and behavior. If the goal is to help children and adolescents, it is important for every adult to keep the emphasis on development. Even some mental health professionals need reminders about the developmental aspects of child and adolescent behavior.

Family relationships have a great impact on kids' behavior and mental health. In addition, contacts with other youngsters and adults from outside the family are important.

Parents and other responsible adults define the youth's problems that they believe need attention. That is, adults decide whether behavior or conduct is troubling or abnormal and whether it requires remediation or intervention.

Often the adults and children disagree about the core problem. It is easy to believe that the difficulty comes from within the child and that the kid needs help. It is more likely, however, that the family needs help in order for change to occur in the child or adolescent. Sometimes the need for change extends to other sources, such as the educational services made available to the youth. The mental health professional should ensure that adults and youngsters alike realize that behavior is shaped systemically – that is, from a variety of sources beyond the child or adolescent per se.

The child is a mirror of the system in which he or she lives. Dishion and Stormshak (2007) emphasize the interconnections between family, school, and the community, recognizing how both genetics and family/ social relations cast the die for the child's mental and physical characteristics – this defines the system. Further, they believe that inherited liabilities for mental health disorders commonly lead to special vulnerability for the child in his or her family, peer, and teacher relationships, concluding: "Psychopathology is not within the child but rather in the child's maladaptation to a set of relationship experiences" (p. 16). They add, "The central idea is that children and adolescents are interacting and developing in multiple settings and relationships" (p. 18), and call for interventions in both the family and school settings.

The foregoing reflects the fact that behavior problems and emotional distress experienced by a child or adolescent actually come from many sources outside the youngster. For example, as I discussed earlier, research supports the assertion that the child who lives with parents who are coercive often learns to cope with these interactions with antisocial behavior (Patterson, Reid, & Dishion, 1992). This finding points to the need for mental health professionals to help the coercive parents as a way of helping the child.

Family members and other responsible adults, such as educators, can help or hinder the young person's development. When a child reaches a developmental milestone, such as moving from elementary to middle school, the child faces stress from the new environment. At developmental transition points, mental health professionals and other responsible adults need to intervene in a way that will stave off behavior problems and emotional distress.

For whatever reason, I believe that many (most?) adults tend to be more interested in a child's behavior problems than emotional conditions. Due to social/emotional factors, if the child does not learn positive ways to adapt, the resulting behavior problems may last throughout life. Being anxious or depressed is potentially as harmful to a child's overall development as learning or behavior problems.

Because of the serious emotional risks involved, it is essential that adults try to prevent a child from being overwhelmed by stressful situations. When stress is inevitable or occurs, parents and caretakers should help with support and seek professional intervention that includes the family and school, and other community resources as well. The professional helper should alert parents and caretakers to the resources that are available.

Who needs help? Everyone in the life of the youngster potentially needs help. When all of the adults involved receive encouragement, support, and motivation, the child or adolescent can learn to cope with developmental stresses and problems. The mental health professional should be a supply source for these fortifying conditions.

Reasonable Expectations

To understand parenthood, a fundamental premise is that each parent expects to gain personal rewards from having a child. The personal reward may be love and companionship, a sense of personal fulfillment, or achievement that evaded the parent. While *Great Expectations* makes a good book title, the term is not appropriate in parenting. It is important that a parent's expectations of a child be reasonable.

Reasonableness is defined by the conditions that are actually present, not what would be ideal. If parents have little commitment to learning, it is illogical to expect the child to hold learning as a primary goal. Of course, there are some children, thankfully, who will, as they mature, become aware of the joy of learning, even though their parents failed to encourage the pursuit of academic goals.

On occasion, parental neglect may not be the source of a child's lack of opportunity. The family simply may not have the necessary resources available. Even though a household cannot financially afford to makes books readily available, parents and others can help the kid discover the school library and become an avid reader. With these families, the mental health professional should scout for educational resources.

The reality of what can reasonably be expected is defined, to a large extent, by the characteristics of the particular child, not just the wishes of the parents. A parent's skill or interest in something does not mean that the youngster will be capable of the same level of skill or be interested in the same things as the parents. The parental task is to help the child cultivate skill and develop interests that are compatible with the kid's true characteristics and opportunities. Of course, the mental health professional and other responsible adults share in this task.

In my parenting, I recognized times when I was pushing one or more of my children toward doing something that I valued or enjoyed. For example, given my interest in music, I routinely practiced musical instruments with my kids. While all three, to this day, have a strong interest in music, only one chose a music career (i.e., he is a professor of music). The other two dutifully participated in music lessons and school ensembles, but eventually music became secondary in their lives (but with those two, it is easy to see how my interests influenced their career choices).

In hindsight, I realize that my children all chose the right pathway, even though it was not my road in life. My payoff was in sharing music with my children. However, I neither needed nor would I have encouraged all three kids to decide to be musicians.

To avoid disappointment, the professional helper should caution parents and other adults about looking for a specific personal reward from the child's achievements. Every youngster cannot be expected to do certain things as well as other children. Measuring the progress of a child should be based on individual potential and opportunity, not on what seems to be the accomplishments of other kids. The best payoff for adults is to relish the experience of a mutually loving, caring adult–child relationship.

There is no preordained formula or even a shortcut to recognizing the developmental characteristics of a given child. As parents, we must simply do our best to cultivate the well-being of every kid. To the best of one's abilities, the effort should be to create opportunities that will yield rewards according to the child's needs and to maintain a meaningful relationship that will continue as both the child and the parents move through the stages of life.

Knowing What to Do

Every adult likely harbors a wish to provide caring, nurturance, reinforcement, respect, and protection to children, so they will develop a healthy lifestyle and enjoy a constructive and rewarding life. Granted, because of their own shortcomings or problems in life, some adults fail consistently to meet the challenge. Some adults, however, flounder in their contacts with youngsters because they simply do not know what needs to be done or how to do it.

Certainly professional helpers have formal training in child development. From their knowledge base, they have acquired expert skills.

Most adults, however, do not have a great deal of textbook information per se. By necessity, they must respond to children and adolescents intuitively.

Although their intentions may be good, without a reasonable amount of knowledge and understanding of the nature of development and influences, adult efforts to help may be restricted. Thus, the mental health professional should routinely alert all adults to information, such as in the mass media, that will help them become better informed about kids. In addition to physical health, for which there is an abundance of information flowing to everyone throughout life, acquiring information about mental health is an essential goal.

What constitutes "mental health" is not as easily defined as a known physical ailment. To offer a highfalutin definition, the US Public Health Service (1999) states that mental health is "a state of successful performance of mental function, resulting in productive activities, fulfilling relationships with people, and the ability to adapt to change and to cope with adversity." Let's pinpoint three core terms: *productive, fulfilling,* and *adaptation.*

If the well-intentioned adult approaches contacts with a child or adolescent with a conscious wish to promote *productive activities,* it will set the stage for a positive relationship. Similarly, wanting a youngster to have *fulfilling relationships* can lead to worthwhile social influences. Finally, *adaption* with the adult and the youngster both pledging to be open-minded, the contacts can help the child (1) learn about what is healthy or good in life, and (2) gain the critical ability to learn from experience, avoid negative situations, and cultivate alternatives for thinking, feeling, and acting. The mental health professional should teach these three principles to those who seem to need guidance.

Starting about a century ago and for years thereafter, our society embraced the so-called child guidance movement (which I mentioned in the Preface). The approach involved the belief that various professions could provide answers to questions or cures for problems found in children, and there should be interdisciplinary communications and efforts to help families deal effectively with child development and problems.

Today, the ready availability of information about children and adolescents allows every adult to learn to provide child guidance. Except for serious problems, it is no longer necessary to turn to a clinic. Indeed, it is often undesirable. However, the mental health professional should encourage adults to make a commitment to bettering their knowledge and skills for child guidance.

Instead, it is best for the parent or responsible adult, with acquired everyday knowledge and common sense, to seek to prevent major problems. When talking to, or doing this with, a youngster, the adult's intent should be to cultivate productive activities, fulfilling relationships, and healthy and constructive adaptations. By adhering to these three principles, the adult will help the child or adolescent avoid, stem, and reduce mental difficulties.

Improved Helping

In becoming a parent, it is a natural inclination for a adult to want to safeguard the child and help the youngster maximize potentials and avoid problems throughout life. Although professional helpers receive formal training for working with kids, parents and other kinds of responsible adults (e.g., relatives, friends, acquaintances, and even passersby) are not formal helpers, yet they have the capacity to contribute greatly to the safety, welfare, and well-being of young people.

The mental health professional should inform others of the following message: A starting point for becoming a parent or other responsible adult is to pledge to improve helping skills. It is important to make a commitment to managing everyday life in a constructive manner. An adult with personal burdens is unlikely to be a skilled helper to children, even (or especially?) to his or her own offspring.

When problems arise, such as within the marriage relationship or in encounters with others, parents and other well-meaning adults should find solutions for themselves. This will improve the likelihood that they can help others, such as the children with whom they deal. However, a professional helper can be an invaluable resource for those searching for solutions.

Everyone's life involves problem situations. When a problem of any kind occurs, it is best to analyze the issues and act decisively. Opportunities for wise and effective problem-solving should not be postponed or missed.

Effective parenting requires good problem-solving skills, including for self-management. Many people fail to use their full potential for problem-solving and living. Lacking confidence can contribute to the reluctance to take charge and bring about a positive outcome. Recognizing personal strengths and weaknesses opens the door to self-improvement. For example, children can benefit from accompanying adults to almost any kind of activity or event, and if the adult senses difficulty in talking or dealing with a youth, a bit of serious contemplation or reading about parenting can bring about better helping. By taking stock of personal values and beliefs – the fuel for stoking self-confidence – the person is better prepared to deal with whatever is encountered in parenthood. The professional helper should help people recognize and evaluate their personal values and beliefs.

Improved helping skills come from striving to live more effectively and developing personal resources, along with creating ways to live in a more productive and healthy manner. If there are unused resources, there should be a plan for putting them to good use. For example, having a child tag along to any kind of activity related to the adult's hobbies or interests yields payoffs for both the youngster and the adult.

Lacking the wisdom and judgment that comes with adult maturity, children need wise adult guidance for how to solve problems well. Children will potentially thrive on a relationship with essentially any adult who offers acceptance, respect, positive regard, and information for better living.

Helping does not have to be done in just a problem-solving context. Pinsof (1995) suggests that an alternative to problem-solving is a *value-centered framework* that leads to the helping being "organized not around presenting problems but around a definition of health, normality, or ideal functioning" (p. 3). For example, professional helpers and other responsible adults would do well to encourage youngsters to engage in socially constructive groups, such as the various types of Scouting, 4-H, Future Farmers of America, school or community musical ensembles, art and drama clubs, church activities, and the list goes on – these groups teach positive values that can help the child or teenage avoid problems.

Logically, becoming a parent necessitates guidance for problem-solving and development of personal strengths (e.g., values and morals) in the everyday communications to, and relationship with, an offspring. The outcome will be a set of parental helping skills that will benefit youngsters of all ages and provide the adult with a priceless benefit of having nurtured children to better living.

3 Fundamentals of Guidance

The primary objective of the preceding chapter was to help mental health professionals understand the nature of parenting and the unique aspects of the parent–child or family relations. Such understanding will increase the professional helper's credibility with anyone (such as parents or teachers) who might rely on professional expertise.

In the preceding chapter, consideration was given to adopting an effective parenting style, with emphasis on the best interests of the child. My opinion is that a positive parental style (i.e., the parent shows warmth and love, concern for the child's needs, and willingness to discuss problems and negotiate solutions with the child) is best; and parenting style needs to be caring, empathic, and supportive, not uncaring, harsh, or rejecting – indeed, use of coercion creates problems. The five areas of effective family management were elaborated, derived from the research (e.g., Dishion & Stormshak, 2007):

- the quality of the relationship that each parent has with the child is fundamental to mental health;
- positive reinforcement is an important principle;
- family management benefits from monitoring; ·
- clear, consistent, and logical limits on child behavior should be maintained; and
- adult–child relationships should involve collaborative problem-solving.

These same five principles are equally applicable to the relationship between a professional helper and a youngster. They are the foundation for guidance of children and adolescents.

For mental health professionals and laypersons alike (e.g., parents and family members), it is important to consider developmental factors, avoid adult (non-child) ideas clouding insights about childhood, and keep all expectations reasonable. There must also be awareness of the social influences that impact on persons of all ages. This chapter explains how children develop, and it provides fundamentals for effective professional helping.

Doing the Right Thing

When my kids were young, how to bring them up to behave properly was almost always on my mind. From working with professional helpers, parents, and other responsible adults, I am aware that I was not alone – all responsible adults want children and adolescents to grow up with certain beliefs, values, and morals, and to behave in a manner that will be healthy, acceptable to others, and constructive to our society.

My quandary led to me to think a lot about my personal beliefs and values. Recall my mentioning in Chapter 1 that Preves and Mortimer (2011) state: "An individual's beliefs shape interpersonal behavior, relationships, and ultimately social institutions. This occurs even if those beliefs are not factually correct" (p. 3). I learned later that identifying one's beliefs and values is the first step for all adults in their effort to provide guidance to youngsters. Unless the adult has a clear notion of his or her own beliefs and values, it is difficult to be consistent and effective in conveying values to a child. This is axiomatic for the mental health professional; the effort extends beyond graduate training and continues throughout one's career as a professional helper.

I also came to realize just how much my personal beliefs and values were evident to all – including my children – in my own behavior. If I slipped into an unwise viewpoint or behaved irresponsibly, I had clearly sent my children a faulty message.

All responsible adults, and most certainly professional helpers, need to monitor and control their own words and deeds for the benefit of youngsters. Children and adolescents are uniquely tuned into adult messages and actions even before their own thinking has matured. If an adult makes profane, vulgar, racist, or narcissistic statements, children take these in – as if by osmosis – and imitate the same behavior.

Although biological factors can influence a child's moral development, responsible adults need to pay close attention to how socialization affects whether a child will have positive and wholesome attitudes, values, and behaviors. Socialization will receive considerable discussion in later chapters (especially Chapter 7).

As they grow up, children assimilate society's rules and values regarding acceptable behavior. They internalize, adopt, and act on what they sense their parents and others accept and reward.

Therefore, if young, impressionable children witness antisocial behaviors that go unpunished (such as by persons in real life or in the media), they may come to model these same socially unacceptable behaviors. Older youths who already have an established set of positive values and behaviors may not be quite as vulnerable, as they can themselves judge the antisocial behavior as unacceptable and potentially leading to undesired consequences – but they are still potentially influenced.

The child's early experiences are particularly important. Infants need good care that is consistent, loving, and nurturing. This enables the young child to feel secure and trust parents and later others encountered in the world. This foundation then allows the child to trust and respect the parents' authority, as parents must inevitably set limits and expectations appropriate to the child's age and needs.

Professional helpers, parents, family members, and other responsible adults have an important say with youngsters, especially with young children, as to the social influences and contacts the children will experience. This means that adults should screen out negative influences that might come the children's way. Likewise, adults should create positive opportunities for kids. For professional helping, creating positive conditions and opportunities for children and adolescents is a primary objective.

If a child shows repeated signs of failing to achieve moral development that is appropriate for his or her age level, the child's chances for a positive life and future are quite limited. Professional helpers, parents, family members, and other responsible adults should heed the warning signs and step forward to help the child.

When adults provide compassionate, patient, consistent, and informative guidance, youngsters learn that they can behave in the right way and still get their needs met in socially accepted ways. With good care and guidance from adults, even bad behavior can be turned around. Consequently, a task for mental health professionals is enlisting support for creating positive conditions and opportunities from all adults within the youngster's life.

The professional helper should help parents, family members, and other responsible adults provide guidance to children and adolescents in the context of love, attachment, sympathy, and empathy. It is not good guidance for any adult to create "feel bad" emotions in the child. Much like avoiding coercion, adults should not be critical or try to instill shame or guilt. Mental health professions should teach relevant adults that shame and guilt are counterproductive.

Child development research supports that giving children opportunities to engage in *prosocial* behavior, such as behaving to benefit others, may be able to repair deficits in moral development that occurred earlier. Along this line, professional helpers and other relevant adults should encourage children and adolescents to participate in the value-oriented programs offered by schools and community organizations. For example, many young people have gained positive values and improved behavior from being involved with mentoring and public service activities.

The bottom line is that, to a large extent, mental health professionals should enable parents, family members, and other responsible adults to lead children and adolescents to the pathway to doing the right thing. Once youngsters are marching forward, adults must guide them toward a positive destination for health and happiness through acceptable and constructive behavior.

Childhood and Adolescent Transitions

Every person's trajectory or pathway through life develops from learning, experiences, and personal choices, all of which may have both positive and negative aspects. Actions are necessary to preserve the positives and eliminate the negatives. Fortunately a trajectory can be changed, but transitions must be created and managed effectively. Trajectory management is essential to professional helping.

By definition, a transition in life involves moving from one condition to another. A transition introduces a shift in thinking, values, beliefs, emotions, or behavior. Likewise, changes in education, employment, and relationships, among many possibilities, constitute transitions.

Transitions vary in importance to the person. That is, a certain type of life event will affect people differently. For example, when a young child starts school, the primary caregiver may welcome or resist the event. When a teenager graduates from high school and plans to go away to college, members of the family may view this event as a time for regret or celebration. In the case of parents' divorce, the offspring may react in different ways, such as one feeling a sense of relief while another feels tremendous sadness or anxiety.

To manage life events, young people need adult guidance, such as from a mental health professional, to understand the situation and consequences. Everyone involved in the transition will likely require adaptations. Making ongoing adjustments is, of course, a normal aspect of life.

No one is immune to transitions. Thus, the challenge is to make the most of the event, namely by finding effective ways of coping and learning about life. Certainly receiving support from a unified family or other responsible adults will be essential to enable young people to become competent to meet life's ups and downs.

Adaptation is not always easy. Research shows that persons who are resistant to change or adaptation may get stuck on a negative path. The goal is for the person to use the life event as a means for increasing social stability. Commonly this means casting it into a positive framework. For example, even a negative event, like a failure in school or loss of employment can be reframed to carry an important message for avoiding failure in the future or as an opportunity to assertively seek more rewarding work.

Some life events, especially those that are tragic, are best understood and accepted by having emotional support from others. For example, the death of a classmate or family member requires discussion of the importance of the deceased to the young person (and adults) affected by the death. Such conversations must allow for expressing and accepting a range of painful emotions, as well as sharing good memories. Professional helpers should help kids deal with traumas and grief; it is part of trajectory management.

Transitions or life events become embedded in a youth's trajectory or pathway through life, and can have a dramatic impact on the substance and direction of life's goals. Everyone must deal with transitional happenings, whether anticipated or unanticipated. In every instance, people gain by learning from the events and using their personal knowledge and strength to make a better life.

Dealing with Traumas

To flesh out how mental health professionals should assist children with traumatic events, let me share a personal story. When I was in the first grade, one of my classmates died suddenly. Since the start of the previous year of kindergarten, all the kids knew that "Dickie has poor health."

But we had no idea that he would die! If any effort was made by the teacher or parents to resolve questions about his death in the pupils' minds, it must not have been adequate. For years, the kids talked about Dickie's death.

Life presents traumatic situations to everyone. Mature adults learn how to accept the inevitability of major illnesses, accidents, or deaths of family members or friends – and their own mortality.

Adults vary in their psychological resilience and coping skills for dealing with their grief or fear. Psychiatric research indicates that, if the emotional effects of a trauma are not pretty well eliminated within a year, the person had a significant mental disorder beforehand.

Being immature, children lack understanding of the traumas in life. When a negative experience occurs, children need support and guidance from their parents or other responsible adults. All adults, and most definitely professional helpers, should tool up for this task.

Due to the omnipresence of the mass media today, children and adolescents now have much greater exposure to images and stories of violence and traumas than did youngsters in previous generations. In our current society more than ever, a child's reactions to life-threatening conditions require help from adults.

One approach is to try to shield younger children from excessive negative images. For example, a school can implement policies that preclude classroom teachers' showing televised scenes of warfare or natural or man-made disasters. However, there is no question that children cannot be totally shielded from awful images on television.

Another approach is for adults to know about resources to help children who encounter a traumatic event. Some schools offer training that will strengthen the children's resilience. In a time of disaster, mental health professionals and other responsible adults implement efforts to provide crisis counseling, such as through clinics social agencies. For example, if a student commits suicide, these days there is often a crisis team within the school system ready to step forward. A professional helper must certainly know what the availability is of community resources for crises management, and communicate this information to key adult sources.

Although it is logical that professional helpers should confront trauma-related problems, parents and other caregivers are in an excellent position to know how to develop understanding and coping skills with their own child. There is, however, no one strategy.

When one father opposed a school's ban on television images of the aftermath of Hurricane Katrina, he asserted, "I want my kid to see what life is really about." His child was in an early elementary grade. This situation raises the question as to what kind of information a particular child can understand. To a large extent, the answer will be determined by the age and maturity of the child.

Remembering Dickie, I believe that it is highly unlikely that children 6 years old could understand medical information about a classmate's illness. Similarly, my classmates and I certainly could not have comprehended the abstract, philosophical, or religious views of death per se.

In the case of Dickie, a suitable explanation came years later: "Dickie's blood was bad, and his body just could not continue to live." (Apparently he had blue baby syndrome, involving low oxygen in the blood.) Also, we could have benefited if the teacher or our parents had let us talk about Dickie and express our own concerns and insecurities. Obviously as a child matures, more factual information is appropriate. By the middle-school grades, most children will be able to understand the meaning and consequences of a trauma.

Finally, children and adolescents need more than just information about the trauma. Perhaps more than an explanation of Dickie's illness, my classmates and I needed reassurance that we would not suffer the same fate.

Evaluating the Problem

Both the mother and father had tears in their eyes as they told me about the problems that their child was experiencing. In school, despite the child's apparent efforts, basic learning did not seem to be occurring in a normal or predictable fashion. In contacts with other youngsters, there was hesitancy and avoidance. Simply put, the child was not flourishing.

The parents' intentions were honorable, and they both appeared to be well versed in how children develop. They could identify strategies that seemed appropriate, such as spending time with the child and helping with learning tasks. Conferences with teachers created a united front, but there were no noticeable positive changes in the child's learning and social behavior. Despite all of these constructive efforts, the parents and teachers were stymied.

With this scenario, there is no missing link per se. However, a solution was unlikely without going back to the most basic issue: What is the problem, where does it come from, and then what can be done about it?

Being on the front lines with kids, parents and teachers (and other adults) can have limited or clouded views. Frustration can lessen motivation and narrow consideration of alternatives for helping the child or adolescent.

Any intervention, whether it is relevant to learning or social behavior, should be based on a realistic and objective evaluation of what is or is not occurring. Seldom will there be a single cause of the problem. Although a medical problem might result from one source, developmental problems in childhood and adolescence usually emerge from a combination of factors.

Certainly the child's biological or hereditary factors will establish certain potentials and characteristics. But often times, how others respond, such as using the power of reinforcement, can circumvent what might seem to be a biological limitation.

An old-fashioned idea was that childhood problems come from certain conscious or unconscious conflicts that the child experienced in the early years. Although an experience (e.g., something traumatic) in infancy or early childhood can impact on the child's responses and resiliency, here again there can be a turnaround by use of positive reinforcement.

The modern view is that a child or adolescent who is demonstrating a distinct learning or behavior problem is apt to be reflecting the conditions that occur within the family system. To clarify, research reveals that a child's witnessing domestic violence between the parents will increase the likelihood of problems; and within the family context, a child who is ignored, overprotected, punished severely, lacking educational stimulation, or subjected to adverse emotionality can suffer negative consequences. In other words, the problem to be addressed is not strictly from within the kid, it arises from the conditions and interactions within the family. In this view, the young person is simply the weather vane, and the problems show which way the wind is blowing.

When it comes to evaluating one's own family, the issues may be too close to home to allow objectivity. Personal defensiveness may be present, and professional help may be needed to overcome it. That is, human nature can lead people to avoid personal responsibility and to point an accusatory finger at someone else, as opposed to owning up the underlying issues. An evaluation of a youngster's problem may, therefore, require an outside professional helper. In any event, if there is a problem, a comprehensive evaluation of the situation should be obtained, with the parents and other responsible adults collaborating in the effort under the guiding expertise of the mental health professional.

Finding Solutions

Being a parent introduces daily dilemmas. Every day there is likely to be a predicament for which there seems to be no answer. Regardless, it is up to the parents or other responsible adults to find a solution. Obviously professional helpers will commonly be an important option within the matrix of solutions.

When it comes to raising kids, there are dozens of books authored by people who claim to have the magic formula for resolving the problems that parents encounter. While claiming to have the ultimate answer may sell books, it is, to quote an old song, "an impossible dream."

A book cannot contain to an ultimate answer for every question involving a child. Why not? Because every child is unique and every family rightfully has its own set of values and beliefs that must be part of the chosen solution for the problem.

Finding a solution to a childhood or adolescent problem is a process. In other words, there is no laundry list of solutions to which the adults can turn and pick and choose discrete options. To find solutions, the adults must engage in a series of problem-solving efforts, and this is when professional helpers are invaluable adjuncts. For example, if a child seems to lose interest in going to school, the adults need to discover what is causing the loss of motivation, and a mental health professional can help sort out the possibilities.

Many things can cause a youngster to resist school. It is possible that the child or adolescent is being bullied, rejected by classmates, or is unable to master the academic substance. As I mentioned, there is no simple list of solutions, there is no cookbook in which to look up a recipe – the adults must ably solve the problem by their own insights and skills, which can be facilitated by professional helpers.

Problem-solving necessitates a realistic appraisal of what is involved in the problem. Often the most difficult thing will be for adults, particularly parents, to recognize, acknowledge, and change what they are contributing to the problem. For example, adults may be unknowingly causing or maintaining the problem or making it worse. Regrettably, some adults unwittingly hamper healthy maturation.

Often other more objective observers, such as a mental health professional, will see what the adults in a child's life are doing differently from what those adults think that they are doing. Self-appraisal, such as by the parents or even teachers, may be through rose-colored glasses or be unjustly guilt-ridden.

After identifying the nature of the problem, there should be a brain-storming process, guided by a professional helper. The adults involved with the child or adolescent should pool their ideas and insights to identify reasonable actions. Hopefully, new possibilities will be recognized, and effective plans will be developed. Commonly the professional helper can further the effort by being the one who writes out a diagnostic-intervention plan, which will, of course, always be subject to modification as the child or adolescent changes.

Once the problem and its various components have been narrowly defined and alternatives for solving the problem have been considered, the parents should continue to seek information and insights. Certain alternatives may be overvalued or undervalued by the adults in the youngster's life. In fact, there may be some options that go unrecognized, and it will be the task of the professional helper to illuminate these options.

All adults trying to constructively guide a child or adolescent should be open to ideas from others. Keeping an open mind also means being able to seek new information and gain insights to find trustworthy sources for new ideas. Yes, the professional helper should be an advocate for open-mindedness (and a model for it).

There is reason to be wary of anyone who claims to know exactly what should be done or condemns the parents in the process. Truly helpful sources will listen, explore, and consider the concerns of both the parents and child, neither placing blame nor prescribing solutions. The role for professional helpers and other responsible adults is to offer clarification and information, not give judgments or dictates.

In addition, mental health professionals should encourage responsible adults to be objective as they consider alternative ideas. Despite my caution against expecting ultimate answers in books, there are fine magazines and books about child-rearing that can provide useful information and guidance. Also, schools and community agencies share a responsibility to help parents handle childhood problems. Certainly the concept of family–school collaboration, presented in Chapter 1, supports an exchange of information and ideas.

The final step in solving a problem is to evaluate the options, choose the best course of action, implement this action, and evaluate whether it works to remedy the situation. Professional helpers should emphasize to the parents and other responsible adults that no one should be tempted to try to pass the buck to others, such as teachers, to "fix my kid." Responsible involvement by numerous adults can benefit the search for solutions to childhood and adolescent problems, and the professional helper can be the recruiting agent.

Straight Talk

Recently a parent told me, "When I try to talk to my kids, it seems like we just go around in circles. I end up not knowing any more afterwards than I did before we started the conversation." That same kind of comment could probably come from almost any adult.

When a child or adolescent is talking to an adult, the youth may not actually focus on the specific topic being discussed. This is not surprising. A less mature mind does not understand situations as clearly as a mature mind, and when pressed for comment, the youngster's response may seem almost irrelevant or incomplete.

In talking to children or adolescents, an adult should first state the purpose of any question or comment. For example, the adult could say, "I have been wanting to talk to you about how things are going at school so that I can know what, if anything, I can do to help you." The purpose "how can I help" gets the emphasis.

In contrast, if an adult starts talking immediately about a negative thing, it is logical that the youngster may respond promptly with defensiveness or tuning out. For example, the adult should not fire off a criticism, like "You are doing awful in school, and it is high time that you and I had a serious talk – you've got some explaining to do." In contrast, a warm and supportive tone from the adult will prime the kid to enter into the conversation.

After the purpose has been stated, the second thing the adult should express is a goal. The child or adolescent needs to know, through tactful and precise words, that there will be a payoff from discussing the topic. By making clear that he or she will benefit, the young person will more willingly pay attention to the topic and the stated purpose.

As a third step, once the adult clearly presents the purpose and goal in a positive way, the next challenge is to think about what will reinforce the youngster's willingness to both explore the issue AND be open-minded to changing his or her outlook. That is, the adult should select a strategy to motivate the child or adolescent to reveal new information and be willing to make things better. In other words, the youth needs to be motivated to express his or her views and want to change. For example, the adult might say, "As we talked about before, your keeping your grades up will be a surefire way to impress the other kids."

The professional helper should be a purveyor of strategies to parents, family members, and other responsible adults that will elicit information that is accurate, understandable, meaningful, and – above all else – truthful. If the child or adolescent is not being candid and straightforward, all that is said is wasted. Just because there is a lot of talk does not mean that the information conveyed by the discussion has any value. For example, a parent or teacher could ask, "What is it exactly that keeps you from paying attention in class? You have told me that you know your grades would be better if you were more diligent."

Although the positive tone is essential to effective communication, it is also necessary to avoid language that may mean less to the immature mind than it means to the mature mind. The concept of maturity is based on the fact the children and adults differ in the way they: (1) perceive or view the world, (2) cognitively process or think about information, and (3) communicate or express information. For example, an adult is apt to think about the payoff that comes from getting a task completed, plan a way to accomplish it, and talk openly to others about it, perhaps for supportive ideas. On the other hand, a child or adolescent might be so bound up in anxiety about doing well or avoiding criticism that the effort is ineffective.

A professional helper should assert that a good rule of thumb is for the adult to speak in a way that will definitely be understood by the particular youth. Statements should be kept simple. Long and complex statements should be avoided. Not only can information about this sort of communication be offered by the mental health professional, he or she can model it in interactions with persons of all ages.

Talking and Listening

Straight talk is something people of all ages value. A meaningful discussion about a possible problem requires a clear statement of purpose, a goal that will be beneficial, willingness to explore new information, and motivation to improve the situation.

To guide children and adolescents, adults need to set a positive tone and by example offer information that is accurate, understandable, meaningful, and truthful. When an adult talks to a youngster, the talk should be geared to the child's age and level of maturity (Woody, 2002).

With any conversation, even between adults, the culture, intelligence, and education of the persons involved will be influential. For example, if those conversing come from significantly different backgrounds, perhaps with cultural or ethnic differences, a loss or distortion of meaning could occur. Or certain words might mean something to one person, but not to another. Therefore, the words (or vocabulary) used must be appropriate. Likewise, one person might be able to follow an explanation that is complex, whereas another person might become confused by it. Although somewhat obvious, professional helpers should remind themselves to adhere to these ideas.

To summarize this issue, the language used has to fit the particular participants in the conversation. For example, while a parent or teacher might tell a teenager, "Unless you marshal your resources and reschedule your commitments . . . ," the same message to a young child might be, "You need to keep your brain on the assignment and stop thinking about video games so much."

How to keep a conversation meaningful can be difficult to determine. Until the characteristics of the person to whom one is talking are known, it is best to keep comments simple and avoid long and complex statements. Although parents and other responsible adults presumably (hopefully) have a solid understanding of the needs and characteristics of a child or adolescent, other less involved adults working with the same kid, such as teachers, may need to focus on increasing their insights about what makes the youngster tick.

Listening can also be challenging. If the other person's comments are difficult to follow or track, it is appropriate to admit, "It is probably me, but I don't understand what it is you are telling me." In other words, it is fine to let someone now that you do not grasp the message. Certainly mental health professionals need to understand everything that is said by someone to whom they are committed to helping, and should be quick to ask for clarification and additional information if a message is unclear.

Being a good listener requires being attentive. The listener needs to let the speaker, be it adult or child, know that what he or she is saying is being heard, considered, and understood. A good way to show this is to reflect back or repeat your understanding to let the person know that your are tracking the message. This is very different from the tendency to listen halfheartedly while planning your response – which, in this type of listening, is often a rebuttal or defensive statement. There should be visible cues that the listener is tuning in.

The listener should also reveal an empathic understanding of the comments. That empathy can be a simple comment that conveys that you understand the speaker's views and feelings about the situation. Considerable research supports the notion that the effectiveness of professional helping is contingent on conveying accurate empathy.

When an adult such as a parent or teacher talks to a child or adolescent, there is potentially a generation barrier; of course, mental health professionals are also commonly in a different generation from the child or adolescent with whom they are working. In the youngster's eyes, the adult has a degree of authority, and the kid may feel second-class. A feeling of insecurity or defensiveness will hamper communication, including with a professional helper of any kind.

By focused listening, adults can promote effective communications that encourage young people to talk about their experiences; the way they think; their feelings, emotions, and moods; and their behavior. Having a positive attitude about listening to the youthful talk, even if it may seem like palaver, will open the door to meaningful exchanges in the future. Here is a simple guideline for any adult, including a mental health professional, wanting to guide a child or adolescent: Let yourself step into the shoes of the youngster.

Questioning

Most of us do not like the feeling of being interrogated. Whether with adults or children, for someone to start probing with questions tends to lead to defensiveness. Certainly the air of authority that adults commonly have when questioning youngsters can result in silence or resistance. Therapeutic interventions depend on communication.

The adult who wants to have a meaningful conversation with a youth should remember that the goal is to get the child or adolescent to talk and reveal potentially useful information. For example, if a mental health professional launches into a lengthy statement, the youngster will not be talking. The silence may set the wheels in motion for the kid to be thinking of a good or right answer – one that may placate the adult but not be 100% truthful. If the adult's comments are primarily questions, it is highly unlikely that the conversation will be meaningful.

Assuming that questions are justified to obtain specific information, the structure of the question should be considered. The basic idea is that a question should be posed to minimize defensiveness and maximize information. For example, a parent could say, "I'll bet the plants are looking forward to your watering them – or have you already got them happy?" Professional helpers should teach parents, family members, and other responsible adults to formulate questions and comments in a way that will facilitate communication with the child or adolescent, not construct barriers to communication. Here are some ideas.

Open-ended questions foster communication, whereas closed-ended questions are problematic. For example, a closed-ended question allows the youth to select between alternative answers, such as "Yes or no, did you get your chores done?" The child or adolescent need only give a minimal response, although there are occasions when a *fixed-alternative* or *multiple choice* form of questioning is appropriate, such as "Do you want to walk with the other kids or ride with me to school?" This format leaves no room for elaboration, although additional information might, of course, be useful.

With many, perhaps most, conversations that call for questions, reliance on open-ended questions yield the most information. The question is worded in such a way that the person is led to answer in his or her own words. For example, the adult might say to a child or adolescent, "What do you think would be the best way for you to get to school today?" The youngster might then say something like, "I believe that I will ride with you because I need to take my trombone today."

Open-ended questions accomplish two things. First, the person responding has a sense of self-determination or volitional control. Second, there is a wider range of possible responses than with closed-ended questions.

To lessen the possible defensiveness to questions, the adult should give the child or adolescent an affirmation for the youth's response. That is, the adult should say something positive about the youngster's importance, strengths, efforts, abilities, or steps to be taken. The fact that the positive reinforcement is coming from an adult, such as a mental health professional, is likely to encourage meaningful conversation. For example, a parent could say to the child, "I'm glad that you are in the school band, you have a lot of talent," or the teacher could tell a pupil, "You did the right thing by turning in that billfold that you found – it really speaks well for your character."

Talking About Kids

Most parents, it seems, like to brag about their kids. There are, of course, parents who also want to talk about the shortcomings of their children.

Perhaps it's the old saying "Misery loves company" that leads friends and family to commiserate about how their offspring are causing problems, not living up to parental expectations or preferences, or behaving in inexplicable ways. The professional helper should convince adults in the life of the child or adolescent that, whatever may be the conscious reason, an abundance of talking about negative child behavior is not necessarily a good thing. Perhaps in a religious context, confession is good for the soul. But for developing improved parenting skills, a confessional does not in itself bring about helpful information.

Sigmund Freud believed that just rambling on and on – what he called *free association* – would help the person work through conscious and unconscious conflicts, which he called achieving *catharsis*. Perhaps in psychoanalysis a lot of directionless verbiage had a payoff, but in everyday life, parents and other responsible adults need information about how to solve concrete problems. Information of this sort comes best from knowledgeable sources, such as mental health professionals. Providing information about guiding children and adolescents, to all sorts of adults is a major function for professional helpers.

What if a parent from family #1 wants to share war stories about his or her child's behavior with a parent from family #2. If the first parent seems to want to express feelings of concern or frustration, it is appropriate for a friend or family member to offer support and empathy. However, if the person continues to seek sympathy, without interest in problem-solving, it would be best for the parent from family #2 to close off the conversation and advise the person to look for solutions.

Isn't that rude? Not at all. By not feeding into an unhealthy motive, the parent from family #2 is showing respect for family #1's integrity and boundaries.

I walked into a store. For no known reason, the owner immediately asked what I did for a living. To play it close to the vest, I said simply, "I work with kids." She launched into "I just got convicted of sexual child abuse, let me tell you about it." I said immediately and firmly, "No, it is not my role to hear about your conviction, but I encourage you to find a qualified therapist." I paid for my purchase and left quickly – and have never been back!

Why was I so abrupt? It was obvious that this was a person who was hoping to get someone with absolutely no personal connection to her to buttress whatever self-explanation she had concocted for her crime. I would have done her a disservice by listening and pretending to be interested or helpful, but it was clear that she needed professional help.

In another situation, a good friend started to tell me about how his wife was not a good parent. Apparently because of my facial expression, he said, "You don't want to hear about it, do you?" With honest concern for his well-being, I responded, "No, as a friend, I cannot and should not be involved in your intimate family issues, but I do hope that you will gain a positive outcome – do you know a family counselor to whom you can turn?" When he said no, I gave him two or three names of qualified counselors. Later, he thanked me, and told me how he and his wife had found one of the counselors whom I had suggested to be very helpful and that in just a few sessions.

The decision point is whether the person is talking excessively about the child to lessen guilt, gain sympathy, or enlist an ally in the warfare against another person, such as a spouse or child. Becoming a third person in a family triangle is very ill advised. Professional helping requires avoiding triangulation.

As I mentioned earlier, if the parent truly wants to talk about the problems being experienced with his or her child or adolescent to gain helpful information, then it is fine to respond. There is a limit, however, to the help that can be offered by friends and family members, whereas seeking professional help, such as from a marriage and family therapist, has much more potential for benefits. Promoting a referral to an appropriate professional source is important.

The One-Parent Home

The demands of modern society make it difficult for many families to have adequate financial resources unless both parents are employed. Consequently, with both parents outside the home for much of the day, the child is at risk of not having adequate adult contact time or supervision. If the parents divorce, the child faces another set of risks.

Divorce is common in today's society. About half of marriages (perhaps even more, depending on the demographics of the spouses) end in divorce. There are about 1 million divorces per year in the United States.

Whatever the justification or reason for a divorce, it has a significant impact on all concerned. According to research, for a period of time, children are especially vulnerable to negative effects when parents go their separate ways.

When approaching divorce, most parents are sincerely concerned about minimizing the problems for their children. Indeed, many couples stay together "for the kids." It is not unusual, however, for a number of these couples to divorce eventually, perhaps after the kids have graduated from high school and are presumably on their own.

Whether due to the advent of *no-fault divorce* or likely a combination of other factors as well, the increasing divorce rate in the past few years has the potential for grave consequences for children, regardless of age. Now, at least in some quarters, the frequency of divorce seems to be stabilizing, and there may even be a slight decline in divorces.

Do today's employment- and divorce-related conditions impact on the quality of nurturing and parenting for the child or adolescent? The answer, of course, is "it depends."

From her research on the intersection of work and family, Halpern (2005) reports the good news: Maternal employment in general seems to have few, if any, negative effects on the children of working parents. She concludes that parents "may be assured by the research findings that children can develop equally well regardless of the employment status of their parents," and she adds, "The home environment is a far more important determinant of how children fare as they grow up" (p. 399). Indeed, the most harmful source of jeopardy for children seems to be living in poverty.

With divorces and certain other adverse values, these days it is not unusual for a child to live in a one-parent home. Most often, the primary custodial or residential parent is the mother, but there is a gradual change toward more fathers having this primary responsibility.

When either parent is out of the home, the child loses in several ways. If the father is gone, there may be a lack of a father figure, that is, conditions that help the child or adolescent develop a healthy view of masculinity. With the sole parent overloaded with responsibilities, there may less parental care and supervision.

Finally, it is known that well over half of poor children living with just their mothers, whose fathers live elsewhere, do not receive child support. It appears that the failure to pay child support is often due to the fathers' limited ability to pay (that is, being underemployed or unemployed), not because of the fathers' not wanting to provide financial support.

Obviously getting out of poverty is highly difficult, perhaps even impossible for those who lack education and other resources or who, by life conditions, have restricted opportunities. The message for professional helpers is simple enough: They should let the parent from a financially impoverished home know that financial aid, such as from government-sponsored benefits programs, is available. Professional helpers of every ilk should be prepared to inform those with financial and other needs about the resources that are available,

Returning to the matter of parental employment, Halpern (2005) states, "The work status of a parent is not as critical a determinant for child development as having a supportive home environment and a warm, loving parent or other adult and avoiding the negative correlates and consequences of poverty" (p. 400). Stated differently, if the child or adolescent has access to care and supervision from other responsible adults, the potential adverse effects of parental deprivation per se would not need to occur.

If the young child is left to a hodgepodge of stopgap attempts at childcare, such as not having stable, consistent daycare or a babysitter or being left alone as a latch-key kid, the likelihood of a problem is greater. Professional helpers should motivate parents, family members, and other responsible adults to do their part for children by supporting efforts, policies, and community programs that strengthen parents and combat poverty.

The Absent Parent

Regrettably, divorce, death, or a host of other reasons result in many children growing up in a one-parent home. In my own situation, my father died suddenly when I was 13 years old. I can personally attest that, to this day, there is a void in my life because of his absence.

From birth to death, parents influence a person's life. Even if a parent is absent from the home, thoughts about that parent impact on the child. These childhood thoughts may be fantasy or rooted in reality or a mixture of the two. Whatever their nature, they can impact on the child's development.

When a child loses a parent during childhood, as an adult, he or she may continue to harbor thoughts about what was or might have been with that parent. I often think consciously about how my father would handle a situation or react to something with which I engage or which I accomplish. In some ways, the absent parent may be just as influential, or perhaps even more so, than the single parent who raises the child.

The mental health professional should help the parent, family members, or other responsible adults who are raising the child harness the influence from the absent parent, and be sure that the ongoing influence is constructive. If a parent abandons the other parent and children, there should be no discernible long-term hostility. The absent parent should not be ignored or the child's loss denied. There should be no attempt to diminish the realistic positive thoughts that the child has about the absent parent. Certainly, professional mental health services for the concomitant issues may be merited.

As relevant to the previous statement about no long-term hostility, no matter what might be the circumstances, there certainly should be no demonizing of the absent parent. Unfortunately, a parent's describing an absent parent in negative terms can happen, especially during or after an angry divorce. Bad mouthing or trying to erase the influence from an absent parent can only impose additional burdens on the child, as he or she struggles with growing up. Because the parents did not get along and split up does not necessarily mean that the absent parent was totally bad for the child. The message to be promulgated by the mental health professional is that all relevant adults should keep in mind that children and adolescents are not immune from the effects of an absent parent.

What the child or adolescent needs is guidance to understand and accept the loss of a parent. If the parent is no longer present in the day-to-day life of the family, the youngster needs mature help in gaining personal insight into the real, versus imagined, qualities of the absent parent. Any negative facts should be acknowledged, but not overemphasized. For every negative fact that is considered, there should also be an effort to identify a positive fact.

To be a healthy adult, the young person needs to go through the maturational years with views about, and feelings for, the absent parent that are realistic. Having realistic views and feelings can help the child or adolescent recognize the benefits that were gained from the absent parent. When an absent parent seems to defy a kind word, even that parent can justly be credited with giving the kid an opportunity to undo the negative by growing into being a responsible adult.

Emotional Divorce

Numerous adults who have divorced parents have talked about how, all through the years, they continued to consciously harbor the notion that their parents would rediscover each other and get remarried. Children, adolescents, and adults all want deeply to think of their parents as having had an idyllic marriage.

Divorce has a powerful impact on the entire family. Consequently, some couples choose to stay together, even though the positive aspects of marriage have diminished or disappeared. That is, they stay together, but live with negative emotions. Their bond of love is eliminated, and toleration "for the sake of the children" becomes the glue for keeping the marriage and family together. Although there is no legal divorce or dissolution of the marriage, there is an emotional divorce.

Just like a legal divorce, the emotional break-up of parents definitely places their children at risk. Moreover, children of any age can feel the impact. That is, adolescents can have negative outcomes as much as younger children. Waiting until the children reach a certain age before divorcing does not necessarily shelter the kids from negative effects.

In some instances, a legal divorce can prove to be less detrimental than an emotional divorce. A marriage without love and devotion can easily become abusive (physically and mentally) and harmful to all concerned. Children who live with parents who are in an emotional war or live as though the other parent is a pariah will sense, at some level, insecurity and will be deprived of the family joy and positive feelings that are essential to helping them grow up to be healthy, happy, and productive adults.

If childhood is spent with parents who are negative toward each other, it is logical that the child will reach adulthood having been exposed to and influenced by poor role models. The outcome may well be that the child's own attachments to others will be difficult and result in less-than-positive relationships, including in marriage.

These views in no way advocate legal divorce. It should be a last resort. However, from the standpoint of benefiting the children, an emotional divorce is not a panacea and may actually prove to be an unwise choice.

If the interests of the children are upheld, the parents should not consider legal or emotional divorce without first seeking counseling from a mental health professional or well-qualified religious source. Incidentally, the potential for harming a child and burdening his or her efforts to learn has led some school systems to establish services to parents with marital problems, such as conducting a group counseling experience for "Improving Your Marriage to Improve Your Parenting." As should be obvious by this point, professional helpers should be competent to deal with disintegrating marriages, as well as the aftereffects of divorce.

Remarried Families

Modern societal values do not place as much of a stigma on being divorced as was true in previous generations. Also, the legal system, with its emphasis on no-fault divorce, has simplified the divorce process. Although these two conditions, social values and no-fault, have seemingly contributed to the surge in divorces in the past 30 or so years, they have also paved the way for ease of remarriage.

Studies show that when a first marriage ends in divorce, a large percentage of the partners will remarry. In fact, most divorced persons do not stay single very long.

Upon remarriage, there is a need for a complex blending of two family systems. While the two new marriage partners may have a lot in common and enjoy each other's company, their positivism does not eliminate the challenge of interweaving the lives of the children from their previous marriages. There is no simple formula for: (1) creating a new marriage that will be free from trials and tribulations or (2) assuring that the youngsters will accept the new stepparent. To provide beneficial guidance to children and adolescents, professional helpers must be aware that the reconstitution of a family life is complex and help those who are struggling with it.

Each parent in the new marriage, whether he or she does or does not have children already, has the social responsibility and legal duty to safeguard and cultivate the development of the children who come to the new family with the other spouse. The new stepparent cannot ignore or avoid parenting the stepchildren. It is immature and irresponsible to try to escape by saying, "They're your kids – you deal with them."

The newly married spouses need to discuss and plan for how each will participate in the care of the children. Usually, the stepparent should not take a high-profile role, such as in disciplining the children.

Before entering into a new marriage, any marital vows should include a shared commitment to the existing children. Such a proclamation could, of course, actually be included in the wedding ceremony. Likewise, many parents include their children in the ceremony, thereby giving a direct indication of their importance to the marriage.

In day-to-day activities, the remarried spouses should consistently carry out the roles that they agreed on as being best for the children. With this unified front between the adults and good communication, their child guidance efforts should be more effective.

No one can predict how a child will respond to the presence and involvement of a new stepparent; however, the child needs to know and be comfortable with the new family roles, responsibilities, and expectations. As with any relationship, both adults should strive to create a positive, supportive, and loving connection with all those, including the children and extended family members, who are part of the blended or reconstituted family. Obviously, assistance from a mental health professional will be useful.

Parental and Adult Radar

Professional helpers should encourage parents, family members, and other responsible adults to maintain a close watch on their children's behavior. The initial motive is to be sure that the children are safe, but there is the added purpose of assuring that children do not do something that adults would frown upon. By using what I call the "parental and adult radar," we can help children develop good values and adopt constructive behavior that would win approval from the family and society.

Despite their best efforts, however, adults are often surprised when kids do something totally unpredictable. To paraphrase a saying by Art Linkletter, the old-time comedian, "Kids say and do the darndest things."

In law, negligent or wrongful behavior can be by omission or commission. With a child who behaves in an unexpected way, it need not be a commission of deceit or lying. Instead, the surprise could come when a child or adolescent fails to tell the responsible adults about something that was happening, such as in school or among, say, teenage friends.

When adults are open, caring, and trusting, this atmosphere tells the child or adolescent that it is OK to talk about what is going on in their lives. Without these qualities, establishing effective communications will be unlikely. Obviously, being able to have frank and complete information exchanges between an adult and a child or adolescent also depends on a long-term bond that is characterized by dignity and respect between all concerned.

Among psychologists, the term *facilitative conditions* is used to describe communications involving accurate empathy, positive support, and mutual respect. Without facilitative qualities, children will not be likely to open up to adults, and the talks between the adult and the child will not contain revealing information. Teaching adults to effectively use facilitative conditions is a critical function for the guidance efforts by professional helpers.

During the teenage years, tuning into the youth's life is particularly difficult. Adolescents, even those who are relatively mature and well behaved, are pressed by their friends to honor the *teenage code.* That is, teenagers expect each other to not reveal to adults what is going on in the teenage world. As a troubling example, it is all too common for a youth intending to commit violence at school to tell one or more classmates about it beforehand, yet the classmates do not always reveal the impending hostile act to parents or teachers, even though this might enable the warding off of the horrible event.

Although understandable, due to the "rebel without a cause" inclination that is associated with adolescence, the teenage code does not deserve to be endorsed by youths, their parents, teachers, or other responsible adults. Sheltering criminal intent because of a teenage code is a mark of a lack of clear values, immaturity, and social irresponsibility. Everyone should make a concerted effort to create an open channel for communications between adolescents and adults, even for things that are far less traumatic than violent acts. The parental and adult radar concept is important, and will be discussed further in the framework of vigilance and adult monitoring.

Defining Moments

In everyone's life, there will be events that have a lasting effect throughout life. For example, when the mental health professional receives a graduate degree or license to practice, his or her career path will be forever different.

For professional helpers and laypersons alike, these defining moments will likely shape all sorts of values, attitudes, and behaviors in the future. In fact, if the event is highly significant, it may even become the primary determinant of how a person acts later on. For example, I realize that after receiving my doctorate, graduating from law school, and completing study at a bona fide law enforcement academy, my values, attitudes, and behaviors relevant to countless issues were changed (presumably forever).

A defining moment can be positive or negative. On the positive side, there is typically great importance attached to events like winning an award, graduating from high school or college, getting married or divorced, having a child, and so on. On the negative side, there are regrettable events, such as when a youth or family member has a serious illness or an accident, gets arrested, loses employment, or is victimized. Of course the foremost negative is undoubtedly the death of a loved one.

When there is a defining moment, the inclination may be to become highly self-centered. That is, the mind wants to maximize the positive as fully as possible (taking pride in or credit for a youngster's achievement) or turning a negative event into a "pity party." This self-concern is understandable but may block understanding of the full meaning of the moment. Certainly professional helpers cannot allow egotism and narcissism to infiltrate professional judgments.

Mental health professionals should alert parents, family members, and other responsible adults to the importance of guarding against a defining moment in the family leading to neglect of, or forgetting about, the children. For example, one mother reported that, upon the unexpected death of her spouse, she became oblivious to the children, and it was long after before she realized that, as she was struggling with her grief, the children were left on their own to try to make sense of their father's death.

Suffice it to say, if a negative defining moment is difficult for an adult, it will most certainly be more difficult, both in the short and long run, for the youngsters. Their immaturity does not equip them with the coping abilities that (hopefully) an adult has acquired through responsible and meaningful life experiences.

If it is a positive defining moment, such as the birth of a child or a graduation, the other children in the family should not be forgotten. The adults should make a point of helping all family members share the glory achieved by the honoree. The professional helper should encourage sharing the glory within the family system.

There are some events that may, at first blush, seem like defining moments when, in point of fact, their significance may be far less. For example, a traumatic situation may seem to cast a pall that will seemingly last throughout the family's lifetime. Instead of succumbing to a burden, the family members, especially the parents, should be stalwart in their commitment to improving their lot in life. By being loyal to and supporting each other, the family members can jointly unravel the negative effects, place the causes and consequences into a realistic perspective, and define a positive approach for moving beyond the event.

Whether the event is positive or negative, parents, family members, and other responsible adults may need a professional helper's support in helping the children deal with or appreciate the essence of the defining moment. To leave family members alone in defining moments is neither helpful nor responsible. Family members should share the good and the bad, and move into the future with a sense of unity. Guidance by mental health professionals includes helping the family deal with defining moments in a way that will prevent problems arising, for all concerned, especially children and adolescents.

4 Dealing with Kids

The preceding chapter provided fundamentals about children and adolescents that the mental health professional should provide to parents, family member, and other responsible adults. It was pointed out that, among other things, adults (including professional helpers) need to recognize their personal values and, with insight, seek to convey positive values to the child. To benefit the child or adolescents, all adults (again, including professional helpers) should monitor and control their personal words and deeds. Failure to do so can lead to unwanted effects on socialization, including the possibility of unhealthy or antisocial behavior.

Early childhood experiences are especially important for the development of security and trust, as well as respect for authority and the rights of others. Mental health professionals should help relevant adults screen out negative influences in the young child's life. Every child and adolescent will benefit from compassionate, patient, consistent, and informative guidance from parents, family members, and other responsible adults. Adults should encourage children to engage in value-oriented experiences, such as those offered by schools and community organizations. These contacts can be particularly useful for the child's moral development. There is no template for values; solutions for value-related questions or problems should be based on the child's and family's unique characteristics, preferences, and beliefs.

Whether this applies to a professional helper or layperson, struggling with problems requires objectivity. Some adults have tunnel vision. Consequently, when parents, family members, and other responsible adults find that they are unable to recognize alternative ways of thinking or acting in their contacts with children and adolescents, it may be time for them to turn to professional helpers.

In the preceding chapter, I also explained the considerations and influences that may arise with the one-parent family, the effects of divorce, and the continuing influence of the "absent" parent. Finally, I offered ideas for developing a parental and adult radar that allows helpful scrutinizing of a youngster's development and behavior in order to take proactive steps to avoid problems in the future. When providing services, the mental health professional should be aware of these considerations and influences.

This chapter focuses on the psychological aspects of child development. Consideration will be given to guidance relevant to personal psychological needs within the family, deciding how to solve problems, gauging maturity, principles for talking to kids, determining words and deeds to influence children and adolescents in a positive fashion, balancing parental/adult and children's psychological interests, gearing up to help children of all ages face problems and change targeted behaviors, and using authoritative (but not authoritarian) guidance skills. As always in this book, the purpose is to prepare mental health professionals for the task of providing effective guidance to people of all ages.

A Full Life

All responsible adults want children and adolescents to have the best of everything. Acquiring material things is not the primary goal. They hope for a healthy, happy, and constructive lifestyle; they want kids to live life as fully as possible.

Living a full life is far more than simply being busy all the time. Likewise, it is more that just avoiding cares and woes, because nobody can achieve that sort of freedom.

Regrettably, at one time or another (or many times?), everyone struggles with problem situations that seem overwhelming. When a child or adolescent lacks the ability to stay on top of a situation, it is time for parents, family members, and other responsible adults to offer assistance – and their efforts can be strengthened by guidance from a professional helper.

The family's structure – what it believes and what it sanctions for living life –should include supporting any family member who encounters a problem. Ideally, a foundation of family love would make one person's problem everyone else's problem; and when a problem arises, there should be an alliance for working together to find solutions for the troubled family member.

A wise and healthy family will fulfill the old adage "An ounce of prevention is worth a pound of cure." That is, before there is a problem, there will be a conscious family plan for dealing with problems that can and will occur.

In raising children, the family plan should include encouragement and reinforcement for positive accomplishments for each member of the family. With this atmosphere, every family member has meaningful life goals. Family resilience will be strengthened by this approach and will help ward off any potentially negative impact from, say, an unexpected misfortune.

Also to deal effectively with problems of living, children and youth (and a lot of adults!) need to develop better *social intelligence.* In other words, life will be made better by being able to think and act according to self-awareness, self-control, and decisive and well-reasoned actions. Developing these cognitive and behavioral qualities should be promoted in the context of mental health helping.

The foregoing stoic and personal qualities will be further strengthened by mature relationships, in which there is sensitivity to each other's feelings, needs, and concerns. In any relationship, there will be richness of life for all involved by having and seeking understanding, mutual need fulfillment, good communication, respectful challenging, the resolution of disagreements, responsible intimacy, openness to influencing and being influenced, avoiding coercion, and being well oriented to the realities of the community and world. These are the qualities that professional helpers will promote.

Using a common example, when an adolescent seems to be losing interest in school, presumably because of an inability to get good grades, the family should focus on what may be contradicting positive attitudes. It may be that the youth is harboring self doubts, lacks friends, does not engage in rewarding activities, or is under the influence of a host of other possible negatives. The parents, often with the help of educators, should engage the teenager in gaining better awareness of personal potentials, identifying ways to bring them into daily life, and taking steps to have greater self-confidence and an improved ability to find support in new ways. For example, joining additional youth activities could provide social motivation, with a possible spillover effect to doing better in academics. If academic failure or dropping out of school seems imminent, the parents should consider obtaining the services of a tutor or professional helper.

Finally, achieving a full life should include having a commitment to social responsibility. That is, the person's life will be better by his or her being a law-abiding citizen intent on making living conditions better to everyone in society, now and in the future. For example, encouraging a young person to do volunteer work provides an important lesson about life.

There is no simple formula for living life fully. Every person needs to find a balance between what is and what can be, and then move with positivism toward thinking, feeling, and acting accordingly. The mental health professional should fortify any relevant person, regardless of age, for this balancing act.

What a Child Needs

As relevant adults face the daunting tasks of helping a child or teenager weather the storm of growing up, a common question is, "What should I be doing to help this kid steer a safe passage to a healthy and constructive life?" Regrettably, there is no simple answer.

Obviously, a child needs consistent protection, care, and the basics of food and shelter. Children of all ages have, however, many other types of personal needs, some unique to the particular child and some quite common to all youngsters.

From infancy, the child is on the path to develop his or her self. The self is a complex notion that is made up of several components.

In the early years, the child learns about the physical self by literally exploring his or her own body. For example, consider how wiggling their toes or how their fingers can pick up things is fascinating to babies.

As the years pass, the exploration becomes more mental, and this is where mental health information becomes more important. The child begins to imagine what he or she can become. Early on, these fantasies are more idealistic that realistic. However, at this early stage, fantasies do not have to be connected to reality, as evidenced by kids pretending to be superheroes.

The child's learning about the world in school becomes part of the self that leads to becoming a competent human being. During adolescence, young people begin to grapple seriously with forming their own unique identity. That is, they start deciding who they are, what their talents are, and how they will gain a place in the world. Psychologists refer to this stage as the child's needing to *differentiate self* from other children. For any age, professional helpers need to assist efforts to differentiate one's self.

Parents particularly, but other responsible adults as well, need to help the child through all of the developmental stages and even into adulthood. Indeed, many psychologists assert that the need for self-understanding is a lifelong undertaking, which is essential to fulfilling personal potential, and feedback from, and interactions with, others (throughout life) can contribute significantly to the effort to gain self-understanding.

All adults need to support children and adolescents in their search to fulfill personal potential or self-actualization. The objective is health. As Maslow (1968) said: "Healthy people have sufficiently gratified their basic needs for safety, belongingness, love, respect, and self-esteem so that they are motivated primarily by trends to self-actualization" (p. 25).

With this summary of child development as the roadmap, parents, family members, and other responsible adults can help children and adolescents gain a healthy maturity by assisting their efforts to form a wholesome and rewarding identity. When discussing theories of personality, Hergenhahn and Olson (2007) state that the need for positive regard is "universal but not necessarily innate," and requires "receiving warmth, love, sympathy, care, respect and acceptance from the relevant people in one's life" (p. 445).

Although there is no simple formula to assure that a child or adolescent receives sufficient positive regard, the responsible adult should try to treat kids in ways that promote feelings of self-worth. Making a statement that seems to be a put-down is not helpful.

Certainly misconduct by a youngster should not be ignored; but by guiding the child to manage his or her own behavior so as to avoid misconduct in the future, the responsible adult turns the situation into a positive learning lesson. For example, a young person needs clear expectations and to understand that misconduct will lead to loss of opportunity and loss of respect from others. Mental health professionals should reinforce this standard.

It is fundamental that a child of any age (and an adult too) needs emotional feeding from others. Berating the child or adolescent for past misconduct carries no opportunity for learning, and may damage self-esteem and contribute to more unacceptable behavior. A youngster who is hurt or stigmatized by harsh criticism may become rebellious, defensive, and quit trying to have a positive life.

In terms of learning, there are certain situations in which, if the child or adolescent cannot receive a positive emotional response from the adult, the kid – in need of emotional reinforcement – will settle for what can be obtained, namely a negative emotional response. This kind of adult–child interaction is not good for positive learning. The old adage "A spoonful of sugar makes the medicine go down" provides a useful guideline in helping young people learn how to manage their own behavior to achieve good results.

Deciding How to Solve a Problem

Childhood and adolescence are, by nature, full of uncertainty. Before reaching adulthood, some youths may see a situation as a problem, although an adult may not view it so seriously. In his popular song about teenagers, "Letter to Me," Brad Paisley sings, "I know at 17 it's hard to see past Friday night." This suggests that youngsters commonly believe that acceptance and enjoyment are urgent matters. For adults, one of the first steps toward helping a child or adolescent with problem-solving is to, with an empathic tone, tactfully point out the true importance of the issue, namely an everyday situation is usually not of grave importance and "these things too shall pass."

Mental health professionals should help relevant adults bolster children's abilities and efforts to solve the problems that arise. Here the focus will be on how adults can help a child or adolescent who is experiencing a problem, such as with a classmate, find a way to eliminate the conflict and get on a more positive footing.

If a problem seems to be emerging in a youngster's life or if a kid is already besieged with a difficulty, adults should decisively step forward to offer support and guidance and help the youth find a good solution. It is best to brainstorm for various possible solutions and then evaluate each. Professional helpers can be a resource for information and skills that will accomplish these strategies.

When deciding what tactics might be the most appropriate, adults and young people should share ideas about what seems logical for family values and for the resources available. Mental health professionals should help the adults decide what intervention and by whom is apt to be the most effective for the particular child or adolescent in the given set of circumstances. For example, if faced with a problem, the professional helper could convene parents and their child, and together decide what can be done and what each family member should or should not do to bring about the desired resolution of the problem. After the deliberations, the parents should not be surprised if their child says, "I want to take care of this myself" – that would be a healthy and preferred outcome (as long as the youngster is capable of handling the situation).

In choosing a plan of action, it is important for the mental health professional to weigh the unique aspects of the particular family. For example, if the parents are divorced but remain mutually concerned about their child, it will be necessary, perhaps with guidance from a professional helper, to collaborate in a way that recognizes how both parents can set aside their personal differences and support the child's views and behavior relevant to the problem. If only a single parent is available, the choices for conflict resolution will be influenced accordingly.

In dealing with problems within the family, the first goal is to improve the relationship between the members of the family, such as finding a course of action that will help the parents and troubled child have a more positive bond. Second, the child needs to experience the benefits of parental and adult involvement; this will enable the child to seek and value adult guidance. The third goal is for both the responsible adults and child to actively engage in problem-solving, sharing and evaluating ideas about how to change and better the situation. When these three goals have been accomplished, the youngster may become more open and communicative in general, and behave in a way that will help prevent similar problems in the future.

Professional helpers should teach parents, family members, and other responsible adults how to show understanding of the feelings and preferences held by a child or adolescent. Nonetheless, given that mature reasoning and judgment take time to develop, the adults should not let the youth be the sole decision-maker – unless a wise course of action is chosen.

The bottom line is that relevant adults and the child or adolescent should collaborate in the problem-solving efforts. Among family members, there should be openness, caring, and sharing, and respect for the values, beliefs, and preferences held by the others in the family. The parents (or caregivers), however, are responsible for guiding the child toward a positive solution. The professional helper can contribute to and facilitate these guidance efforts.

Gauging Maturity

As my three kids were growing up, it was common to hear them chide each other about "being immature" or, when one acted uppity, the other two would poke fun, saying, "Oh, aren't you so mature!" Likewise, throughout childhood and (especially) in adolescence, youngsters' arguments will claim maturity as a reason for parents to allow special privileges (such as hanging out at the mall, staying out late, driving the family car, etc.).

Although *maturity* refers to completed growth and development of mental, emotional, and physical qualities, it is far more. The mature person can effectively manage the self, such as in demonstrating self-awareness and self-control and making decisions that lead to positive outcomes. The mature person has a realistic knowledge of strengths, self-worth, and limitations, and understands how emotions are experienced and expressed. Also present is a wish to continually improve one's lot in life, which means being prepared to solve problems and overcome obstacles.

Mature persons can be trusted to uphold personally and socially relevant standards (honesty, integrity, decency), manage impulses or emotions so they do not disrupt their lives, cope with stress constructively, and be open to new information, ideas, and ways of doing things. Their actions take into account their life goals and being responsible for what they do. They are assertive without resorting to negative aggression.

Maturity is not a given; it has to be demonstrated in relationships with other people. The truly mature person engages with others and in creative ventures, including various activities and types of social relationships.

Professional helpers should advocate that, before being able to help children and adolescents, it is essential for adults themselves to be mature, that is, they must be capable of being aware of feelings, needs, and concerns, whether with a child or another adult. This requires treating others without bias (defined as an inclination, tendency, or preference based on other than the facts at hand); preordained ideas jeopardize the full potential of a relationship. These adverse conditions are quite appropriate for therapeutic interventions.

The awareness of another's qualities must be communicated. For example, the young person needs to know that the parent or responsible adult understands and cares. Views and preferences must be stated clearly and respectfully, along with a willingness to explain or negotiate any differences that occur in the adult–child relationship.

Social relationships involve intimacy, that is, a mutual or interpersonal emotional closeness. This sharing promotes trust and appropriate affection. In any sort of relationship, there should be a mutual influence. A demand by one person to control the other person will likely produce negative results.

Maturity also requires an understanding of the other person's world, such as the nature of the youth's social activities. Mature adults are in a good position to guide a child or adolescent to becoming a constructive member of the society or community, having respect for the rights of others, and abiding by social rules and laws.

People do not mature at the same rate. There can be slowness or delay, perhaps due to neurological, biological, or hereditary factors. There can be a crisis (e.g., a highly disruptive event in a child's life) that stunts the progress toward maturity. Thus, there are no definite age-related benchmarks for gauging or determining the level of maturity.

So when a child or adolescent claims maturity, a professional helper should assist the relevant adult(s) reflect back over the preceding ideas. Consideration should be given to how both the adult and the youth demonstrate self-management and handle relationships.

Talking with Kids

Many adults, including some well-trained professional helpers, find it very difficult to talk in a meaningful way with children and adolescents. Thus, it is no surprise to hear parents lament, "I try to talk to my kids, but they just clam up – I can't get anything out of them."

If the speaker, such as a parent, is sensitive to the mental ability, vocabulary, and verbal ability of a child, the language used must be understandable to the child. Good communication, however, is more than words.

Within the family and the classroom, the relevant adult has to convey that talking openly will be beneficial to both the youngster and the adult. Good communication calls for the adult to be sincere, open, caring, and sensitive. Without these qualities, the child or adolescent will not likely feel heard or understood and may go silent. The adult should talk *with*, not *to* the child or adolescent. For mental health services, these guidelines are essential when the topic of discussion is a problem that involves the young person. The following are some strategies that can be used by the professional helper.

After developing a positive relationship with a child of any age, the adult can explain the reason for the conversation, and seek the child's personal views about the situation and the need to talk about it. In a sense, this stage is for the definition of the problem or purpose.

Once the discussion is underway, the adult should avoid being a conductor of the comments. In general, the less direction from the adult, the better; however, the adult can set the stage for helping a kid learn how to solve problems.

An important step is to brainstorm for solutions by considering a variety of options, encouraging the child to express opinions about possible solutions. Of course the adult can offer ideas too. The discussion can then move to evaluating which of the options are feasible and likely to bring a good outcome. For example, if the youngster is prone to think that a negative condition can be eliminated by wishful thinking, the adult should listen and discuss the idea, but then guide the child to taking concrete actions to resolve the problem.

Ideally the responsible adult and child will agree on a decision and plan to implement it and see how it works. They would also agree to keep talking about whether the solution worked or other options should be tried. When an opportunity arises, the mental health professional should talk with them, regardless of age, about problem-solving and concrete actions,

An old adage says, "Silence is golden." When it comes to helping kids, this is a false notion. First, when a young person, particularly a teenager, becomes silent in the presence of an adult – especially an adult who is trying to talk to a youngster about a problem – the silent kid is likely anxious. The child becomes silent as a way of dealing with the source of the stress. Second, if the adult–child relationship is to be helpful, there must be communication. Yes, silence communicates, but its message is that a barrier exists.

Words and Deeds

At any age, communication with youngsters is challenging. This is especially true if the message is critical. No kid likes to hear about shortcomings, and most will resist demands to change.

Even if well-intended, not every responsible adult is able to overcome communication barriers with youngsters. Everyone knows that, to recall a line from the movie *Cool Hand Luke,* there can be big problems when there is a "failure to communicate."

As every mental health professional knows, conveying a message is not a simple thing. For example, while the parent may want to make a particular point to the child, the youngster's response to the parent will depend on more than just the words of the message itself. The relevant adult needs to be clear on the underlying intention and anticipate how the child or adolescent will perceive or interpret the message.

Let's assume that a child has misbehaved or has not been performing well in school. To attempt to improve the situation, the parent or teacher needs (perhaps with the help of a mental health professional) to plan the message, including what should be said, perhaps almost word for word. But more is needed.

The child will benefit from guidance, but only if the parent, teacher, or other responsible adult uses terms that can be understood by the child. For example, it is best to organize the bits of information in a way that will both teach and persuade, with the end result being guidance toward improved behavior or performance by the child or adolescent.

More than mere words are needed. Youngsters, as with all persons, are sensitive to the manner or tone of the speaker, as well as the accompanying nonverbal cues or actions.

There is much truth to the old adage "Actions speak louder than words." Mehrabian (1981) discusses the relative importance of verbal and nonverbal cues and concludes that, for the liking-effect of a message, 7% comes from the verbal (chosen words) elements, 38% comes from the vocal (intonation, projection, and resonance) elements, and 55% comes from the visual (facial and body expressions) elements (see pp. 75–80).

This research certainly supports another old adage: "It is not what you say, it is how you say it." In other words, if parents and other responsible adults want a child to hear and accept the message, they need to capitalize on communicating with the youngster in a way that offers positive vocal and visual reinforcement both in words and deeds.

When trying to help children and adolescents improve behavior or school performance, adults should create a positive framework for the information that is offered. Showing warmth and caring is essential; and this is communicated by the words, tone, and mannerisms of the adult. In addition, the total message should convey respect and sincerity. Finally, it is important to state the behavior that is the concern, and not to criticize or label the child or adolescent. In this way the adult and youngster can then pinpoint the desired behavior and collaborate on ways that will help the kid achieve it.

All of the foregoing ideas and principles are appropriate for the helping context. Mental health professionals commonly use teaching, insight, and reinforcement to help others, regardless of age, achieve these competencies.

Focus on the Kids

After spending a week in the mountains with two kids, 3 and 5 years old, I had a renewed awareness of the demands of parenting. Those two youngsters never stopped moving or talking. Their fast-paced activities created a blur. They darted here and there, got into things that they should have left alone, cluttered the house, and demanded immediate attention. They jabbered constantly, asking a barrage of questions and expressing opinions about everything imaginable.

When the week was over and they departed with their parents, all that came to mind was: "Whew, thank goodness it was just for a week!" And then I thought about how their parents were not getting a respite from the demands of child-rearing.

Many family problems arise because the parents are worn out by the rigors of taking care of the kids. Some parents hold up better than others. It is known that people vary in their resilience to stress, such as that which might be caused by taking care of the kids. Also, people vary in their motivation to want to take care of children.

Being a stepparent introduces the issue that, when the pairing with the parent occurred, the child was part of a package deal. However, the biological parent had bonded with the child from birth, and the stepparent may have to cultivate motivation to be involved in the raising of the child.

Even birth parents may flounder in their motivation to put the child ahead of their personal preferences or needs. However, the nature of an adult–child relationship demands that the adult consistently safeguard and nurture the child to the best of his or her ability. This is true even when the child is not part of one's immediate family. These conditions may call for involvement by a mental health professional.

For some reason, I am reminded of the time that, for several weeks, my neighbors and I joined forces to fence the perimeter of each of our acreages. It was hard work, and at times, we thought the job would never be finished.

By sunset each day, we were exhausted. Each evening, we would sit together, sipping a cooling drink, talking about the day, and poking fun at each other for not getting a post straight. We found that we were replenishing our energy, spirit, strength, and motivation.

By the next day, we were prepared to set more posts and stretch more wire. Eventually the job was completed, and to this day, when the three of us come together, we share memories of the experience and pride in our accomplishment.

After a hard day of child-rearing, every adult – some more than others – needs to replenish energy, spirit, strength, and motivation for the parenting role. For example, allowing each parent to have some personal time is essential to being prepared for the next day of parenting.

When a parent engages in rest, recreation, and creative activity, there will be benefits for both the parents and the children. Also, doing something that is just plain FUN contributes a great deal to the reservoir of resiliency demanded by parenting.

When it is a two-parent family, the professional helper should advocate that each parent should routinely take care of the kids to give the other parent some time out, whether it is actually going out alone to be with friends or family or staying home and having some personal space. For the one-parent family, the same principle applies. For example, two single parents can work out a swap, with one single parent taking care of another single parent's kids to allow relief from childcare.

Through it all, the key message is simply: "Because I am an adult, the kids come first." This should be a conscious idea. By focusing on the kids, their development leads to positive outcomes, and the rewards of parenting will increase. Later on, the parents, like my fence-building buddies, will share memories of the experience and pride in their accomplishments.

Learning to Trust

Each week on the television show *The X-Files,* the agent warned, "Trust no one." Although building suspense for television viewers, distrust is not a healthy quality to promote. If the skepticism or "paranoia" is too entrenched, the person can create barriers that lead to separation from others or from meaningful activities.

Everyone needs to realistically evaluate situations and people to decide whether they are trustworthy and safe. Certainly there are risks and dangers in the world, and there are people of whom we should be wary.

The challenge is to accurately assess and judge the conditions that are present. Professional help may be needed to gain these assessment and judgment skills.

From birth, the child faces the challenge of developing trust. Parents who provide consistent and empathic nurturing enable the child to trust, not only parents but the world. If they fail to give proper care and protection, the child may suffer and grow up believing that people will not be dependable in relationships. Trust in others is the basis for confronting the challenges that the child faces at various stages of development through adulthood. Developing realistic trust, which is essential for healthy and constructive relationships, is often an ongoing theme in mental health services.

It is during adolescence that young people begin to move toward being independent and wanting to make their own decisions. There is, of course, good reason to cultivate the child's ability to make decisions. In fact, a primary purpose of parenting is to help the child grow into being a self-determining adult who can make wise decisions.

Before a child can be allowed to be self-determining, parents want to see signs that the child can consistently and accurately recognize what is occurring or could happen, and consider the alternatives. As cognitive development progresses, the adolescent is better able to move toward analysis of, thinking about, and judging situations before making a decision to take an action.

By giving guidance to the child, relevant adults help promote this level of mental processing. For example, they should let the child or adolescent know the family and societal values and how they apply to the life situations that the youngster faces.

I'll bet that almost all adults have heard a child say, "You don't trust me!" This common refrain likely occurs when the child wants to do something that the parents oppose. It is a ploy to make the parents feel guilty and to cave in to the preferences of the child.

By definition, guilt is a feeling of discomfort elicited from the sense of having hurt, harmed, or disappointed another person. When offering guidance to a child, there is absolutely no reason for a parent or other responsible adult to feel guilty. On the contrary, the adult should sense pride in making a good faith effort to help the child develop into a healthy adult decision-maker. Of course, the adult should be open-minded to information that might improve the quality of what is said to the child or adolescent, such as discussing certain concerns with knowledgeable others, such as professional helpers of every kind.

As for the "you don't trust me" assertion, a reasonable answer is, "It is not a matter of not trusting, it is a matter of safeguarding you." If said with love and caring, with no negative tone, the child will recognize the blessing of having a responsible parent or other responsible adult(s) in his or her life.

Outside Influences

Knowing how and when to guide children and adolescents requires more than just monitoring for blatant problems. Certainly, parents and other responsible adults need to keep a wary eye on how the youngster is behaving, and be ready to take steps to reduce any observable emotional distress or problem behavior. It is also necessary, however, to focus on the daily interactions that the child has with caregivers, siblings, other youngsters, and teachers and so on and assess the external influences that are in the kid's life.

The surrounding environment influences the child's daily interactions and motivations to change. The issue for the adult is to evaluate whether the child's interactions with others are constructive or destructive and whether the motivations that are evident suggest that youngster is developing in a positive or negative manner. Effectively confronting this challenge may require assistance from a mental health professional.

A child does not talk or act the same way with everyone or in every place. To some degree, the child will determine by the context what to say and do. For child development, *context* refers to what the child witnesses in the everyday events that occur and the conditions that are present in given situations. Contextual factors influence the child's thinking, judgment, learning, and other mental processes.

When adults help children, regardless of age, they should contextualize the experience. The resources that are available from the family, the school, and the community (e.g., social service agencies) construct the context for helping. Within the limits or realities afforded by the context, the child should be encouraged to seek self-regulation.

Self-regulation is important because children and adolescents are constantly exposed to temptations to think and act in ways that could prove to be problematic. The proper goal is for the child to be able to exercise independent thinking and decision-making in accord with the positive values, beliefs, and morals of the youngster's family and society. The foregoing is a tall order, and certainly justifies potential involvement by a variety of professional helpers.

If the child or adolescent is allowed to move into a negative context, say associating with peers with antisocial values and conduct, the influences will contradict the positive intentions of the parents, school, and community. Although there will always be external contextual influences that are beyond full control by relevant adults, a stronger family can become dominant in the child's development by emphasizing appropriate values, beliefs, and morals to create a positive familial/social culture. The challenge is for adult wisdom (1) to assist the youngster in being aware of the negative consequences that may arise from the context, and (2) to guide the young person toward a more constructive and healthy context.

For adults who sense they need assistance, professional helpers (e.g., educators and other human service workers) can help promote parental leadership, as well as family management and strengths. Of course, other types of professional helpers (e.g., in education, mental health, health care, social service, and law enforcement) can be important allies and provide supportive guidance as well.

Judging Influences

Two major aspects of effective parenting are protecting youngsters from bad influences and helping them have positive experiences. Therefore, it is appropriate for parents, family members, and other responsible adults to exercise judgment about what a child of any age does or does not experience. Simply because there is an opportunity to do something does not necessarily mean that the young person should do it. It is up to responsible adults to evaluate whether the activity is age appropriate for the child and positive and constructive.

Influence can occur simply by a child being exposed to something. Mere exposure is the underlying principle of advertisements. For example, if a person, whether an adult or a child, passes a billboard each day that touts a product or has a picture of an attractive person, the elements of the portrayal are implanted in the person's mind. The young mind is highly impressionable. In contrast, an adult's mind commonly has better-developed values and beliefs by which to evaluate influences such as an advertisement, and decide whether to accept or reject it.

The frequency of exposure also enters into the effects of a message, such as in an advertisement. Whether for an adult or a youth, seeing or hearing the same thing over and over and over increases the likelihood that the message will take hold. Research supports the idea that even if the person encounters a neutral stimulus or message, repeated exposure will increase the person's acceptance of it. Why? Because the person develops an understanding, which may be realistic or unrealistic, about the various components of the message, and that detailed understanding leads the person to be prone to having a positive reaction to it.

Among other possible influences, parents and other responsible adults should be aware of the models to which a child or adolescent is exposed. At any stage of life, the power of *social modeling* can lead a person to adopt values, beliefs, preferences, and actions demonstrated by others to whom he or she is exposed. This is, of course, readily evident in the use of beautiful and high-status celebrities in marketing.

Beyond celebrities, the effects of social modeling are present in commonplace encounters in daily life. The old adage "You are known by the people with whom you associate" targets the influence that comes from encounters with other people. Here, again, responsible adults should exercise their judgment about which personal contacts will offer children and adolescents positive influences.

Adults should not be hesitant to monitor children's exposures to influences. Any notion that the child should be self-determining is illogical. Indeed, throughout life, anyone can potentially benefit by having another caring person point out that certain influences seem to be impacting on the situation.

Until a youngster gains cognitive and emotional maturity, relevant adults have the responsibility to monitor possible influences, offer guidance, and in some instances, impose behavioral controls, such as when a kid refuses appropriate adult guidance. Sometimes adults must resort to saying, "No, you cannot do that!" In those instances, the adults should also offer the child or adolescent an explanation for the decision and the concern about the influence. Responsible adults, especially parents, should continue to show love and support, even when saying no, and propose other opportunities that will introduce more positive influences.

All of the goals described in this section may be difficult to fulfill. Therefore, the mental health professional should fortify those who face these challenges, regardless of age, to gain a positive outcome for these issues.

Helping a Child Change

Telling a child or adolescent that he or she had "better change or else" is most likely a reflection of the adult's frustration. Rather than an emotional threat, good child guidance takes a rational approach, accepts that change is difficult, and involves helping a child learn how to make changes. The first step is to recognize when an attitude or behavior is creating a problem for the youngster. The relevant adult(s) should not sermonize about the potentially problematic attitude or behavior.

Since people of any age are prone to rebel against demands or directives, it is best to let the child or adolescent describe the situation. Indeed, some people, when told that they cannot or that they must do a particular thing, quickly exhibit "psychological reactance." This stance means they go ahead and do the opposite of the demand. For helping young people, triggering psychological reactance would be an undesirable outcome

By personally talking about the attitude or behavior, the kid is more likely to accept that it is his or her issue to handle and understand its characteristics and possible consequences. The potential problem is then "owned" by the one person who can do something concrete about it, namely the youngster.

During the various developmental stages, adults can help children start to identify the likely consequences of attitudes or behaviors. After a bit of consideration and discussion, the child will typically contemplate in real terms whether change to avoid the situation is justified.

It is the adult's responsibility to help a child know the behavior that is expected and why it will bring a good result for the youngster. For example, it is common for a child to resist change, saying something like "I don't want to do it that way," and to be resistant to adopting a new kind of behavioral response. Again, the relevant adult is in a position to assist the child in identifying what the new behavior will look like, why it is the best way to behave, and what will be the likely outcome.

There can be a discussion about what will help the young person achieve the behavior and how effort and progress will be monitored. The child or adolescent should, of course, play a major part in determining, evaluating, and controlling efforts to change behavior.

It is important to maintain any change. Once there has been even a small accomplishment of change, adults should consistently reinforce the child's decisions and attempts to change. Praise, linked to particular positive efforts, will help establish the new behavior until the youngster begins to sense his or her own internal reward or pride in the accomplishments.

At some point, the desired attitudinal or behavioral goal will be achieved. The child or adolescent should be credited with the success. Parents, family members, or other responsible adults should not try to take away the accomplishment with a comment like "I knew that you could do it because you are my kid." Instead of an "I told you so" response, every adult should express sincere respect for the child's commitment and ability to change.

Authoritative Parenting

Just prior to the second year of life, the infant becomes aware of his or her image in the mirror. Thereafter and for the rest of life, the individual constantly explores personal identity and the image that he or she presents to others. Sometimes the image that we have of ourselves is realistic, but sometimes it is not accurate, because of a lack of self-understanding.

There are two major aspects of the self that the child develops in relation to the parents' care and style of child-rearing. First, there is a sense of relatedness to others. This means that the child feels secure, loved, and valued, and therefore can and does trust others, feeling close and connected to them. Second, there is the sense of autonomy or a sense of the ability to be separate – to value one's own uniqueness and competence, and be self-determining.

Both relationships with others and autonomy are central to developing a self-concept for healthy functioning in childhood and adolescence, and throughout adulthood. Feeling adequate in both of these aspects of the self means that the youngster will experience much-needed self-esteem.

Parenting style can be a factor as to how a child develops the self. *Authoritative* means parents have and enforce rules, but they also allow the child to exercise a reasonable amount of freedom within the rules of the family. To be sure that the child does not make a faulty judgment, the authoritative parent provides and discusses the reasons for the rules of the household, and thus what is expected in the conduct of the youngster. In addition, authoritative parents show warmth and support and also encourage the child to contribute to defining the boundaries for behavior. To structure their own behavior, kids need both love and specified boundaries from their parents.

The authoritative parent should not be confused with the *authoritarian* parent who has rules and boundaries that are rigidly administered without explanation, guidance, or love. This pattern of parenting is not helpful to the self-concept. Commonly, authoritarian parenting hinders the child's development of positive self-esteem.

Equally detrimental is the overly permissive parent, who takes little interest in the child, expresses few expectations of the child, and lets the youngster be more self-determining than is justified by the child's level of maturity. With overly permissive parenting, the child often develops an exaggerated sense of self-importance and entitlement. Both authoritarian and overly permissive parents tend to produce low self-esteem in their offspring.

Without adequate self-esteem, the child will have doubts, which can lead to a lack of the internal discipline that is necessary for maturity and achievement. There will likely be a negative impact on learning and social relations that will lead to a less rewarding life than would otherwise be possible.

Self-esteem must, of course, be rooted in reality. Developing an unrealistic notion about one's capabilities can be unhealthy. Recognizing that there are limitations to personal resources, qualities, and characteristics is not the same as low self-esteem. On the contrary, knowing what can and cannot likely be done in the classroom or elsewhere can instill a confidence for entering into a situation or relationship in a healthy fashion. Assisting the child develop realistic self-esteem should be a goal for parents and other adults who wish to help kids.

Professional helpers should assist all relevant adults to support and implement authoritative parenting. When offering guidance, certainly, mental health professionals should steer relevant adults away from authoritarian and overly permissive ideas, and teach them how to adopt authoritative qualities.

Separation Anxiety

Professional helpers need to prepare relevant adults to anticipate changes in a child's emotions and behaviors. For example, parents may find the challenge particularly great when it involves their first child. Also, the years of early childhood, such as when the child is preparing to enter school for the first time, can bring on a rapid-fire series of developmental changes – for both the child and the adults in his or her life.

By reading about child-rearing, parents can gain awareness of how a child develops and what may be coming next in terms of emotions or behaviors. In addition, it makes sense to talk about children's growth and development with family members, neighbors, friends, and especially other responsible adults with special training. Teachers are, of course, an excellent resource for information about child development, and every parent should seek to establish a strong connection with each teacher who enters into a child's life, which will enable effective family–school collaboration.

When a child enters preschool or kindergarten, it is normal for both the child and the parents to have mixed feelings. On the one hand, it is a new adventure that can give the child priceless experiences in learning and social relations with other children. On the other hand, it still means that "the baby bird is leaving the nest," even if it is for just a few hours.

The change in the almost constant contact between parent and child can create uneasiness. Both a parent and a child can be anxious about being left alone. The move to independence is part of normal development, and should not bring on alarm or even negative thoughts. For example, to immerse the child in a parent's anxiety will likely lead to what psychologists call *separation anxiety disorders*. Yes, an adult can have the same sort of disorder, and an intervention by a mental health professional may be needed.

It is essential that a child develops a sense of being able to handle situations, and this includes separation from parents or other caregivers. (Throughout this book, self-management is emphasized.) Obviously a parent or other responsible adult will not, throughout life, always be at the child's elbow ready to step forward to protect against bad judgments or missteps. Venturing out alone into the safe environment of the school, the child progressively learns how to handle things that were previously taken care of by watchful adults. Without these experiences, the child's development will be fraught with problems.

When young children have not had ongoing experiences of being briefly absent from parents or other caregivers, they may not be ready for school. A child who does not want to leave home can develop an unrealistic fear about being without parents or caregivers – even for a few hours.

If a child is fearful, cries, or refuses to go to school, adults should be consistently supportive, listening to the child's concerns while also continuing to take the child to school and leaving him or her with the teacher. When the adults take this stance, the child then has the consistent opportunity to adapt and cope with the new situation.

Parents and caregivers who are ambivalent and allow the child to stay home do not help the situation and may be revealing their own worries about the separation. In some cases, professional help may be necessary to help the child overcome extreme anxiety, as shown in acting tense and being worried, unable to concentrate, and fidgeting. Research supports the conclusion that the preferred professional intervention would involve the parents and caregivers being included in the services provided to the children. However, the parental/caregiver involvement needs to be tapered off, otherwise it would be a continuation of unhealthy attachment.

Giving Advice

When someone else is having a problem, most outsiders have 20/20 insight into the cause and cures. If the person with the problem is someone with whom there is a caring connection – such as a family member, a neighbor, a fellow worker – it is common to want to step into the situation and try to solve the difficulty. The first impulse is to offer the solution that seems obvious. Of course, to the one with the problem, the solution is not so simple.

Giving advice involves offering another person a prescription (what should be done) or a proscription (what should not be done). For the outsider, the answer may seem clear and undeniable, which may lead to a directive. The person receiving the advice, however, may interpret the comment as being a demand that takes away self-determination – an "I know more than you do" put-down, or a smart-aleck response.

Clint was locked in a battle with his teenage daughter, Brittney, over her refusal to abide by family rules. It had reached the point where any verbal exchange between them ended in a shouting match, a battle of wits, or neither hearing what the other was trying to communicate.

Since Clint was the father and had characteristics of being strong willed (some might say he was set in his ways), he was not about to let any other family member tell him how he should treat Brittney. At the same time, he was well aware that, although he hesitated to admit it, he was at his wits' end.

When approaching another person in a deadlock situation, the parent or other relevant adults must accept that, despite the undeniable hurt from, and irresponsibility of, the teenager, the youngster needs understanding and help. There can be no victory by conquest, only by assistance, information, and love.

Family members and friends (as well as mental health professionals) who wished to support Clint would likely accomplish more by offering him information than by giving advice. In other words, Clint needs more knowledge and skills, which will be learned, accepted, and implemented only by his self-determinations.

When talking to Clint, plain-folks language is necessary. First, he should hear an acknowledgement that he is the decision-maker: "As Brittney's father, you certainly know the things that go on better than anyone else, certainly better than I could ever know."

The next step is to offer Clint information that has been helpful to oneself. For example: "Everyone is unique, but I remember when I was having problems with my son, Juan, I had to bite my tongue many times and even though I thought he was the one who should apologize to me and do what I say, I found that he eventually responded when I took the first step toward putting the argument behind us – in fact, now that I think about it, I took many, many first steps, but I guess that's what being a parent requires."

By receiving information in a sharing and nondirective way, Clint is more likely to give it a second thought later on. Although not said openly, speaking in the informational manner also accomplishes modeling – that is, letting Clint see how he could talk differently to Brittney to get her to be open to change.

Whether it is a professional helper or a layperson trying to help anyone solve a problem, there is a need to empower the person to make more effective decisions. Information is the basis for all decisions, and the helping person should provide support for analyzing the situation, identifying possible actions, and taking steps toward change. These same principles apply to any relationship, whether is adult–youth or adult–adult; moreover, they apply to parent consultation by a mental health professional (Holcomb-McCoy & Bryan, 2010).

Breaking Through

Although Jeffrey's parents had divorced, each had regular contact with him throughout the years, but when each remarried, Jeffrey was never comfortable with either of the new stepparents. More and more, he lived with his paternal grandparents, who were very attentive to his every need.

Jeffrey had always been a good kid, conscientious about the feelings of adults and other kids alike, a mediocre but erstwhile student, and seemingly following a positive pathway toward adulthood. Then he changed.

After graduation from high school, Jeffrey dropped out of his courses at a community college, broke up with his long-time girlfriend, got fired from several fast-food jobs for mouthing off, and became unmotivated for anything. He stopped looking for a job and had no wish to go to college. Then he started having money that he received from unknown sources, seemed belligerent and was sleeping a lot, was caught in numerous little white lies, and began alienating everyone, including his devoted grandparents.

Obviously drug use was suspected, but it was impossible to talk with Jeffrey about it or what he was experiencing. Ill feelings were destroying all lines of communications. All of the adults in his extended family wondered, how could barriers like this be overcome?

First, when there is a clear problem, it is important to keep talking and talking and talking, but always in an understanding and listening sort of way. However, there should be no condoning or reinforcing of bad behavior. When family members give support of any kind, they should expect the youngster to earn it by responsible actions.

Second, each adult must own up to being in a helping role. This often means setting aside one's own pride to help the troubled youth. For example, when grandpa was so insulted by the belligerence and lying that he quit talking to, and started avoiding, Jeffrey, this was contradictory to helping. A professional helper reminded Grandpa that he was of critical importance to "saving" Jeffrey, which meant being the one to take the first steps toward rebuilding a positive relationship between the two of them. (Grandpa told Jeffrey, "There's no excuse for the bad stuff that happened but the past is behind us. Let's both start being more positive.")

Third, in this sort of disruptive scenario, everyone in the family, and often friends as well, is affected by the problem. In other words, what impacts on one person will influence everyone else in the family system.

Although it is logical that those closest to Jeffrey, such as the grandparents and biological parents, would seemingly have the most potential for helping, others, such as the stepparents, should not shy away from helping in appropriate ways. For example, the stepparents should not bad mouth the kid or demand that their spouses disown Jeffrey; rather, they should offer their spouses behind the scenes support for their efforts to help him.

Fourth, if or when it becomes apparent that guidance from a professional helper is needed, the adults – again, all of those in the family system – should offer individually to be available in whatever way the professional believes would contribute to the therapeutic intervention. Unified support for each other, as well as for Jeffrey, might prove to be the key to a successful outcome.

Fifth and finally, it is necessary to move on from the negative experiences, just as Grandpa proposed to Jeffrey (at last report, things were going better – Jeffrey went on to become a US Marine!). Obviously, most people would remember, say, an angry outburst from a loved one or some abusive act, such as lying. But it is not a matter of forgetting – it is a matter of forgiving. Learning from the bad experience can help family members teach what to avoid in the future and what to try to maintain in the family relationships.

These five strategies involve complexities. Consequently, when there are disruptive situations along these lines, that may be a clarion call for invention by a mental health professional.

5 Preparation for Learning

In Chapter 4, numerous important principles for dealing with children and adolescents were presented. The intent was to alert mental health professionals to the sort of information they should be sure is known by the parents, family members, and other responsible adults.

A major theme was that everyone is motivated by psychological needs; beyond protection, care, and the basics of food and shelter, each person has a unique set of needs that seek fulfillment. At the different developmental stages, one's self-concept is formed, and support from parents, family members, and other responsible adults will help the child mature and move toward self-actualization (for the needs of achieving safety, trust, belongingness, love, respect, and self-esteem).

Regardless of age, a person needs emotional feeding from others. If deprived of positive emotions from, say, parents or other caregivers, some children will resort to misbehavior because they sense that a negative emotional reaction (e.g., anger) is better than no emotional reaction at all.

The professional helper needs to assist adults in understanding and accepting that communicating with youngsters is not always easy. It is not unusual for an adult to try to talk with a child about an important matter, only to have the child clam up. In both Chapters 3 and 4, I offered some ideas that provide for effective communication skills with kids, such as matching the language to the child's mental and verbal abilities, and being supportively in tune with the child (by being sincere, open, caring, and sensitive). Professional helpers should teach these techniques to relevant adults. Since it is so important, communication is discussed throughout this book.

When it comes to solving problems, it is best for adults to explain the reason for a communication (i.e., define the problem or the purpose); talk *with,* not *to* a youngster; and encourage the kid to express opinions about possible solutions. I mentioned that, contrary to an old adage, silence is not golden.

Whether directed toward childhood or adolescence, adult guidance is highly demanding. Regardless of age, everyone needs to replenish his or her spirit and energy through rest, recreation, and creative activity. Dealing effectively with kids well requires that the relevant adult(s) have strength and energy. Incidentally, this applies to professional helpers as well; they must be on guard against so-called professional burnout.

Recognizing that the kids come first, adults need to help youngsters learn to realistically trust others and develop their own problem-solving skills. At any age, a child should play a major part in determining, evaluating, and controlling efforts to change his or her behavior. The adult alone cannot accomplish change.

Parenting and other forms of child guidance should be authoritative, but not authoritarian. Praise from an adult, linked to positive efforts by the youth, will help establish new behaviors until the child or adolescent can experience internal rewards from personal accomplishments. An end objective is for adults to guide youngsters to have healthy differentiation and separation. This is a defining dimension for the helping process provided by mental health professionals.

For a child or adolescent to be on a positive developmental track and progress into maturity, there must be effective learning. In this chapter, I will describe how to motivate kids to want to learn new things and how to sort out good and bad influences.

Reducing the Speed

From the time that children can get their balance and start to be mobile, until they achieve some degree of maturity, they do not seem inclined to walk – they seem to always travel faster than the eye can follow. In fact, the toddler stage could be more aptly named the "speeder stage."

Since parents (and other caregivers) have so many responsibilities, they have to always be multitaskers. Arriving home from work, parents need a few minutes of down time, such as for reading the newspaper or catching the evening news on television. They would like to have time just to relax their minds, maybe indulge in a hobby, nap, a soak in a hot tub, or just be free of demands for a few minutes. Instead, they must do routine chores, like cooking and cleaning, and be continually aware of what the children are doing.

Parenthood and caretaking impose a constant demand to monitor all of the child's activities. The safety and welfare of the child must be foremost in the adult's mind. The guardian or caretaking role is not made easier by the child's indulgence in fast movements and a never-ending need to be active.

Every child benefits from being active, at least to a point. Doing physical and mental things stimulate learning and development. The inactive, reclusive child needs to be motivated. However, hyperactivity can prove to be too much of a good thing.

Parents and teachers are particularly aware of children who cannot sit still, are always wiggling or getting out of their seats, making distracting movements, and who are unable to stay on assigned tasks. If not modified or if maturity does not eliminate it, hyperactivity can have a devastating effect on socialization, academic learning, and general quality of life. For severe and chronic problems, there are professional interventions or treatments, including medications. Mental health professionals should be well versed in how to deal with hyperactivity.

For kids who seem to do everything fast, most will grow out of it. In the meantime, of course, the weary parents and caregivers are left to their own devices to try to reduce the speed. Doing so will help the child and potentially allow the adults to enjoy more time in activities that they need for their own good. If the adults' resources are exhausted, everyone's interests are in jeopardy.

To slow children down, it is important for the parents and other responsible adults to agree with each other about what seems to trigger excessive activity. It may be something as simple as a bad diet, such as ingesting too much sugar and caffeinated drinks.

Professional helpers should teach parents how to explain to the speedy child that haste make waste and is not good for either the child or the adults. The adults need to know how to tell the child the rules of the road, such as "If you are leaving the dining room or family room to go to your bedroom, you must walk – you must not run." When a child breaks the household speed limit, the adults must consistently admonish the child in a firm (but caring) tone of voice. There should be no negative emotion, such as anger. Likewise, frustration should not be revealed.

Without emotionalized badgering or negative criticisms, adults should require that the child repeat the route, such as walking to the bedroom to which the child had previously run, and show approval of this accomplishment. If the child inappropriately resists these adult directions or becomes obstinate, the situation has moved to a problem level, and it may be time for the family to receive guidance from a mental health professional.

To address the problem, parents and caregivers should give the child calm but frequent reminders of the adverse effects that pandemonium has on both the child and the adults. Also, the child should be disciplined in an appropriate way, such as losing a privilege.

When the child starts to control his or her helter-skelter pace, a reward, such as a privilege or positive comment, should be used. Children react well to praise for changes in their behavior.

All of the foregoing goals are suitable for mental health services. Professional helpers should not shy away from reinforcing the parents, family members, and other responsible adults to be control agents for kids.

Being Motivated

When my three kids were young, I often thought about what I could do to motivate them to do constructive things. I especially wanted them to learn new things.

I tried not to be too heavy handed when I restricted their watching mindless television. For most programs, they had to do some task to earn viewing rights. They had regular chores around the house, which could bring them a chance to do something they wanted to do.

Even when they were young, it was obvious to me that my offspring governed their own efforts. If there was no wish to cooperate or to act responsibly, my wishes and intentions were thwarted.

Child psychologists would say that my efforts were to promote intrinsic motivation – the child's own desire to be curious, think, and have an interest in the world, to want to learn about numerous topics and do stimulating activities.

To accept an idea, like learning or doing something new, children must believe that there is a direct or indirect benefit. This is where parents and other responsible adults come into the picture.

Guiding children and adolescents involves two things: helping the youngster be competent and helping him or her recognize personal ability. Young people who achieve and recognize their competence will deal effectively with the learning environment, which is necessary to survive and thrive. These accomplishments can then lead to further success in tasks and activities. A personal sense of competence becomes part of an identity that can persist and cope with difficult circumstances.

Every child is unique, but there are some common trends found with most kids. Research tells us that, as children get older, they may tend to be less positive or optimistic about their capabilities, and their motivations may change. Whereas young children are eager to learn new things, older children may start to decline in motivation to learn school subjects.

By the teenage years, external values, such as messages from parents and family members, become less influential, and the child's internalized values take over. This means, of course, that all through childhood, the relevant adults should be offering guidance. For example, a warm and supportive home life will help shape the child as he or she gradually becomes self-determining.

Although some children, especially during the teenage years, may question or criticize their parents' or family's values, research shows that, as they move toward adulthood, they often accept many parental or family values, even if they may not demonstrate them exactly as their parents or family members do.

With my kids, who are now adults, I can easily see how they listened to and accepted the parental messages. Each seems to reveal values much like mine – for example, commitment to work and openness to new learning.

Information for Kids

Being concerned about behavior problem children, I have been searching through research reports for practical ideas about how to keep kids on the straight and narrow. As my three youngsters were growing up, I came to realize how each one would come home with ideas that were not heard from me. They were getting information about life from all sorts of sources: the kids at school and in the community, neighbors, and especially what they saw on television. I came to realize that the term *parental guidance* was of great importance to my effort to be a responsible parent.

Psychologists who study influences on children and why they turn out the way they do emphasize the type and quality of the information that the child receives. Whether in a classroom, at home, or watching

TV, what the youngster learns will determine beliefs, values, morals, motives, and most of all, judgment in problem situations.

Research now makes it clear that exposure to violent TV, movies, and video games is related to actual violent behavior. The American Psychological Association (1996) studied the matter, and concluded that a steady diet of violence on TV increased the viewer's fear of becoming a victim, desensitized the viewer to violence, encouraged some viewers to become more involved in violent acts, supported ideas that aggression and violence could be used to obtain things, and (with R- and X-rated videotapes) increased sexual aggression in some males.

Allowing a child to watch an R- or X-rated video with images of violence and degrading of others cannot be justified. It seems unlikely that any responsible adult would want a youngster to grow up believing that violence is okay or other people do not deserve respect. A harmful view about violence and dealing with others would, of course, promote the possibility of criminal conduct, racism, sexism, and other sorts of antisocial ideas and actions.

It is inappropriate to totally ban depictions of violence on TV and in movies. Under our Constitutional rights, adults should not be prohibited from having access to information, except under extreme conditions. There is, however, solid reason to believe that responsible adults, especially parents, must consistently monitor the information that children and adolescents receive, and provide ongoing guidance to assure the development of healthy and constructive beliefs, values, morals, motives, and judgment.

Recently, there has been increased professional interest in "whether video games may be put to some good use or are just games in the end" (Ferguson, 2010, p. 66). Olson (2010) provides a revealing analysis of social motivations for video game play, such as using video games for peer interactions with a shared teaching component, developing friends, opportunities for leadership, regulation of feelings ("forgetting problems and coping with loneliness" and "video games can do more than purge negative feelings; they can provide fun and stimulation to promote a positive mood," p. 182), and intellectual and expressive motivations. However, the potential for adverse affects from the appeal of violent and mature content still merits strong concern, especially among mental health professionals, and deserves consideration in professional helping.

Creative Play

During several holiday seasons, I have wandered through toy stores and been struck by how many of the boxes had language that bragged about the learning that would occur. I commonly come away wondering whether playing with a toy for sheer enjoyment has become secondary to learning with a toy.

Adults certainly want all children to be, as Garrison Keillor says about the folks living in his mythical Lake Wobegon, "all above-average." However, adults should want them to enjoy being children too. Playfulness is a valuable personal quality (including for adults).

Mental health professionals need to educate adults, regardless of their connection to children and adolescents, that "kids are not mini-adults," "kids will be kids," and "all work and no play" is unhealthy (for people of any age). There are two ways to combine play and learning for a child, namely through socialization and creativity.

Playing alone is fine up to a point. It allows a child to explore how things work, which can lead to new ideas. Every child can, however, benefit from play activities involving other kids. By socializing with others, especially of the same age, a child observes behaviors and their consequences. An adult's watchful eye can assure that inappropriate behavior is not rewarded during playtime.

From studying healthy people, Maslow (1968, 1970) noted their "greatly increased creativity." Being creative does not require being an artist. Few of adults will be blessed with becoming a master of a musical instrument or of painting, sculpture, dance, photography, and the like. Just experimenting with everyday things is helpful to the person.

Years ago, I worked in a mental hospital in the United Kingdom, studying the effects of psychotherapy versus occupational therapy. Somewhat to our surprise, the research supported that often a person, such as someone wallowing in depression or posttraumatic stress, experienced as many or more gains from working with crafts as from seeing a psychotherapist.

So it is with toys. By playing and experimenting with toys, the child begins to learn that there are often different ways to solve a puzzle. The child may or may not be aware of the creativity that goes into the problem-solving, but the child is enriched by the underlying creative component.

Also, creative play has been proven to bring on good emotions. Accomplishing a task, such as getting the final piece of a puzzle in place, leads to a sense of pleasure. Being in a good mood leads to better learn-ing than being down in the dumps.

To make creative play especially useful, the professional helper should encourage relevant adults to share the activity. For example, a parent's presence in playing a game is a priceless complement to the child's learning and development.

With my kids, I found that the learning activities not only helped them, I enjoyed playing like a child (yes, adults need to be playful too). Which brings us back to the toy store. I wonder how many toys are bought for the children and how many are bought because the adults want to play with them? Ideally, the toy should be appropriate for the child, but when an adult plays with a child and enjoys a toy or game, the adult's life is enriched too.

Being on Time

Anyone who is routinely and inexcusably late to an appointment casts a negative net over the encounter. When there is a specific time for meet-ing someone, failing to be on time is potentially insulting. Certainly a professional helper should NEVER be late to an appointment with a client.

A person kept waiting may accept the tardiness the first time, but even then, whatever occurs may be tainted by feelings that impact communi-cations and the relationship. Put politely, the scheduled meeting is off to a bad start.

Consider a visit to a physician or dentist. Assume that you have an appointment for a specific time, and the practitioner is "tied up with an-other patient" until well past the designated time of your appointment. If this sort of faulty service delivery occurs, you will not likely view the practitioner positively.

For what it is worth, I have a general rule, if I have an appointment and the physician is late beyond 30 minutes, I cancel the appointment, walk out, and write a letter to the practitioner criticizing the inefficient scheduling – to me, tardiness is an indicator of nonprofessionalism. Moreover, a disgruntled patient can write a letter to or file a complaint with the practitioner's state-level licensing board. Or if the services are within, say, a hospital, the patient can write a letter of criticism to the administrator of the health care facility.

The foregoing comments emphasize the violation of a patient's rights. The above example also indicates that timeliness reflects efficiency, whereas tardiness reflects inefficiency – and is potentially insulting to the patient and a sign of poor professional functioning.

Contrary to what some health care practitioners would like patients to believe, there is absolutely no reasonable excuse for habitual tardiness. If a physician is too busy to see a patient for a particular appointment, the physician is apt to provide substandard health care.

An efficient person plans for being on time. The possibility of a delay is anticipated and built into the mental schedule by which the person operates. There can, of course, be an unexpected event that makes it impossible to keep to a schedule. However, an unforeseeable barrier is the sort of thing that should be the exception and not the rule.

Now let us apply the issue of timeliness to raising children and connect it to learning. A simple example is when a child has a homework assignment. The teacher expects that the assignment will be turned in on a designated day and at a particular time. If the child fails to complete the task on schedule, it is logical that the teacher will give the child a low grade or no grade at all. Consequently, the parents will frown on the child's unimpressive report card.

Like so many things, effective guidance of children and adolescents requires that relevant adults set a good example. Within the context of parenting, if a parent cannot get things done as planned, the message to the child will not be a good one. For example, if the parent agrees to pick up a child after school at a certain time, the child should not be kept waiting.

Another challenge is for adults to keep track of or monitor how well children fulfill schedules. If a child does not consistently meet a deadline, there should be adult guidance about planning, prioritizing other activities, and ways by which the child can more efficiently accomplish assignments.

Adults should reinforce or praise the child's getting things done on schedule. When adults cultivate timeliness in childhood, they are preparing the child for rewarding experiences in the work world, and in social and family relationships. It is important that professional helpers model and reinforce timeliness to children, adolescents, and adults alike.

The Cluttered Room

Another message for mental health professionals to convey to everyone is that an important goal is to help all children grow up to be efficient in tasks. For anyone, child or adult, getting the job done requires being able to make full use of resources, implement a plan, and monitor the success or failure of the effort. The payoff from being efficient is pride and satisfaction in an accomplishment, which leads some people to believe that work is its own reward.

What keeps some people from being efficient? There are two types of personalities to consider: disorganized and organized. Figuratively and literally, the disorganized person allows blocks to occur that will impede accomplishments, whereas the organized person keeps the road to achievement clear of debris.

By the way, although the word *debris* is usually associated with objects that have no usefulness, it is possible for the disorganized person to harbor mental debris as well. In other words, the disorganized person may hold on to ideas, attitudes, and beliefs that have no usefulness and end up cluttering the mind – resulting in inefficiency.

The disorganized person is prone to let things go unattended. That is, the disorganized person ignores the old saw "Don't put off until tomorrow what you can do today." As a result, when there is a task to complete, the process is slowed down, perhaps even stopped, by all the disarray in the person's lifestyle.

In contrast, the organized person is committed to accomplish the most from any effort. To grease the skids, the organized person makes sure that there is no blockage.

When my kids were in their preteen years, they and I were taught an important lesson by the way they kept their respective bedrooms. One child discarded clothing, books, toys, or whatever over every square inch of the bedroom floor. In the bedrooms on either side of the seemingly disorganized child, the other two of my children kept tidy rooms. With those two, generally everything was in its place, and all objects were well ordered. Comic books had to have plastic covers and be filed in sequence. Even articles of clothing were folded and placed in their proper places in the chest of drawers.

At first blush, it would seem that the cluttered room would be an indicator of a disorganized personality. Indeed, at the time that was probably true. However, with maturity, the disorganized child eventually came to realize that an organized life would be beneficial and more enjoyable.

Today, thankfully, all three of my offspring, now adults, seem to enjoy clear sailing. There is no clutter in any of their houses. Each throws away any object that does not have a good reason for being retained. Consequently, they seem to make the most of the tasks and efforts needed for careers and family life.

The point here is simple. Adults should do their part to set a good example and guide children and adolescents toward getting jobs done efficiently. Even if the effort does not pay off in every childhood event, more often than not maturity will lead the youth toward better organization, which will eventually be supported by self-imposed values. Needless to say, mental health professionals must guard against slipping into disorganization and inefficiency, which will surely lessen professionalism.

Doing Homework

"Mom, Dad, I need help with this homework!" This plea is a common occurrence in households that have kids in school.

It is fundamental that a mental health professional will encourage adults to help children and adolescents with all sorts of tasks and problems. The question here is: When it comes to assigned homework, what should be the adult's role?

To form an answer to that provocative question, the first step is to consider the reason that homework is assigned. Simply put, homework is intended to promote learning for the child or adolescent. Consequently, homework usually has a connection to what is going on in the classroom.

This framework means that the student, not an adult, should complete the homework. The student's learning will not increase if an adult provides the answers; in future class sessions, the student will be stuck.

The decision of how to help with homework depends on the age and competency of the child. Although children of all ages, including youths in high school, need help from responsible adults, younger children are most likely to require adult involvement with their homework.

An adult, such as a parent or caregiver, may help the young child best by simply offering support and encouragement. Of course, those same positive efforts by adults will buttress the teenager's attempts as well. Also, if the child has any known limitations, such as problems with reading comprehension or written expression, the adults can provide guidance or instruction to overcome the barriers.

Experts say that parents or caregivers can help by creating the best conditions for the child's success with homework. This means having a regular and quiet place and space for the child to work, and making homework a priority. For example, the parent or caregiver and child should have a clear plan as to when to do homework in relation to activities, such as playing outdoors, visiting friends, practicing a music lesson, and watching TV.

As mentioned, adults should not just do the assignment for the child. Even when the child is stymied by a problem or badgers an adult, saying, "Just do it for me," it should be remembered that homework is to enhance the youngster's learning. Having the adult solve the problem to simply complete the assignment does not help accomplish the purpose of improved learning.

What is helpful, however, is for an adult to check to see that the child understands and has all the materials for the assignment. The adult can also stay long enough to see that the child can get started and is on the right track.

When it comes to homework, the mental health professional should instruct the relevant adults to conceptualize their role as being like a coach. To help the athlete perform well, the coach provides information, instructions, and guidance, and conducts practice sessions. However, the coach stays off the playing field, and only the athletes play the game. Afterwards the coach offers praise for achievement and effort, and helps them analyze the game, and think of other strategies they could have used to improve their performance the next time. Using the same coaching techniques, parents and other responsible adults can equip children of all ages to achieve better performance and be winners in their learning.

Owning Homework

As might be inferred from the preceding section, many parents and other caregivers dread their kids' homework assignments. This section goes further, describing how professional helpers can promote children owning the homework tasks.

Students often find homework to be daunting and try to avoid getting started and finishing. As I indicated, there may be halfhearted attempts, excuses given, or repeated requests for help from adults. Youngsters are skilled at avoidance tactics, such as alleged ailments and reciting a list of other things that demand attention.

Wearied by all of the evasive maneuvers from the kid, the professional helper should encourage a relevant adult to not give in and not start doing the homework. At first, the child may seem to be working with the helpful adult, but soon the unsuspecting adult discovers that the offspring has gone elsewhere and is expecting the adult to complete the homework ("My favorite TV show is on, why don't you finish this for me?").

Although this scenario is common, anything along this line is unacceptable. The adult who accommodates the child's avoidance or lack of responsibility can be sure this nonlearning behavior will continue.

What are the purposes of homework? As mentioned earlier, the goal of the assignment is to teach the youth – such as about how to organize tasks, acquire new factual knowledge, develop analytic and writing skills, and gain a sense of motivation for achievement. When an adult takes over the assignment, many purposes of homework are lost.

The responsible adult, such as a parent or a teacher, should approach the homework as though it will, in fact, be a learning experience for the child or adolescent. It should never be thought of as being simply a demand imposed by the teacher.

Going back to the previously stated purposes, the mental health professional should teach the relevant adult(s) how to help the youngster recognize what is required for completion of the project, such as what materials need to considered; what information should be discarded or kept; what would be best the structure for the response or the order of the information that is to be contained in the response; and how the answer can best be expressed.

The concerned adult's role is as facilitator (e.g., motivating effort and eliminating distractions), not provider of answers or responses for the homework. Ideal responses from the adult are encouragement, gentle probes that will lead the child or adolescent to identify what options or information to consider, and advice here and there about the adequacy or correctness of the youngster's responses. In some instances, the adult may suggest specific alternatives to what the youth has selected as a response, but the young person should make the final determination of the answer or response.

There will be times when the relevant adult(s) may be aware that the choice made by the child or adolescent is not wise or may be incorrect. However, the learning process justifies allowing the youth to go ahead and self-determine the final answer or response. It is possible to learn from a mistake.

One particular pitfall occurs when the youngster engages in plagiarism. Responsible adults need to be alert to this issue and offer the child guidance. The term *plagiarism* refers to the wrongful taking of work done by someone else and presenting it as though the writer created it. Simply making an occasional citation of, or reference to, the original source does not eliminate the possibility of plagiarism.

While ideas from another source can and should be discussed in an answer or response to a homework assignment, exact wordings from someone else's work should not be used without quotation marks and a citation of where the work appeared. This problem is singled out for emphasis because the availability of materials on the World Wide Web seems to bid welcome to the easy way out, such as doing a cut-and-paste response. It is plagiarism to copy the work of someone and present it as having been done by the student. It cannot be condoned by anyone.

What seems like plagiarism may actually be naiveté about how to paraphrase and cite the ideas published by others. Students need to learn how to properly cite the sources of information they use in their answers or responses to homework.

Perhaps the greatest dividend of doing homework is for the child or adolescent to sense academic achievement. Research supports the idea that fulfillment of the need to achieve will have far-reaching positive effects on a person's overall life.

Whether the outcome of completing homework results in high or low grades is not the total story. Obviously a high score is desirable, but the sense of ownership of the completed homework is highly important for the youth's learning and development.

6 Character Development

As suggested in the preceding chapter, being an effective learner is essential for a healthy, productive, and law-abiding life. From knowledge, the young person develops abilities for problem-solving and decision-making.

Children and adolescents are more self-determining than some adults (especially parents?) like to admit. Consequently, adults need to help kids grow into responsible independence. In the process, youngsters develop characteristics that will govern their decision-making.

Mental health professionals should, of course, promote these goals. Further, they should assist parents and other responsible adults help children, regardless of age, become competent and able to realistically recognize personal abilities. Kids who have strong academic achievements and appreciate their competence deal effectively with the learning environment and situations they encounter in life, which is necessary to survive and thrive. Regrettably, some youngsters have difficulty and will need support from the adults in their life; in turn, these relevant adults will often need professional services to improve their handling of the kids.

As children get older, they may tend to be less positive or optimistic about their capabilities, and their motivations may change. In the teenage years, external values, such as messages from parents, become less influential and the child's internalized values take over.

The earlier chapters have explained how children and adolescents are constantly getting information about life from all sorts of sources, such as the kids at school, neighbors, people in the community, and especially what they see on television. Whether in a classroom, at home, or watching TV, what the child learns will determine beliefs, values, morals, motives, and most of all, judgment in problem situations. At all stages of childhood and adolescence, guidance from professional helpers, parents, and other relevant adults is of great importance. Before moving on to character development, I would like to review four important ideas about learning.

First, as the old adage warns, "all work and no play" is not a good thing. I have mentioned that there are two healthy ways to combine play and learning for a child, namely through socialization and creativity. To make creative play especially useful, an adult should share the activity.

Second, disorganization and tardiness can impede learning. Anyone who is routinely and inexcusably late is being inefficient; for example, homework should be done on time. The organized person is committed to accomplish the most from any effort. Whatever the task, the job that is done requires being able to make full use of resources, implement a plan, and monitor the success or failure of the effort.

Third, when it comes to homework, the best role for adults is helping or facilitating children and adolescents doing the homework. The decision of how to help with homework depends on the age and competency of the child. An adult may help the young child best by simply offering support and encouragement. It is also helpful for an adult to check to see that the child understands the assignment in general or a problem specifically, and has all the necessary materials and a suitable place to do the homework (e.g., free from distractions).

Fourth, when it comes to any learning task, including homework, the adult's role (as stated previously) is facilitation, not being the provider of answers or responses for the homework. I believe that the ideal responses from the adult are encouragement, gentle probes that will lead the child to identify what options or information to consider, and advice here and there about the adequacy or correctness of the child's responses.

Some adults find it is difficult to grasp and implement the foregoing four ideas about learning. Here again, this is where the mental health professional can become an important ally.

This chapter will discuss how to help children and adolescents develop positive character traits, make good decisions, and become effective in self-management. This is a developmental process, and how personal qualities are formed depends on the age and maturity of the child. Like so many aspects of child and adolescent development, character development does not come easy, and professional helpers will need to promote self-management for this purpose.

The Golden Rule

There is a valuable message for children (and all adults as well) in the old adage "As you sow, so shall you reap." Another old adage, known as the Golden Rule provides the solution: that is, "Do unto others as you would have them do to you."

It is common during early- and middle-childhood development for children to be self-centered, even as they should be moving to a more mature stage. Sometimes this characteristic leads teenagers (and adults) to take unfair or inappropriate advantage of others.

All adults have seen children try to be persuasive or, some might say, manipulative. That is, youngsters want their way, even though this preference may not be logical, fair, or in their best interests. This is when guidance from professional helpers, parent, and other responsible adults is needed.

Without empathy (i.e., sensitivity to the needs of another person), an individual of any age has the potential to behave badly and trample on the rights of other people. Children who mature appropriately will able to understand and empathize with the needs of others. They realize that they are not the center of the universe.

Whether a child or adolescent, if the youngster seems uncaring about the rights of others, such as by bullying, his or her parents and other responsible adults need to take a close look at the youth's character and moral development. They need to try to understand why the child or adolescent has to denigrate another person to feel a sense of personal worth. If these negative attitudes and bad conduct are present, help from a mental health professional may be necessary.

The Golden Rule captures the meaning of the quality of empathy. If a person can step into another's shoes figuratively and understand the other person's feelings and needs, the person will gain the capacity to live by the Golden Rule.

In the context of parental or family guidance, mental health professionals should help the adults in the life of a child or adolescent accept responsibility for structuring the child toward living by the Golden Rule. They should be taught how to remind the child or teenager that "what goes around comes around." Adults should realize, however, that children do not learn this aspect of character simply by telling them the Golden Rule. Learning to be a decent respectful human being starts in early childhood.

Adults teach empathy by the way that they behave with their own children, family members, friends, and others in need. For example, how the parents treat each other will impart critical messages to the children. In the context of normal family life, the parents can then also teach the moral value of compassion and living by the Golden Rule. This principle is applicable to all types of adult–child relationships.

As they become more mature and independent, teenagers will continue to need help in identifying and avoiding the tendency to treat others poorly. If they see put-downs going on all around them, such as among their friends, they may forget lessons about morality that they learned as children in the family. Parents and other responsible adults need do stay alert for how children behave toward others, even after they are on their own.

When it comes to the Golden Rule, the bottom line is that all adults should practice what they preach. Specifically, adults should model polite and respectful ways of dealing with others in social relations. It should go without saying that the conduct of professional helpers must reflect these same empathic, polite, and helpful qualities.

Finding Opportunity

Mental health professionals should help adults understand the importance of character development, and how they can help children and adolescents develop it. Character development involves acquiring values and morals, which lead to beliefs and actions. The first step toward positive character development is self-control and making decisions that will bring about desirable outcomes.

When things are not going well in life, human beings are tempted to look for an excuse. Whether for a youngster or an adult, when life's road gets bumpy, the final responsibility to make change remains with the individual.

It makes sense, however, to look for support from others. Certainly, friends and family members can help a person bring about changes that will lead to a happier, healthier, and more constructive life. Of course, services from a mental health professional may be needed to accomplish critical aspects of character development.

Often the person who is stuck in a problem cannot see any options. In such a situation, a friend, family member, or professional helper can reinforce the person's efforts to become more open-minded, gain useful information, and evaluate options. Nonetheless, the individual must be in charge and make the choices. No one else should be in the driver's seat. Helping a person accept responsibility for one's decisions is certainly a primary objective in mental health services.

When a person tries to help someone with problems, the goal is to improve the self-management and decision-making by the person with the difficulty. Egan (2007) indicates that the intent is to enable and empower the troubled person to manage problems in living more effectively, as well as recognizing and developing unused or underused resources and opportunities, and become more competent at self-help.

An initial step toward improving daily life is to decide what is a problem AND what would be a more desirable outcome – that is, the person should target what would eliminate or could replace the conflict. More will be said about this task later.

As mentioned, there is a link between resources and opportunities. Therefore, a strategy for change requires a reconnaissance of unused or underused support services. In other words, the person with a problem should think about what people and conditions might improve the situation. For example, one parent said, "I had never really tried to talk to either my Mom or Dad about my kid's problems. I guess I didn't want to admit my shortcomings to them. When I did share my problems with them, I was surprised at how understanding and helpful they were."

After recognizing the resources that are and are not available, the person with a problem should seek to locate other resources. Even a small boost can be helpful, especially when it can be cultivated or increased. For example, one teenager, who had few friends, tended to read a lot. After he mentioned to the local librarian that he was interested in trying to decide on a career, she often had a book set aside for him when he came to the library. Not only did he get useful information that would strengthen his vocational planning, he formed a positive relationship with the librarian, which resulted in his having a rewarding social experience with a helpful adult. In his senior year of high school, he ended up working part-time in the library.

Helping children and adolescents develop positive character qualities includes guiding and teaching them how to solve problems. Learning this important life skill enables the child to be his or her own agent of change for life. Certainly adult guidance and assistance is essential. Nonetheless, in the long run an important objective is for every kid is to be mature and logical, and exercise sound reasoning and judgment. An adult can promote this goal by guiding the child to learn how to solve problems, which is better than the adult's take charge of solving the problem.

Making Good Decisions

As adults think back over the years, it is common to experience regret about something that occurred, and say to oneself, "What was I thinking?" It is likely that most adults can recall some decisions that proved to be unwise. Or an adult may realize that he or she escaped bad consequences by "the skin of my teeth." What was occurring was the development of character. Certain thoughts or actions, whether wise or unwise in retrospect, led to progressively mature evaluation and acceptance of the values and morals that became guiding forces in adulthood.

All of us, regardless of age, should learn from our own experiences. This is, of course, why the training of mental health professionals commonly includes opportunities to gain self-understanding. By benefiting from experiences, a person of any age – and children and adolescents are no exception – will improve in making wise decisions and avoiding pitfalls.

Increasing self-understanding is not a simple undertaking. In guiding youngsters, parents and other relevant adults need to do the most when the children are young. The hope is that they can then exercise good decision-making when they have more independence, namely during the teenage and adult years.

Many sources influence a child's decision-making ability. Aside from certain genetic endowments, such as temperament, the child's intelligence and willingness to learn are important factors. Adults who put a premium on learning, such as by having children's reading materials available and engaging in shared learning activities with the child, provide a strong boost toward good intellectual development and judgment, the precursors for positive character.

Turning specifically to character development, acquiring moral values and standards occurs throughout life, but particularly in early and middle childhood. Some professional helpers believe that the teenage years have a far greater impact on moral development and judgments than is commonly recognized. For example, Harris (1998) offers a convincing argument for believing that parents matter less and peers matter more in determining the way that a youngster turns out.

Influences on character development come from countless sources. And parents and other responsible adults have the challenging job of deciding which experiences the child or adolescent can have and which must be off-limits. Professional help will often be needed.

It is not an easy decision for an adult to say that certain friends of a child are "bad apples" and to simply forbid contact with them. With an older child, there needs to be discussion and watching behavior before deciding on a course of action. The mental health professional can help adults develop judgment and communication skills for effectively meeting this challenge.

Through self-thoughts, called cognitions, children start, in the early elementary years, to understand and decide what they consider to be good and bad behavior. In forming their own views, children gauge the motives and intentions reflected in the behaviors of adults and other children.

What the child sees to be the consequences to other persons, whether there is reward or punishment, has a strong impact on childhood evaluations of behavior. Parents, teachers, and other responsible adults can help by talking with the child about these situations – whether they occur in real life or are depicted in the media. In this way, the youngster is guided toward accepting correct and constructive messages, while rejecting wrongful ideas conveyed by these other sources.

In early and middle childhood (say, ages 6–11), children gain an understanding of fairness. Also, certain emotions related to moral develop emerge, such as guilt and sympathy. The child should begin to share with other children, offering them help without any payoff per se. And if the child misbehaves, there will be self-imposed criticism.

As children move toward middle school (say, ages 12–13), they increasingly consider circumstances when evaluating their own behavior. In other words, at this stage children begin to acquire self-control and consequently base their judgments on what particular circumstances they will accept or reject. The best example is probably how a child acts in school versus at home – different rules apply in each setting.

By the time that children reach the upper-elementary grades and junior high school, most children have usually developed so-called conventional morality. They have opinions about good and bad, law and order, and interpersonal relationships (sharing, trusting, and loyalty), which they consciously use in their decision-making.

If adolescents (say, ages 14–18) do not recognize, accept, and abide by rules, they may behave badly and face sanctions. These are the youngsters who are disciplined or punished by parents, the school, or the juvenile justice system.

Although moral development continues on into adulthood, such as during the college years (with strong influences from other college-age students), a teenager should have a sense of conscience allowing for responsibility to self and others.

An adolescent with healthy moral development adheres to rules and conventions, even if there is no punishment per se. Healthy and responsible self-regulation is dedicated to a positive life.

Now for the issue of the youngster's making good decisions. Every parent and other responsible adult must face issues like when a child or youth should be allowed to date, stay out late, go places without a chaperon, drive a car, own a firearm, be employed, and manage money – to name but a few of the countless decisions that occur in every family.

The answer to all of those questions is the same: The child or youth must demonstrate consistently that he or she can manage the self and act in a responsible manner. This ability is termed *effective self-regulation.* Without this degree of maturity, parents and other responsible adults should not relinquish decision-making to a child. I will say much more about effective self-regulation later in this chapter. For now, suffice it to say that professional helpers need to embrace self-regulation as a critical principle with all – yes, ALL – persons to whom they provide services.

Adult–Child Time

It is critical that mental health professionals help parents and other relevant adults accept that they need to commit adequate time to just being with the children and adolescents for whom they have responsibility. However, since adults have to work and satisfy many other aspects of their lives, setting aside time for youngsters is often a difficult undertaking. Schoor (1992) points out that the average American today spends 163 more hours working per year than a counterpart 20 years earlier. For families, this means that a parent today could spend over 20 additional workdays away from his or her children each year.

Consider when both parents work. In addition to possible work overload, they may each have a long commute between home and job. In addition to the job itself, the driving time, essential to maintaining employment, keeps family members apart.

The mental health professional should encourage parents especially, and other relevant adults as well, to keep track of how much time they are away from the children and how they are spending their time together in the home or wherever they are together. The next step is for the professional helper to try to change the routine so that there will be more adult–child time and healthy shared activities.

When adult–child time is limited, consideration should be given to having good organizational conditions. For example, parents need to look closely at how the household is organized. Is everyone helping with the essential tasks that need to be done? If both parents are in the home, do both help organize and carry out the daily routines? Are children involved appropriately in household upkeep? When all family members work as a team, there can be more time for leisure, fun, or just being together.

Children benefit from different kinds of time and interactions with adults. Good conversations can happen when adults and youngsters are together doing chores, housework, and errands. Also, adults should ensure that they engage in games and outdoor play with the kids, which may be as simple as watching family-type television shows together – but communicating with each other in the process.

Good times and rewarding talks happen when adults ask about children's activities, listen and pay attention, and treat each other with a sense of affectionate humor. In the midst of these kinds of interactions, there is character development because the adults can share their values, express praise and love, and help the kids find their talents, dreams, and hopes. In the process, the adults learn to make the most of the time that they and the young people have together.

In our fast-paced modern society, time is limited. Nonetheless, adults can choose, perhaps with help from a mental health professional, to make changes. Commonly the goal for adults and children of all ages is to "slow down and smell the roses."

Aggressive Kids

In one of the university classes that I teach, I was surprised at how many of the undergraduate students indicated that they had been in a physical fight. The numbers were about the same for males and females, so I had to revise the old notion of the "gentle" or "weaker" sex. The statistics on the amount of violence encountered by kids of all ages (e.g., weapons brought to school and physical fights between students) are frightening. Borum (2006) notes that: "Since the mid-1980s, youth violence has increasingly gained recognition as a significant public health problem... Beginning around 1985, reported rates of violence committed by juveniles began a sharp and substantial increase" (p. 190).

Our society has become extremely aggressive, which leads to being mean-spirited. Mills (1997) captures the negative mindset that is so common in our society. He warns that the "new meanness" present in our society is reflected in style and attitude, and "meanness without guilt" (p. 17). Obviously, this trend bodes ill for having a peace-loving society.

When a child repeatedly acts in an antisocial, destructive, or violent way, mental health professionals consider such behavior to be a conduct disorder. Regrettably, conduct disorders are persistent behavior patterns that are difficult to turn around.

With parents and other responsible adults, professional helpers should cultivate an ability to help children and adolescents avoid inappropriate aggressiveness. Of course, all adults must be committed to promoting healthy values for young people. The first step for an effective intervention is to recognize the warning signs of a potential conduct disorder.

Although there are various degrees and forms of inappropriate aggressiveness, telltale signs are attempts to bully, threaten, or intimidate; initiating physical fights; using any object as a weapon; demonstrating cruelty toward people or animals; stealing; and forcing sexual activity. In addition, adults should be concerned when a child or adolescent destroys property, is deceitful, or violates rules set by parents, teachers, or the law. Immaturity does not justify any conduct of this nature.

Sometimes parents and other responsible adults must pay attention to a given child's overall attitude toward people and life. For example, the child who is routinely defiant, oppositional, negative, or hostile is not on a healthy track.

If there is an indicator of a conduct disorder, adults should not shy away from taking responsible action. For example, if parents see this kind of behavior occurring in the home or if teachers report it, it is time to collaborate and arrange for needed professional guidance that may involve school mental health specialists or other professional helpers. In addition, other children should not tolerate the kind of behavior just described – they should immediately report it to parents, teachers, or law enforcers.

Kids Gone Wild!

I received a letter from a fellow who works in a large store. He said: "As I walk around the store, I see how parenting has gone downhill. Unsupervised children are running around the toy and electronics departments. I see them stealing stuff out of the packaging – I see it every day! Just in the past couple of weeks, we have had several incidents of unattended young children falling out of shopping carts and getting hurt, one even broke a leg. Parents let the kids go off alone into the store, and they run wild."

Those unsolicited criticisms of parents started me thinking about the reality that some parents and other relevant adults are inattentive, if not irresponsible, and how this governs the character development of a youngster. It is possible that some of children's difficulties would never develop if they were under the watchful eyes of responsible adults, particularly their parents.

Take bullying on the playground. Consider kids who shoplift, curse, and use drugs and alcohol. The list goes on and on, giving witness to the fact that some of this misconduct might never start if there were closer adult supervision.

This sort of maladaptive behavior is indicative, of course, of socially flawed character development. Most certainly, it will lessen the youth's chances of attaining healthy and constructive behavior and all the rewards that would otherwise come with exemplary character development.

It impossible to always have an adult being the proverbial policeman at the elbow everywhere the child goes. Young children, however, need almost constant attention from an adult.

For character development, adult attention is critical in helping every child and adolescent develop the wherewithal to make strong moral and social judgments. Until the youngster has shown consistently that he or she has the ability to think and act in a safe and responsible manner, adult oversight is mandatory.

Mental health professionals should advocate that meaningful involvement with children and adolescents in many activities is essential for healthy development, and this imposes a social responsibility (and with parents and other caregivers, a legal duty) on all adults. Such close ties enable adults to be sensitive to the types of thoughts or behaviors that are potentially problematic for a child or adolescent. With an awareness of the youth's particular needs, the adult can help guide the child or adolescent to healthy and socially appropriate actions, both by teaching and modeling the values that will lead to positive self-control.

Kids gone wild in a shopping center certainly points a finger of blame at the parents or other responsible adults. In this day and age, there is a high risk when young children are left unattended in any public place. When the child is so immature that independent judgment is unreliable, the responsible adult is, frankly, negligent in not always being with the child in a high-risk situation. Here again, this is a message that should be conveyed by professional helpers to everyone, regardless of age or role in society.

Often these days, people seem prone to take a live-and-let-live attitude when they see some sort of conflict or problem occurring, such as a parent who is leaving a toddler unattended in a shopping cart or screaming at the child in a verbally abusive way or using brute force to yank a kid around. Passersby are commonly tempted to not get involved. From social psychology research, it is known that bystander interventions are influenced by the information about the situation that is available and a wish to avoid defining dangerous situations as emergencies. Others being present diffuses any sense of personal responsibility for taking a helping action, while being in a good mood increases helping (Franzoi, 2009). As mentioned, accepting social responsibility should be reinforced by mental health professionals.

In a responsible society, adults should be prepared to step forward and seek a remedy for any situation that creates jeopardy for another person, particularly for a youngster. There is no reason to have a confrontation with the adult who seems to be mistreating a child, but there is certainly good reason to report the situation to store security or law enforcement.

Self-Monitoring

If asked, "What do you want for your child (or adolescent)," most parents would probably respond: "I just want my kid to grow up to be healthy, get a good job, stay out of trouble, be happy, and make good decisions." Obviously, while this goal sounds simple, this is a powerful challenge for anyone.

Living in our modern and complex society, any youngster (and any adult as well!) will be hard pressed to create a surefire plan for achieving the positive and constructive life that his or her parents would prefer. This exalted outcome depends upon the youth's ability to be aware of potential pitfalls and decide on a route that will keep him or her on the straight and narrow or to have his or her feet planted solidly on terra firma. When effectively engaging in self-monitoring, the child or adolescent is accurately and consistently processing values, morals, and beliefs relevant to character development.

Mental health professionals should advocate that self-monitoring is part of the key to success. Throughout life, a person needs to be sensitive to how he or she fits into situations involving other people. The social situation may be direct, such as in a relationship with another person, or indirect, such as abiding by the laws of society.

Self-monitoring is more than simply forming ideas about one's strengths and weaknesses. It is also more than identifying personal characteristics, such as being attractive, likable, intelligent, and persuasive, and/or recognizing motives and needs that chart the course for daily life.

Among people, there are profound and countless types of individual differences. Self-monitoring can be thought of a youth's ability to alter behavior according the particular situation that appears. The term *adaptability* also comes to mind. In other words, the youngster needs to analyze each encounter with someone or some set of circumstances and decide how to act. This kind of conscious awareness should help the child or adolescent to recognize that there are options, to evaluate the alternatives, and to come up with a wise decision in which benefits outweigh negatives – this is the epitome of character development.

Self-monitoring and making decisions can also involve judging whether a situation has many potential benefits. For example, to challenge someone to a game of chess because of friendship, with no regard to the opponent's ability for the game, could be positive and enjoyable; however, engaging in a game of chess with a player known to be as good or maybe even better could also offer the added opportunity for a new learning or enriching experience. New learning or enrichments can lead to a better chance of success in reaching life goals.

Clearly adults can do more than just wish that kids will grow up with health, productivity, and the like. They can help children of all ages learn personal skills for living in an effective and healthy manner, such as being able to exercise wise problem-solving and decision-making that will lead to positive opportunities and experiences. Self-monitoring is part of these skills as young people learn how to calculate risks and rewards as part of making choices. The choices obviously have relevance to the values, morals, and beliefs that the youngster accepts into his or her character development.

Effective Self-Management

So far, this chapter has stated bluntly that character development is a difficult undertaking for youngsters and adults alike, and is commonly an important part of mental health services. Since immaturity is no excuse, children and adolescents must own their shortcomings. However, parents and other relevant adults are also linked to youthful failures in moral and social judgments, as well as certain unacceptable conduct. Attention can now be given to the saving grace: effective self-management.

Every youth encounters many danger zones, and good decision-making and self-control provide a safety net. It would be comforting if children and adolescents could readily move through their developmental years with effective self-regulation; however, much learning is involved in achieving this goal. It is the responsibility of parents and other adults to support this learning for, and development toward, positive adulthood. Often these adults will need help from mental health professionals in fulfilling this challenge.

As youngsters grow up, they need to be able to evaluate situations, weight alternatives, and choose actions that bring good outcomes. This ultimately is a process of problem-solving, decision-making, and self-regulation. Precious few children and adolescents can perform these functions well consistently, and many will need guidance from professional helpers. Trial-and-error learning is inevitable, but parents and other responsible adults should step forward to teach and guide young people with support and compassion.

At any age, children will vary in these self-management skills, depending on what they have learned in their family, in school, and from peers. Parents have the earliest and most important responsibility to help their child learn to be increasingly responsible for self-management and accountable for behavior and decisions.

For various reasons, some youths do not seem able to be responsible, and they fail to choose behaviors that support healthy and safe development. As a result, parents and other relevant adults are often puzzled as to how to motivate a child or adolescent toward a healthier and more positive track.

Professional helpers should advocate that all adults realize that, first and foremost, they need to take a close look at how they are involved in a youngster's life. How much time do they give to the child or adolescent? How much listening do they do? Do they participate in the youth's interests and activities? Do they offer clear expectations for conduct? Do they monitor and supervise? Do they teach and guide, and help the child or adolescent meet expectations? Do they praise the kid for accomplishments in self-management? Do they apply consequences when the young person neglects responsibilities or blames others instead of owning to what happened?

Besides these active roles on the part of adults, children and adolescents also learn from watching how the adults, especially their parents and caretakers, manage their own lives and make decisions. It is an understatement to say that parents and other responsible adults are role models for young people, including for effective self-management.

Adults are likely to become concerned when they have seen several instances when the child or adolescent has made a poor decision or behaved in an irresponsible manner. Unfortunately, worry and anxiety within the adult often leads to anger, criticism, or preaching.

One teenager was rather lackadaisical about both studying and getting a part-time job. Instead of trying to guide or encourage the youth, the father took a condemning approach, constantly belittling the adolescent. To make matters worse, the mother sided with the teenager, and the whole family was adversely affected. Suffice it to say, emotional reactions are not likely to help the child or adolescent move in a positive direction, and do not contribute substantially to developing effective self-management skills.

It is fundamental that parents and other responsible adults can motivate change in the child or adolescent by offering empathy or understanding and support for coping with what is being or will be encountered. Of great importance, the adult should provide information for the youth's consideration, and as it is being considered, point out the strengths and weaknesses of alternatives.

Recall the lackadaisical teenager mentioned earlier. After meeting with a mental health professional, the parents became united and began talking with the adolescent about being more interested in school and work, gave information now and then about jobs that would be realistically possible for a teenager to obtain, and supported the youngster's interests – eventually the adolescent began to seek a part-time job and became more aware of the consequences of not studying.

As the child or adolescent begins to demonstrate motivation for change, the parents and other responsible adults should express admiration and praise for the youngster's efforts. With a positive framework established, the adult can then offer additional information and comments that will facilitate the youth's considerations of the costs of not changing versus the benefits that will likely flow from implementing changes.

As the child or adolescent makes gains in self-regulation and achieves desired changes, the relevant adults can supplement the admiration and praise with concrete rewards. No, this does not mean expensive gifts or the like. Rather, the rewards should produce a pleasant experience (e.g., attending a movie, preferably attended by the entire family or other caring adults). By giving the reward soon after a discussion about the youth's attaining a sought-after goal, and without a lot of fanfare, the mere linking of a reward to the motivation for change will be reinforcing of future efforts to change.

In any event, it is essential that the motivation for change be placed on the youngster's shoulders. Although adults should continue to assist the kid's effort to accomplish needed changes, the success of the effort must remain with the child or adolescent. That is, the motivation for change and the outcomes are about the youth, not about the adult. The youngster needs to experience ownership of failing to, or benefiting from, change.

7 Social Development

The preceding chapter explored the difficult challenge of character development. The old sayings "As you sow, so shall you reap" and "Do unto others as you would have them do unto you" were recognized for offering useful guidance to children and adolescents. These principles should be relied upon by mental health professionals.

Maturation is not a smooth process. The vicissitudes of growing up present challenges to youngsters and responsible adults alike. The task of character development is particularly demanding. Aside from certain genetic endowments such as temperament, the young person's intelligence and willingness to learn are important factors for character development.

Children and adolescents need help in identifying and avoiding any tendency to treat people poorly. The nature and complexity of this objective points to professional helpers, whether working with children and adolescents or their parents, family members, and other responsible adults. Empathy is a cornerstone for positive character, and adults should be aware that they teach empathy by the way they behave with their own children, family members, friends, and others in need. Helping children be empathic comes down to the parents' and other responsible adults' practicing what they preach.

Acquiring moral values and standards occurs throughout life, but particularly in early and middle childhood. The teenage years also have a far greater impact on moral development and judgments than is commonly recognized.

In the early elementary years, children's thoughts or cognitions lead them to deciding what they consider to be good and bad behavior. Children are influenced by what they observe. What the child sees as the consequences of a particular act by other persons, whether there is reward or punishment, has a strong impact on childhood evaluations of the given behavior.

In early and middle childhood (say, ages 6–11), children gain an understanding of fairness. This is also the stage when certain emotions related to moral development emerge, such as guilt and sympathy. When children reach middle school (say at ages 12–13), they increasingly consider the circumstances of a situation when evaluating their own behavior. That is, they become more reality oriented and develop so-called conventional morality. They have opinions about good and bad, law and order, and interpersonal relationships (sharing, trusting, and loyalty). At this age, they start using their knowledge and opinions for decision-making, becoming self-monitoring and self-determining and increasingly having control over their behavior.

An adolescent with healthy moral development does not need the threat of punishment to adhere to rules and conventions. If character development has been on a positive track, the adolescent will engage in effective self-management.

Parents and other responsible adults can help by having adult–child time and constructive interactions with kids. If the youngster reflects poor judgment or limited behavior control, the adult should give him or her feedback and suggestions for improvements. Many adults need a mental health professional to teach them how to communicate the foregoing message in everyday language (and in their behavior as well).

Regrettably some children and adolescents do not develop mature judgments and they act in an inappropriate manner. Kids who are overly aggressive (e.g., bullies) or have conduct disorders are at high risk of major life-adjustment problems. For these problem-prone children and adolescents, adult supervision is critical for helping them, regardless of age, develop strong moral and social judgments and acquire behavior controls. Unfortunately, some children and adolescents never develop positive moral and social judgments, with all the negative consequences that go with being out of step with society (e.g., these are the kids who may be charged with crimes).

Maturity brings an ability to wisely evaluate situations, weigh alternatives, and choose actions that will lead to positive outcomes. In other words, the developmental goal is effective self-management. As with so many aspects of helping children and adolescents, parents and other relevant adults may require professional guidance about how to bolster their youngsters' attempts at self-management.

In this chapter, the emphasis is on how youngsters develop qualities for relationships with other people. As discussed throughout this book, socialization or social development is critical to many aspects of life, and mental health professionals must be prepared to help people of all ages know how to achieve effective social maturity, a constructive set of social relationships, and social skills for maintaining and improving relationships.

Needing Other People

In her performances in the movie *Funny Girl,* Barbra Streisand, in the song "People", sings: "People, people who need people, are the luckiest people in the world. We're children, needing other children and yet letting our grown-up pride, hide all the need inside, acting more like children than children." Is she correct? Yes, indeed. The pithy musical message identifies a critical factor in human development: There is a need for emotional bonding or attachment that leads to fulfilling another need, namely belongingness.

Starting with the emotional bond that develops between an infant and caregivers, children have an instinctive need to be connected to others; their very survival depends on this. Bowlby (1969) speaks of attachment as being an evolutionary process among species, meaning that it is part of genetic heritage. This essential bond of the infant with the parents makes survival possible.

As children develop normally, they will want friendships and other kinds of relationships. Some of the attachments that they form may be positive, and some may be otherwise.

A secure attachment style is the ideal that results from good adult care. With this, the child feels trust, no concern about abandonment, and a sense of being valued and loved. Unfortunately, all children are not blessed with secure attachments – such as kids who are neglected or abused. Consequently, some children are avoidant and stay out of relationships, or anxious and ambivalent about a relationship with another person.

Much of what shapes a child's expectations about relationships is due to early experiences in the family. Parents and caregivers differ in their ability to be caring and offer nurturance in child-rearing. Emotional maturity is essential for being an adult who effectively helps kids, and unfortunately all adults, such as parents, are not mature and well adjusted emotionally – and they are in need of services from professional helpers.

Culture also influences a child's attachment style. Americans grow up with a myriad of messages encouraging individualism. Certain other cultures, such as those in Asia, give more endorsement to collectivism, that is, valuing the group, not only individuals.

Why is attachment style important? How a child approaches relationships will influence his or her adult relationships, including those that are romantic in nature. For example, a person who has an avoidant attachment style rarely finds "true love." One who is anxious or ambivalent about relationships tends to be preoccupied with whether love will last or be gratifying enough.

Stated bluntly, the insecure, anxious, or ambivalent child is likely destined for adult relationships that are filled with problems. On the contrary, a child who experiences positive, secure family and other adult–child relationships is most apt to grow up with a sense of security in relationships and have a happy love relationship.

By assessing their own attachment style(s), parents and other responsible adults can seek personal changes that will improve experiences for the child. When parents and caretakers themselves feel a secure bond with a spouse or significant other, the child reaps the benefits, and is more likely to grow up and create positive, happy relationships with others. Consequently and in accord with the previous comments about cultivating social maturity, mental health professionals must be prepared to help people of all ages, including adults, develop positive bonding with others.

Belongingness

Within the human condition, there are many needs that seek to be satisfied or fulfilled. Need fulfillment is essential to survival, health, and happiness.

Every person, regardless of age or background, has a need to affiliate with others. The importance or power of the need to affiliate does, however, vary between individuals. Because of circumstances or personal characteristics, people differ in how they affiliate: some people have a lot of social contacts, while others have very few; and some form highly intimate relationships, and others pursue more superficial contacts. There is no one formula for determining affiliations – the chosen framework for affiliations is and should be constructed by individual preferences and the opportunities that are available.

Belongingness is a need that allows a person to have social contacts, some of which may lead to positives (e.g., friendly acts) and others may be aversive and lead to negatives (e.g., arguments). It is human nature to seek at least some stable, ongoing relationships, in which there are shared mutual interests; being connected to each other allows both parties to sense a reward.

Choosing or being forced to be isolated from other people is not a healthy approach to life. For example, a person who is in a job that does not bring at least some personal contact with others commonly senses loneliness. Even the person who chooses or is forced by circumstances to be a loner may experience a gnawing wish to have human interaction. Substitutes, like having a pet or reliance on vicarious contacts (e.g., watching television), may be his or her solution.

If a need of any kind goes unfulfilled, the person suffers. Granted, the need to belong or to be connected with another person can, as mentioned, differ considerably, but a thwarted social connection can be oppressive to the human spirit and impact on the quality of life. Moreover, research has documented that people who are alone are more apt to experience physical and mental health problems than people how enjoy a solid social network.

As an aside, it should be noted that, despite working with people daily, some mental health professionals tend to become isolated socially. Regrettably, since the daily contacts are with clients and patients who must be served within strict legal and ethical boundaries, the mental health professional could become at risk of a boundary violation if he or she did not gain healthy social feeding from appropriate personal relationships.

The mental health professional should strengthen all adults' abilities to help children develop and enjoy positive relationships, that is, to belong to a social system. Adults who as teenagers were involved with athletic teams, musical ensembles, or clubs or other kinds of groups, often reminisce years later about how much pleasure they derived from those shared experiences or their sense of belongingness in being a member of the team, ensemble, or group. With youths who are reluctant to join into social situations, the parents and caregivers should encourage and reinforce them to engage in shared social activities and cultivate a sense of belongingness. Of course, all adults in the community who have even secondary contact with youngsters share the foregoing mission.

Returning to Barbra Streisand's message about "people who need people, are the luckiest people in the world," there is no doubt about the benefits of belongingness or the detriments that can occur from isolation.

Avoiding the possibility of friendships and social contacts is an illogical way of behaving. And it should be remembered that professional helpers are not immune from needing people.

Helping for Longevity

I once observed a charismatic minister whose slogan was "it's nice to be nice." The colorful fellow, who wore long robes and a crown-like headpiece, may or may not have realized that his simple statement was conveying an important health message.

From early childhood and on throughout life, social values support that a person should be considerate of other people. Indeed, everyone is encouraged to help others. Social psychologists refer to helping others as prosocial behavior, which Myers (2005) defines as "positive, constructive, helpful social behavior; the opposite of antisocial behavior" (p. 408). He also points out that the research reveals that prosocial behavior promotes altruism, that is, having unselfish concerns and wanting to benefit others. Of course, professional helpers epitomize prosocial behavior.

From a personality viewpoint, a healthy person's makeup should include prosocial behavior, altruistic efforts, and conscientiousness. According to Kern and Friedman (2008), being conscientious includes "organization, thoroughness, reliability, competence, order, dutifulness, achievement striving, self-discipline, and deliberation" (p. 505). If thought is given to each of these factors, most of them describe behavior that involves respect for others and concern not to inconvenience or impose on others.

These helping behaviors provide self-rewards to the helper as well. The helper's needs (such as altruism and nurturance) will be fulfilled; he or she will be viewed positively by others and have a sense of being a constructive contributor to improving society. But there is even more – the prosocial person has a chance of living longer!

In research that linked personality with health, Kern and Friedman found that "conscientiousness measured in childhood could predict longevity decades into the future" (pp. 505–506) and that "individuals higher on conscientiousness are less likely to die at any given age than those lower on conscientiousness" (p. 510). They cite numerous other research studies that offer strong support for their notion that personality factors like responsibility, self-control, and traditionalism connect to healthy behavior.

The message is simple: To help children achieve and maintain health, parents should reinforce prosocial behavior, such as (but certainly not limited to) being conscientious. Life expectancy for the child or adolescent is likely to be increased. Moreover, just as an unhealthy habit such as smoking cigarettes or substance abuse can be stopped, it is never too late for parents and other adults to adopt a conscientious approach to relationships with other people. In addition to being role models in daily encounters, professional helpers of every ilk should consciously promote prosocial behavior in all people, regardless of age, characteristics, competencies, or social roles.

Kids and Social Adaptation

Success in life depends on being able to get along with other people. Having healthy and constructive social relationships involves give and take. The people in the relationship must sense that there is a positive exchange. In other words, by giving to each other, both receive a payoff.

Helping a child develop good social skills is an important goal for parents and other responsible adults. Although the school can and commonly does help the student develop acceptable behaviors and skills for engaging with others, all other adults in the child's life need to pay attention to whether the child or youth shows the ability to get along well with others.

Getting along refers to "social adaptation," which means that the child senses the expectations of a situation and lives by the rules that apply to behavior in a particular context. For example, policies and laws define conduct in school. In contrast, kids who do not get along, behave in ways that bring conflict with others, whether at home, school, or elsewhere.

At the different stages of development, certain red flags may signal difficulty with social relationships. With early childhood, a tendency to be overly and inappropriately aggressive is a warning sign. On reaching middle school, the socially maladaptive child may resort to forms of antisocial behavior, as seen with kids who bully others or engage in lying and stealing. Adolescents who cannot maintain positive social relationships often engage in risky behaviors, such as using alcohol, tobacco, drugs, and clandestine antisocial behavior in the presence of similarly inclined other youths. If other serious maladaptive behaviors emerge, such as truancy and criminal behavior, encounters with the legal system may follow.

Emotional distress and internal symptoms, such as depression and anxiety, may affect some youths who cannot sustain positive social relationships. Does emotional distress cause social maladaption or vice versa? Actually, either can be both a cause and an effect and exacerbate the problems being experienced by the youth.

Adults should be sensitive to situations in the everyday life of a child or adolescent. They should listen carefully to how the youngster talks about others and if there is a sense of friendship and belonging. They should also observe closely how the kid behaves in a variety of social situations with peers, family members, other adults, and especially around persons in authority.

An adverse impact on social adaptations can come from health problems, divorce, unemployment, or poverty in the youth's family. Similarly, within the child or adolescent, low self-esteem and learning problems can lead the youngster to resort to socially maladaptive behaviors. For example, the child who demonstrates a tendency toward being shy, reclusive, hostile, or aggressive might be signaling a need for help from responsible adults. In childhood or adolescence, poor social adaptation often leads, of course, to the youngster's being referred to a mental health professional for help.

It is noteworthy that social adaptation may differ between what is seen at home and what is observed at school. Consequently, responsible adults need to seek information about the child or adolescent from multiple sources. For example, talking to only one parent might not provide a teacher or mental health professional with a complete picture.

When planning an intervention for a child or adolescent who seems unable to initiate or maintain positive social relationships, it is prudent to create a plan that will evaluate and influence the existing caregiving system that is available to the youth. Consideration should also be given to possible sources of negative influence, particularly deviant peer groups.

All adults who have contact with a socially maladapted youth should be enlisted to be a contributing member of a supportive team effort. Although the parents and caregivers are first in line to offer a remedy, educators and other responsible adults should be ready to provide help as well. When focused family- and school-based efforts are not working, referral to a professional helper may be advisable.

For a socially maladapted youth, certainly professional mental health services should be sought, often from multiple sources in a coordinated effort. If so, the entire family should stand ready to engage in the intervention endeavor.

Setting Goals

Every family has tales from the past that get repeated over and over. Family therapists call these stories the *family's narratives,* and recognize how the past influences the present and future.

In my household, a popular recollection is how the entire family was awakened in the middle of the night by the excited barking of Buffy, our Siberian Husky. One of my sons, a toddler, had awakened, decided that he wanted cookies, gone downstairs alone in the darkness, and somehow climbed on top of the cabinet to reach the cupboard containing the cookies. Buffy knew something was amiss and sounded the alarm.

To say the least, my son was (and is now as an adult) highly goal-oriented. He gets something in his mind, maps a strategy for getting it, and embarks to fulfill his wish. Regrettably, seldom (if ever) is a plan for achieving a goal foolproof, and risks may be present.

Although infants have inclinations about wanting something from as early as 2 months, by the age of 8 or 9 months, they have definitely become goal directed. They recognize unfilled needs, and start reaching, grabbing, and crawling. They watch and imitate others doing things – and they follow suit. As they grow, infants become better able to get what they want, such as toys or food.

When it comes to human nature, behavior is highly purposeful. The person wants a payoff, and like my son when he climbed the cabinet to reach the cookies, identifies a course of action that will help achieve the goal. Because of their immaturity, youngsters benefit in their efforts to achieve goals from having a guardian (whether human or animal [☺]).

As kids reach school age, a wide variety of goals connect to classroom learning and socializing with other students. For example, research suggests that placing high priority on social relationships may hinder academic achievement.

Children and adults alike want to do well, but people differ in their reasons. Some people emphasize *mastery,* which depends on learning and acquiring new knowledge or skill. Others prefer *performance goals* that rely on appearances and are fulfilled by favorable acknowledgement from others.

Mastery and performance goals should both be present in children. Certainly mastery without performance, or vice versa, would likely have negative consequences. Also, coordinating or juggling several goals takes focus and concentration. The degree of emphasis on mastery versus performance goals has to be determined by the family's values and preferences.

Parents and other responsible adults are in an ideal position for helping children develop a healthy balance between mastery and performance goals, and to decide on appropriate ways to achieve satisfaction of their personal needs. Adults should teach children about the enduring benefits of learning to do things well, and the limited payoffs from superficial qualities. In addition, adults can help children think about long-term goals, making stable decisions that will lead to a good life and chosen career plans. Children and adults alike can benefit from professional help with this challenge.

Just as Buffy summoned the entire family to get my son back on solid ground, adults need to bring children's goals to realization. Patience and understanding will be necessary.

Childhood Influences

Raising a child is not an easy task. Parents and caregivers try to guide their offspring to be constructive citizens. However, other people and sources counteract the influence of even a conscientious adult.

In the past, it was thought that child development was essentially determined by genetic messages (i.e., the *nature assumption*) transmitted from the parents to the child, as well as the type of parent–child relationship (i.e., the *nurture assumption*). Sigmund Freud even went so far as to say that, by age 5, the child's psychological destiny was pretty well determined.

Modern research reveals that the nature and nurture assumptions alone are inadequate explanations of child development. Instead, it appears that children are more influenced by social contacts, such as friendships, than was previously thought. In other words, the *social learning assumption* holds that children are apt to become like the people with whom they associate or observe (including in the electronic media).

For decades, professional helpers have focused on peer relationships. For example, educators and school psychologists recognize that classmates can influence both learning and behavior. When children with similar characteristics, such as being the same age or in the same grade, are together, they are considered to be peers and have considerable influence on each other.

A major step for effective guidance of children and adolescents is to not allow the young person to get involved with someone who may not be a good influence. Outside of the school, the monitoring of peer or other social relations rests with the parents and other responsible adults. Stated bluntly, adults should control with whom a child spends time (or is exposed to in the electronic media).

No responsible adult wants a child's behavior to be harmful to others or in violation of the law. However, some adults, such as parents and caregivers, are prone to give little time to supervising a child's contacts with other children and adults.

The modern era has introduced powerful influences beyond those of neighborhood kids per se. For example, there can be adverse effects from allowing a child to spend hours watching television or playing video games. Not only can the video messages, such as violent depictions, move a child toward negative consequences, time in front of a television or spent playing a video game deprives the child of more healthy experiences.

The best alternative is to guide children of all ages into diversified activities, such as sports or the arts. One parent said, "When I hear my kid playing the guitar, I know that there is nothing bad going on."

When a youngster does engage in activities, it is important for adults, preferably parents and caregivers, to be involved as well. Extracurricular activities should not be viewed as alternatives to childcare. An adult and child who share a positive experience will both be enriched. Professional helpers should reinforce shared experiences by adults and youngsters, and offer guidance about how to weed out negative conditions and locate positive sources.

Choosing Friends

Friendships provide fun, as well as other enriching benefits to youngsters and adults alike. When children have trusting relationships with kids outside the immediate family, they gain information about how to behave and relate to others. Due to differences among children, sometimes a message is constructive and, regrettably, sometimes less than constructive.

There is an old adage that says "you can't pick your family, but at least you can pick your friends." Parents and other responsible adults need to help children and adolescents continually develop their abilities for selecting constructive friends and developing positive relationships. There seem to be four fundamentals that mental health professional should encourage all adults to remember.

First, adults should honor a child's need and right to select a friend, and should not try to dictate with whom a child can develop a friendship. For example, if a parent tries to foreclose another child from being a friend, this might actually serve to reinforce the friendship.

Second, the child must realize that a friendship requires giving in order to receive. In a friendship, there is an exchange of social rewards. From the early to the advanced stages, a friendship must provide both persons with benefits, such as caring and sharing.

Third, when children share, friendship is enhanced by emotions. There must be a trusting exchange of intimate details about oneself. Cultures vary on emotional openness. As a society, Americans tend to share personal information rather more freely than, say Asians, probably because of valuing individualism and gaining satisfaction from sharing personal uniqueness. In general, emotions should flow freely between friends. However, since culture influences the values aligned with behavior, the principle of emotional sharing must be passed through the relevant cultural filter. Being too closed or too open according to the relevant cultural values could become problematic.

Fourth, for whatever cultural or biological reason, girls are more apt than boys to engage in emotional sharing. Also, when establishing friendships, boys tend to rely less than girls on physical touching; positive touching can be a strong indicator of friendliness. Thus, boys may need special help in acquiring social skills, particularly for being tender and affectionate. Again, when it comes to gender differences, there are cultural issues to be considered.

Based on these four fundamentals, effective parents and other responsible adults encourage children and adolescents to explore possible relationships with other youngsters. They also help kids learn how to analyze when a relationship with another person, child or adult, is going to be constructive. Of course, these adults may need professional guidance in knowing how to handle these situations.

Children and adolescents should be helped to realize when aspects of a possible friendship are destructive or disproportionate in benefits. Ideally, both people in a relationship should experience equal benefits. From a young age, adults need to help children develop their sensitivities to what is occurring in a relationship of any kind.

The framework is that the youngster must be the decision-maker. That is, with adult guidance, the child or adolescent must decide who will be a friend. If the young person makes a poor choice, responsible adults should accept that it is time to talk again about how to understand, cultivate, and evaluate friendships.

Making Friends

Knowing how to develop close friendships is a common dilemma for children and adolescents (and many adults too). Justly or unjustly, some young people believe that they are incapable of having close friends. If there is self-doubt, the youngster may adopt an unhealthy belief of "I don't deserve friends." Clearly parents and caregivers, along with other responsible adults (such as teachers), should counteract this sort of negativity, and offer guidance that will help every kid learn how to create appropriate friendships. These adults may need professional help for these challenges.

As mentioned earlier, friendship is primarily to satisfy a person's need to affiliate or belong. Of course it also provides other benefits, such as feedback about personal characteristics and a sense of identity ("my friend thinks I have a good sense of humor"), positive social reinforcements ("when we're together, I feel more confident"), opportunities to model after the friend ("my friend knows how to act in any situation"), opportunities to engage in shared experiences ("now I don't have to go to a school dance alone"), and potential resources ("my friend has a car and I don't").

When a friendship starts, there is often *ingratiation*. This does not mean being sneaky or deceitful, it means showing appreciation for the other person. The person intuitively senses a possible mutual attraction, and acts in a manner that will promote a social connection. Although this is especially important at the start of a friendship, it continues throughout the friendship. When a friendship ends, whatever may be the reason, it is usually because circumstances or diminished attraction no longer allow for an honest expression of appreciation.

Contrary to the old adage that "opposites attract," modern research supports the suggestion that "birds of a feather flock together." That is, people form friendships because of having things in common. People differ in what is of individual importance. Whether the commonality is age, religion, economic background, career, education, aspirations, or whatever, the two people need to share characteristics for a friendship to develop. And a lasting friendship requires continuing compatibility. Being similar promotes liking; being too dissimilar leads to a lack of reasons for being connected.

Research also supports the *matching hypothesis*. The principle behind this is that a person tends to pair up with another person who is equally attractive. Somewhat surprising, the reliance on physical attraction for being open to a friendship seems to be powerful and emerges in all sorts of situations. Thankfully, attraction is more than skin deep, so friendships develop between people who have other positive qualities that are attractive, such as values, beliefs, likability (warmth, charm, compassion), talents, and so on.

Friendships tend to develop and continue because the two people gain something positive. In other words, both people sense a benefit from their association. This and the foregoing aspects of attraction are basically applicable at any age, from childhood through adulthood.

Professional helpers should guide parents and caregivers to teaching and raising a child or adolescent to feel capable and worthy of having friendships, become able to evaluate friendships (especially with any particular person), and pay attention if a friend begins to depart from the family's accepted values and standards for behavior. Adults have to ably help a youngster facing a conflict situation in a friendship. Discussion and dialogue can help the youth voice concerns about the pros and cons. Helping the young person do this kind of evaluation, rather than just ordering the end of the relationship, can be a valuable learning experience for the parents and child alike. Children and adolescents can consider what they value in a friendship, as well as what is positive and what is not in a troubled friendship.

Guiding Youthful Relationships

Adults are often puzzled by a child's great concern about being liked by others, and may need professional help to know how to fit the pieces together for a solution. Sometimes without being aware of it, well-intentioned parents and other responsible adults give too much emphasis to the situation, and end up being critical. If adults harshly criticize the child's motives, efforts, and choices of friends, the kid may cope with the social stress and painful feelings with inappropriate behaviors (including rebellion).

Dictatorial parenting or guidance can trigger an unhealthy clash of wills in the adult–child relationship. The youngster can become caught between wanting both adult approval and the acceptance of peers. When the child or adolescent is forced by the circumstances to choose between parental and peer influence, there can be negative consequences. For example, if the parents declare that "hanging out with your friends at the mall is a bad idea," the sense of loss of personal control may lead the youth to retort with "you can't tell me what to do." Such an unresolved standoff can impede the parents' future attempts to offer guidance.

Instead of trying to dictate relationships, mental health professionals should prepare parents and other responsible adults to develop and maintain keen sensitivity to the nature and qualities of the relationships formed by children and adolescents. With this awareness, they may be able to shape the relationships to be compatible with the family's values, the needs of the child, and the child's need to become self-determining. To have these insights, adults need to consciously think about their own and society's values, as relevant to a youngster's development and well-being, and be willing to patiently guide the child or adolescent through the maze of relationships to create a healthy degree of self-determination. Nonetheless, when obvious risks to the youth are involved, the parents and other responsible adults can attempt to use reasoning and compromise, as well as setting limits appropriate to the child's age and maturity.

Other people influence everyone's development. Every person is subject to the influence of social relationships. Fiske (2004) describes the all-pervasive way that others impact on one another, even to the point that the mere presence of someone can lead a person to act in a manner that would not have commonly been accepted.

It is noteworthy that the influence can come from someone who is actually present, as well as someone who is imagined or implied. For example, people of all ages tend have mental pictures of people who are not actually present, but that imagined presence is still influential. Earlier, I mentioned that it is common for an absent parent (because of divorce, death, or whatever) to still influence the way family members feel and deal with each other. So a parent who is not present in the child's life can have a positive influence, although he or she is not actually with the child about to make a choice. Professional helpers can assist in identifying the sources of influence.

When youths consider forming or maintaining a relationship, they have some notion of how the relationship will bring a payoff, such as self-esteem or approval from others. Young people will differ, however, in how they weigh overall the costs and benefits of a given relationships.

Responsible adults should aim to listen and have a real dialogue with the child, rather than preaching or dictating. They can speak of their concern and care for the child's welfare and future. They can state their opinions and worries, while also listening to the young person's view of the relationship. When there is no meeting of minds, one option is allow a trial period and then come back and talk further.

Parents and other caregivers have the ultimate responsibility to set limits when negative outcomes appear to be likely, even if the youngster resists. The old adage "You are known by the company that you keep" should be a filter that the adults use to help the child or adolescent know how to assess, select, and maintain positive social relationships.

Balancing Peer Influence

Raising children is like traveling through the woods without a compass. You think you know the direction, only to discover that something changed the course and you are standing knee-deep in a swamp.

Responsible adults want to shape kids to have good morals and values, grow up to be intelligent, have a good income, and be constructive citizens. Too often, honorable child-rearing goals are contradicted by other influences.

Even at an early age, a child sees the toys or clothing of other children and thinks how nice it would be to have the same thing. Research makes it clear that a child's behavior changes by observing how other children act.

It is ill advised to try to shut out influences from peers. First, it is impossible to shield a child from influences from outside the family. Second, not having friendships and social relations with other children would deprive the child of experiences that are essential for maturing in a healthy fashion.

Instead of condemning outside influences, responsible adults should make an effort to identify what the child is considering and if a specific information source is involved. Then comes the important step: Adults should talk with the child about the positive and negative aspects of the issue and raise other alternatives if the child's desired action is unacceptable or unwise.

Most children and adolescents respond well to thoughtful, unemotional, and caring discussions with their parents and other responsible adults. If there is blatant rejection of adult ideas, the responsible adults should do a self-assessment regarding how they might approach the topic differently with the youngster; professional guidance for accomplishing that self-assessment may be necessary.

Since all humans, regardless of age, respond to reinforcement, responsible adults can and should purposefully create learning experiences that will allow children and adolescents to learn about, decide, and experience positive values and activities. That is, the kid should be guided into enjoyable interests, hobbies, and friends who share the family's values. Research has shown that it is important to know the parents of a child's friends; that is, the characteristics (e.g., values) of the friend's parents or family members inevitably are reflected to some extent in the youngster.

With teenagers, responsible adults must be cautious of being overly critical of friends and classmates. The adolescent stage often brings on a tendency to be a rebel without a cause. Rather than criticizing, adults should have discussions (not lectures) that encourage the young person to identify consequences of a particular choice and alternatives. When adults actually listen in these conversations, rather than being negative or hostile, the youth is more likely to also listen to the adults' position.

Obstinate thinking by the young person should not cause an adult to be angry. In adolescence, self-determination is a necessary part of growing up. Adult emotions must be held in check, with love, understanding, and support being the modus operandi. However, when necessary to protect and guide a youth, responsible adults must set the necessary limits as well as monitor and supervise the youngster's activities. Clearly, as children get older, they need to be ready to do these things for themselves. Many parents need professional help for accepting self-determination by an offspring.

Avoiding Bad Situations

Parents and caregivers need to help their kids avoid situations that can lead to problems. Simply telling them to "stay out of dark alleys" is not enough. The child or adolescent needs to form a self-governing way for ambiguous and complex situations.

Regardless of age, when a person is with another person, it is tempting to think that any behavior that is evident is due to the relationship between the two people. Likewise, it is easy to assume that the characteristics of a youngster's personality produce his or her behavior. Both explanations are, however, only partially correct and are overly simplistic. Extensive research reveals that a response to a social situation is influenced much more by the context than is commonly assumed.

The term *context* refers to the place and its features, and the circumstances that are present when an event occurs. To some extent, people simply respond differently in different contexts. For example, a youth's speech and behavior at home can be much different from what he or she says or does in a classroom.

Where a meeting happens can influence the reactions of two people. Influenced by the context, an exchange between two people can come from an error in judgment, since people tend to rely on easily obtained information; this is why the old adage "You can't judge a book by its cover" makes sense.

One big, strapping fellow, a university student, told me (with a smile), "I avoid going to bars because, being tall and muscular, too many people want to fight with me, even when I'm minding my own business – I'm a lover, not a warrior." In other words, the outer appearance (being physically large) and the situation (being in a bar) combined to produce behavior from others that was not actually relevant to the person's characteristics. The fellow recognized that it was wise for him to avoid the situation or context.

Instead of paying attention to the situation's influences, people sometimes overestimate their own personal characteristics and judgment. Many a youngster has regretted unacceptable behavior that was out of keeping with his or her presumed values, for example, certain outlandish behavior by a teenager at an out-of-town raucous event, say at Mardi Gras in New Orleans, that the young person would never have done in his or her hometown.

To some extent, when a person acts in a manner that is inconsistent with professed values and past behavior, the influence of context may have been involved. Certainly the situation is potentially influential. Regardless, the person's self-concept is always present as well. The self-concept is always changing, and the situation can, therefore, modify previously held attitudes, values, and beliefs.

Mental health professionals should be prepared to guide parents and other responsible adults in explaining to children and adolescents how important it is to know thyself. Self-understanding will define and solidify the youth's thoughts, feelings, and behaviors in a manner that will help detect situational influences that may prove to be unacceptable, unhealthy, dangerous, or reprehensible.

Young people have to learn how to observe their own behavior, much like an outsider might, and use the information to make their decisions. Through talking and listening, adults can help a child or adolescent be clear regarding values and goals and to judge whether a situation is an affront to the young person's preferred way of being.

Freedom from Prejudice

Social development can be marred by faulty messages about discrimination. To strengthen social development, the adverse influences from prejudice and discrimination must be counteracted.

In the last half century, considerable progress has been made internationally in shaping societies to honor human rights and dignity, and enforcing personal values and governmental laws that contradict and restrict discrimination against certain classes of citizens. Although there continues to be room for improvement, civil rights have become a hallmark for modern government, and even "repressive" societies are being challenged to change on these issues.

Regrettably, human nature sometimes relies on prejudices and stereotypes. A discriminatory act arising out of prejudice is an indicator of poor character. Franzoi (2009) provides an important distinction. *Prejudice* means "attitudes towards members of specific groups that directly or indirectly suggest they deserve an inferior social status" (p. 202), whereas *discrimination* refers to "a negative action toward members of a specific group" (p. 203). Discrimination is the action is caused by prejudice the attitude.

Responsible adults should help all children and adolescents be free from prejudices. There are good reasons to eliminate prejudice. First, in this day and age, discrimination can be a legal matter. To avoid running afoul of the law, people at every stage of life must deal with others free from prejudice, otherwise they risk becoming involved in a situation that might jeopardize, for example, their employment. Second, prejudice takes a toll on the individual and reduces psychological health. Third, throughout the life cycle, people need positive relationships, and these can best thrive when prejudice does not set up barriers.

A message for all professional helpers must be that responsible adults, especially parents and caregivers, should help every child and adolescent get rid of stereotypes. A stereotype comes from putting people into categories, and believing that those in a particular category are all alike – that there is no individual variation. Stereotyping often involves trying to stigmatize the other person, namely discrediting the person in the eyes of others.

Prejudice often comes from childhood experiences. For example, if the parents use derogatory language, such as about racial groups, it is almost inevitable that the child will adopt both the same derogatory language and the underlying prejudicial beliefs.

Unfortunately, there are still people who blatantly hold negative stereotypes. For example, so-called old fashioned racism reflects an unjustified belief that one's own group is superior, that others are not equal, and that there is no right to protection under the law.

In the modern world, a person thrives though interacting with the diverse sectors of society. Avoiding persons with cultural characteristics different from those in one's own culture is stultifying.

Responsible adults can best help children and adolescents develop open and healthy minds by modeling support for cultural and racial diversity, and nondiscriminatory beliefs and behaviors. This means that all adults should avoid derogatory labeling of others on the basis of stereotypes. Adults should encourage all youngsters to have contacts with any person who deserves acceptance and to express understanding about, and respect for, differences among people. The objective is for the child and adolescent to grow up to be sensitive to both the good and bad aspects of another person that are based on the person's actions, not on prejudice that leads to penalties from discriminating against others.

8 Maintaining Health

In Chapter 7, it was emphasized that everyone needs contacts or relationships with others, and helping professionals should promote this objective. Social isolation is potentially harmful; and a caution was issued about how some mental health professionals incur the risk of boundary violations from being too socially isolated. Further, being able to establish positive attachments can actually contribute to mental and physical survival. Regrettably, some children and adolescents tend to be socially avoidant or unable to develop positive social relationships.

The social development of youngsters is subject to parents and caretakers differing in their ability to offer nurturance. The adult's own attachment style(s) will influence the child's approach to social relationships. If the adult's social development has been impaired, the same can occur with the children whom they influence; assistance from a mental health professional may be needed.

Cultures differ in what is reinforced. American culture is much more individualistic than collectivist cultures around the world. Being an individualist has its virtues, such as self-sufficiency in a time of need, but having a commitment to collectivist ideas, such as serving others and thus gaining social paybacks, can also be useful. When considering social relations, information should be placed in the context of the particular culture in which the child, adolescent, or adult lives.

Social adaptation and attachments require that the child or adolescent be able to give and take with others. Kids need to learn to get along with all sorts of other people.

The socially mature person senses the expectations of a situation and lives by the rules that apply to behavior in the particular cultural context. This wins favor from others, and gives the mature person an important sense of social accomplishment.

Low self-esteem and learning problems can contribute to a youth's resorting to socially maladaptive behaviors, such as being overly aggressive (e.g., bullying). The child or adolescent who demonstrates a tendency toward being shy, reclusive, hostile, or aggressive might be signaling a need for guidance. Parents and other responsible adults need to help these youngsters achieve more positive social relationships; to fulfill this helping role, some of those adults may need assistance from mental health professionals.

Human nature is very purposeful. Unfulfilled needs lead a person of any age to being highly goal-oriented. The person gets an idea about achieving something, maps a strategy for getting it, and embarks to fulfill the wish or goal.

Mastery depends on learning and acquiring new knowledge or skill. *Performance* goals rely on appearances and are fulfilled by favorable acknowledgement from others. Although people differ in their mastery and performance goals, everyone possesses and develops them during childhood and adolescence. The emphasis placed on mastery versus performance goals is determined by the family's values and preferences. There should be a healthy balance between seeking mastery and performance outcomes.

Beyond genetics (the nature assumption) and the shaping that occurs in the family context (the nurture assumption), children are apt to become like the people with whom they associate or who they observe, including in the electronic media (the social learning assumption). Parents and other responsible adults should control with whom a child or an adolescent spends time or who he or she observes.

The best alternative for assuring positive social learning is to guide the child into contacts with other young people who hold the values and ideals endorsed by the family and society. It is also helpful for the youngster to engage in diversified activities, such as sports or the arts, with other people.

Parents and other responsible adults should encourage every young person, regardless of age, to explore possible relationships with other kids (particularly in the same age group). They should also help the child learn how to analyze when a relationship with another youth is going to be constructive, which will offer equal and healthy opportunities for development to both of the youngsters.

Parents and other responsible adults need to help every child and adolescent learn how to select friends and develop positive relationships. In a friendship, there is an exchange of social rewards. Friendship is enhanced by emotions, and there must be a trusting exchange of intimate details about oneself. Emotions and trust are important tools for a positive life.

If the child chooses someone to be a friend who is or may be a poor choice (e.g., a friend who the parents believe would potentially be a bad influence on their child), the responsible adults should accept that it is time to talk again about how to understand, cultivate, and evaluate friendships. Peer influence must be balanced. It is ill advised to try to shut out influences from peers. It is, however, quite appropriate for parents and other relevant adults to monitor and shape peer influence. When needed, mental health professionals, of course, should provide these adults with guidance.

Most children and adolescents respond well to thoughtful, unemotional (nonrejecting), and caring discussions with their parents and other responsible adults. If there is blatant rejection of parental preferences and ideas, the parents should do a self-assessment regarding how they might approach the topic differently with their offspring – again, professional help may be advisable.

Rather than criticizing, the relevant adults should have discussions (not give lectures) that encourage the young person to identify the consequences of particular choices and alternatives. When adults actually listen carefully and considerately in these conversations, rather than being negative or hostile, the child or adolescent is more likely to also listen to the mature position.

Social development can be marred by faulty messages about discrimination. Any discriminatory act arising out of prejudice is an indicator of poor character. Effective parents and caregivers should help every child, regardless of age, avoid prejudice. It is especially important for the adults in the youngster's life to be positive role models. For example, if adults use derogatory language, such as about racial groups, it is almost inevitable that the child will adopt both the same derogatory language and the underlying prejudicial beliefs. It should go without saying, but no professional helper should, in any way, condone discrimination (e.g., there should never be joking about any person's characteristics).

With this social backdrop, this chapter gives consideration to how mental health professionals can guide parents and other relevant adults to maintaining both mental and physical health for the child. As will be presented, maintaining health is another child development issue that rests squarely on the shoulders of the parents and other responsible adults, but its substance and complexity often justifies the adult turning to a professional helper for information and support.

Expecting Health

Throughout this book, it is emphasized that (1) without mental and physical health, a child's overall quality of life will be lessened; (2) parents and other responsible adults need to guide youngsters into healthy behaviors, such as by providing information about diet, exercise, etc.; (3) adults need to practice what they preach, and be good role models to children and adolescents for healthy attitudes and behavior; and (4) family–school collaboration, along with use of other community resources, can facilitate healthy and constructive development for children and adolescents. In each of those four areas, the mental health professional has a potential role.

Throughout this book, five principles of communication have been mentioned, each of which is derived from extensive behavioral science research (e.g., see any basic textbook on developmental or social psychology) and are applicable to developmental health. First, in adult–child relationships, the adult and child should both be receptive to new ideas from the other person(s). Second, the youngster should be an active participant, and dominating or dictatorial messages from adults should be avoided. Third, efforts to change bad health practices should be framed in optimism for gaining a healthy lifestyle, that is, positive outcomes should be expected. Fourth, for any age, resistance to change is commonplace, but should not be tacitly allowed to decrease the adult's commitment to helping a child or adolescent adopt healthier attitudes and behaviors. Fifth, since resistance is to be expected, the adult and child should talk openly about strategies for change.

With the foregoing foundation, the culminating idea is that positive expectancies have the potential to provide cures for certain health problems. There is research to support the idea that taking steps to express positive expectancies, such as by *affect regulation strategies* (e.g., talking to friends, exercising, engaging in hobbies) will reduce negative emotions. When negative emotions are reduced, the body and mind respond with movement toward health. Clearly, mental health services embrace alleviating and eliminating negative emotions.

The actions that will work best (i.e., regulate affect) depend on the particular person. For one person, exercise might help. Someone else might respond best to socialization (e.g., supportive sharing of emotional ideas with friends or family members). Being creative is stimulating and therapeutic (e.g., practicing a musical instrument or pursuing a hobby).

One particularly useful technique involves expressive writing. Langens and Schüler (2007) talk about "coping with stressful experiences through written emotional expression," with their research indicating that "emotional expression may work to the extent that it induces high positive expectancies, which then lead to improvements in well-being" (p. 181). Research into emotional expression through writing shows that those "who elaborated traumatic experiences both cognitively and emotionally subsequently reduced their number of health center visits," and "written emotional expression also has beneficial effects on blood markers of immune functions, general functioning, and subjective emotional well-being" (p. 174). Stated simply, by taking time to write about emotions, such as in a diary, a person can develop positive expectancies and achieve improved healthy behavior.

The foregoing concept can be extended to thinking and talking in a positive fashion about emotions. For decades, there have been advocates of the power of positive thinking. Modern research offers convincing support for the idea that adopting a commitment to positive expectancies will promote healthy attitudes and behavior. As has been mentioned before, there may be cultural differences (including family values) relevant to how to best deal with emotions, and the context in which a person lives is always important. A mental health professional can assist in the process of identifying helpful strategies appropriate to the given person.

Modeling Health

Every parent and responsible adult hopes and prays that a child will be born without mental or physical problems, and throughout life, be as healthy as possible. Regardless of age, a person with poor health may miss the full range of opportunities in life.

Since a child is dependent on adults for protection, it is logical that parents and caretakers must give special importance to helping every child stay healthy and safe. Thus, the adult–child relationship can be central to helping a child avoid disabilities and limitations.

Adult guidance, particularly efforts from parents and other relevant adults, is essential to the goal of helping young people maintain health. In practical terms, adults try to instruct and guide children and adolescents through providing health-promoting information and experiences. For example, with these experiences and encouragement, children can learn the value of a proper diet, physical exercise, and healthy, positive attitudes.

To get kids to be mindful of health, the threshold issue for adults, again particularly parents and caretakers, is to practice what they preach. There are two reasons this guideline is critically important.

The first reason is to gain credibility with the child or adolescent. As an example, if a physician is known to be a smoker, his or her medical advice to get patients to quit smoking will be less persuasive than if the physician is a nonsmoker. In other words, it is human nature to believe people who both "talk the talk, AND walk the walk." This principle applies to all adults who want to instill healthy ideas in the minds of young people. (Of course, no mental health professional should reveal any non-healthy behavior.)

The second reason, somewhat similar to the first, is that every adult is a potential role model for a youngster. With parents and caregivers, this is particularly true. Consciously or unconsciously, adult behavior reinforces certain values, attitudes, emotions, and behaviors in young people. Just like the physician who smokes, an adult who chows down on junk food, consumes too much alcohol, smokes, abuses drugs, does not pursue weight control, and so on will definitely be a model for others who they influence, such as family members. Unfortunately, it will be a reinforcing model for the youngster to engage in the same unhealthy behaviors.

Some adults have good intentions about getting kids to adopt healthy ideas and behaviors. They will try to motive children to accept the importance of healthy living and provide information (such as magazine articles) for understanding the importance of self-control for health. Although worthwhile, this attention alone is not likely to be effective. Adults who disregard healthy behaviors in their own lives need to change and be a positive role model for young people of all ages. "Do as I say, not as I do" is an unacceptable message.

Motivating Kids to Be Healthy

As noted several times, there is no doubt that parents and other responsible adults are critically important in helping children and adolescents develop healthy lifestyles (Woody, 2002). Through adult–child guidance efforts, especially by parents and caregivers, youngsters can gain positive values and practices for healthy behavior.

Although adults can teach ideas and themselves model healthy behavior, the ultimate decision to adopt a healthy lifestyle belongs to the child or adolescent. Even though adolescents are expected to progressively make many of their own choices, younger children also have to sort through health-related messages and either reject or adopt them.

Today professional helpers are giving more recognition to the principles of *motivational interviewing*. This approach has relevance to adult–child guidance about health (and other issues as well). The mental health professional should consider conveying the following six guidelines to all adults.

First, the adult must create a relationship with the youngster that will establish receptivity to new ideas. The qualities or spirit directed at receptivity will depend on the nature of the relationship. For example, the child's relationship with a teacher would understandably be different from the relationship with his or her parents. In any event, the first step is adult–child collaboration and mutual respect, with a focus on supporting and benefiting the child or adolescent.

Second, the youth should be an active participant. A dominating or dictating adult will not motivate a kid to change ideas or behavior.

Third, the effort to bring about change, such as accepting health information or establishing healthier behaviors, should be framed in optimism. That is, the adult should convey that positive outcomes are possible and expected. With no hesitancy, both the adult and the child or adolescent should talk openly about being optimistic.

Fourth, the adult should recognize that human beings often resist change; this is true regardless of age of the person. If there is resistance, it should be acknowledged. Lessening the press for immediate change and taking time to discuss the pros and cons of more healthful living is a useful strategy. Stated differently, effective adult–child guidance requires that the adult roll with the resistance (Carey, Leontieva, Dimmock, Maisto, & Batki, 2007).

Fifth, the discussion should include strategies for change. Part of the teaching process is for the adult to get the youth's ideas about health and healthy behaviors. For example, the parent can also say what he or she, as parent, will do to help with change, such as buying healthy snacks instead of junk food. Changing the home environment can be a motivating factor that leads a child or adolescent to be open to personal change.

Sixth and finally (and as stated earlier), adult–child guidance depends upon the helping adult's having credibility. Since kids are impressionable and readily influenced by what they observe and experience, adults should consistently take advantage of their potential to be powerful role models for health.

These six guidelines should be useful to an adult who needs to personally follow a health lifestyle. The fact remains, a child or adolescent is, to a large extent, the product of his or her social situations involving peers, family members, and friends (as well as what is viewed in the media). For the best results, everyone in the youngster's life should accept ideas that promote health and put these ideas into practice in everyday life.

A Safe Haven

To my chagrin, I watched a 4-year-old scamper up an open staircase outside the banister. As he was perilously perched aloft, his response to my attempts to coax him down was, "I just want to touch the ceiling." In the next few minutes, he was running pell-mell across the porch with a pointed stick! These are clear examples of how impulse leads the immature child to make an unwise decision and to blindly move into dangerous activity.

When children are around, responsible adults know that constant vigilance is necessary. Regrettably, minor problems and major tragedies can occur when adult protections lapse for even a brief time. Prompt action was needed to get the 4-year-old off his dangerous perch and to remove the sharp stick before he fell.

Mental health professionals should teach that, in addition to being vigilant, parents and caregivers should take steps to child proof the home and other areas such as the yard, garage, or barn. This principle is especially important when there are young children. Effective child proofing is required when there are kids who, regardless of age, may or tend to act impulsively without any caution.

Children and adolescents should be kept away from dangerous objects, at least until such time as the adults believe that their safety is assured. With young children, many steps are necessary, such as putting child-proof plugs in electrical outlets, keeping objects (like a pot of hot water or a heated iron) out of reach, keeping medications locked away or at least in a closed container, and removing knives and tools.

By virtue of immaturity, a child or adolescent is not capable of adult-level reasoning and judgment. No matter what may be the kid's level of intelligence, how many assurances are given, or how much pleading occurs, responsible adults must steadfastly provide safeguards for young people against potentially dangerous situations or objects.

As has been mentioned earlier, a practical method to help the child or adolescent become aware of safety is for parents and other influential adults to practice what they preach. For example, an adult working around a noisy machine, like a lawn mower, should wear earplugs and goggles. Taking the example a bit further, the adult can enhance the modeling effects by taking all sorts of precautions with power tools, such as demonstrating the importance of meticulous care in using and maintaining the equipment properly.

Regardless of the age of the child or adolescent, there should be special concern about keeping firearms safe. (Note: I am not anti-firearms; in fact, I am a certified instructor in firearms safety and an avid shooter.) Trigger locks should be used. Ammunition should be stored away from the firearm. Gun cabinets and storage boxes should be fastened in a manner that allows only a properly trained adult to obtain the firearms.

When firearms are involved, with older children, the parent should constantly explain the importance of safety, such as "always keep your finger out of the trigger guard until you are ready to fire" and "don't ever play with a gun or knife." (For information about educational materials and training aids pertaining to firearms, contact the National Rifle Association at (800) 336-7402 or http:/www.nra.org/)

Prudent parents and other responsible adults should carefully plan what safety measures are needed in their particular family or caretaking situations. After agreeing on the sources of risk, such as the fact that there are potentially dangerous power tools or firearms accessible to the youngsters, the adults should educate the children and adolescents in precautions and enforce the rules.

Rules for safety are no less important than other rules of conduct that are expected from young people of all ages. As maturity increases, the rules may vary, but a firm commitment to maintaining a safe home environment should always be present.

Being Vigorous

"Gee, I feel awful, I'm down in the dumps all the time and I think that I have every ailment in the book." When someone says something of that nature, my usual first response is to be empathic, as in "I sense your discomfort." And I might even express a bit of sympathy, such as "I regret that you feel that way." However, if the person is making no effort to turn things around, my view changes to being less supportive.

An important message for professional helpers to convey is that being responsible for oneself is a fundamental of achieving mental and physical health. To paraphrase an old TV commercial: "You gain health the old-fashioned way – you earn it."

If a person wants to be as healthy as possible, there must be a strong commitment to physical fitness. Research is convincing that maintaining a good diet, keeping weight down, and conditioning the body produces physical and mental health and, indeed, longevity.

With physical health, mental health is strengthened, whereas physical complaints lead to negative feelings, such as depression. With mental health, positive emotions occur, such as happiness, joy, pride, and love. These conditions strengthen the person's overall life.

Combining physical and mental health, the individual, regardless of age, gains vigor for living. There is energy for favored activities such as sports and recreation, and motivation for being involved in social situations. Socializing yields important rewards, as well as improved opportunities for accomplishing work, family, and personal goals.

Some professional helpers recommend the *broaden-and-build* model for positive emotions. With physical strength, emotional energy, and cognitive (thinking) liveliness, the person gains three things (Shiron, 2004). First, physical strength results in a high level of energy for daily tasks. Second, there is emotional energy for being capable of relationships. Finally, the person feels mentally agile.

The word *vigor* may not be in a person's everyday conversations. It means active strength of body and mind, with an intensity to take appropriate actions. For persons of all ages, vigor is certainly a desirable condition to seek (Shiron, Toker, Berliner, Shapira, & Melamed, 2008). Parents and other responsible adults who pursue vigor will be able to pass the health-related goal on to children and adolescents. As a reminder, mental health professionals can be positive role models relevant to health by seeking healthful living and vigor for themselves.

Emotional Kids

As should be apparent from the preceding discussion, a definition of health includes both mental and physical well-being. Also, it is known that there is a reciprocal influence, that is, emotional factors can influence physical factors, and vice versa.

Almost in tears, a parent said, "I don't know what has happened to my child – cheerfulness has been replaced with irritability." Another parent told me, "The least little thing leads to an outburst of temper, and it didn't used to be that way." Regrettably, many children shift from one primary mood to another one, which is sometimes just part of maturing but is sometimes due to a critical problem.

Everyone has up and down emotions. With children of all ages, but particularly teenagers, the steps toward maturity sometimes lead to exaggerated concerns, especially with worries about how other kids view them. For example, an adolescent may feel easily offended by a peer and then turn the feeling into a catastrophe.

Every adult, especially a parent or caretaker, needs to be careful to not overreact to the emotions revealed by a child or adolescent. In other words, a mountain should not be made of a molehill – it could be that an outburst of emotion is nothing to worry about. The old advice may be true: "Don't worry about it, the kid will outgrow it."

Nonetheless, it is wise to be sensitive to how a child or adolescent feels. If something seems to be troubling a youngster, efforts should be made to help the kid put the source of the bad feeling into a realistic perspective. Often an adult can accomplish this by simply being available and talking with the child or adolescent in a caring way about the bothersome issue.

Major shifts in childhood emotions deserve special attention. When the child or adolescent seems significantly different emotionally, adults who deal with the kid should also look for changes in appetite, sleep, energy level, self-esteem, decision-making ability, concentration, and expectations (anticipation replaced by hopelessness). If there is a sudden change in emotions and for no known reason, it is time to look into the matter.

If the adult's efforts to uncover the reasons for the continuing emotional changes do not work, it may well be logical and wise to contact a mental health professional. Since emotions have both physical and psychological bases, the first step may be to consult with a pediatrician or family medicine practitioner, but the facts of the situation might point toward another type of professional helper.

Assuming that the source of the irritability is not medical (i.e., physical) in nature, the parents and other responsible adults should try to get the child or adolescent to explain what has been going on in his or her life. For example, the kid should be encouraged to reveal thoughts and concerns that might lead to grumpiness. An adult should not just ask "why" questions. It is important to have ongoing conversations about the youngster's everyday activities. With this kind of talk, the child or adolescent may naturally and more openly share concerns. Then the discussion could focus on evaluating the concerns and how best to deal with them. There may be, of course, more to the situation, and professional mental health services may be necessary.

Although perhaps difficult for some adults, especially parents and caregivers, to face, a young person is, in many ways, a barometer of the emotional climate within the family or social system. For example, a father and mother who are warring with each other, even if they try to keep the dispute and rejection out of the presence of the children, are likely to cast a blanket over positive emotions for all concerned, and the kids will suffer. In this scenario, it is obvious that the parents, not the youth, may need help from a mental health professional.

Moody Kids

In the same realm as emotional youngsters, a parent told me, "My child is a puzzle to me. It seems like there is a 'mood of the hour,' from being down in the dumps to sitting on top of the world." What that parent was describing is a possible red flag for a mood disorder.

In normal child development, every young person struggles to understand what life is all about, such as what to expect from other people (especially peers), the meaning of things that are said or events that are experienced, and whether he or she can deal with everyday events. Since thoughts trigger emotions, it is not unusual for the uncertainty that swirls around in a child's mind to cause a wide variety of emotions.

By definition, a *mood* is a short-lived emotional state. Typically a mood is not intense or disrupting. Of course, if the emotion is prolonged and extreme, it is another matter.

Some drastic and reoccurring changes in moods merit concern by the adults who deal with the kid, and help from a mental health professional is often logical. For example, parents and other relevant adults should monitor if a child or adolescent often shows swings in moods, such as shifting quickly from happiness to sadness and differing intensity in similar circumstances, such as from a "whatever" attitude, to rage when directed by a teacher to do something.

Moods are not the same as emotions. VandenBos (2007) provides an example of the difference, noting that moods lack a specific object or trigger: "the emotion of anger can be aroused by an insult, but an angry mood may arise when one does not know what one is angry about or what elicited the anger" (p. 591).

If a negative mood continues, even if it is not particularly disrupting, it is likely that the youngster has developed and maintains a predisposition for how to think, feel, and respond when someone says something or when an event occurs that brings out emotion. Obviously, a predisposition can restrict a full-range of responses. If preordained by moodiness, the response may be inappropriate; if determined by open-mindedness, the response is most apt to be appropriate. In other words, it is much better for a person, regardless of age, to be able to react realistically to the particular communication or event, rather than processing the event through a restricted or preordained mood filter.

Although adolescence is often characterized as a period for unexpected moods, the adolescent stage per se does not eliminate the need for responsible adults to monitor the conditions that surround the moodiness. At any stage of life, it is a sign of health to show accurate and appropriate responses to a given situation, whereas a pattern of negative moodiness increases the likelihood of an unhealthy way of dealing with life.

Swings in moods and intensity may be warning signs of possible emotional problems that require professional mental health services. For example, a mental health professional could help the family members assess whether the youngster has adopted a restrictive or adverse predisposition, whether individual or family therapeutic interventions could help the child alter the predisposition to a more positive one, or whether a physician-prescribed medication is called for to help stabilize the mood.

Eating Problems in Childhood

Overall, people living in civilized societies are blessed by living in a land of plenty. In fact, some people believe that modern society affords too much for the person's own good. Such a caveat can certainly be applied to over-reliance on food.

For crass commercial reasons, mass advertising appeals to everyone's appetite, and tries to create and maintain a craving for foods. All too often, the products, packed with fat, sugar, and other non-nutritious substances, are not particularly healthy.

Young girls are especially vulnerable to unhealthy eating. Media ads subject them to adverse food ideas, as well as bombard them with images and suggestions that every girl should have the perfect figure. Many girls take this message to mean that they must look like a thin and trim teen model to be attractive.

Young boys are also vulnerable to poor eating habits and notions about having to look like a teen hunk. The scandal about steroid use by professional athletes reveals negative role models foisted on children and adolescents (and adults as well).

As with so many aspects of helping children, it is for responsible adults to create an environment that will help every young person develop healthy nutrition habits. Surveys reveal that there are literally millions of American youths, both males and females, suffering from eating disorders.

An eating disorder can take many forms, such as compulsive overeating, anorexia nervosa (self-starvation), and bulimia nervosa (a bingeing and purging pattern). With compulsive overeating, a youth may show signs of obesity. Symptoms of the last two disorders can include intense and irrational fear (with physical discomfort and anxiety) about weight, extreme diet restrictions, vomiting, and misuse of medications (such as laxatives and diet pills).

Not only can an eating disorder lead to permanent physical impairments (such as heart arrhythmia, electrolyte disturbances, low blood pressure, and so on), it can lead to death – yes, even with children.

When an adult suspects or observes serious symptoms of an eating problem, the first instinct is to help the child or adolescent. However, with parents and caregivers, this often takes the form of arguments and nagging about food and meals. It is important to know and accept that eating disorders commonly require professional help.

There are more general symptoms to which responsible adults should pay attention. The child may convey feelings that he or she is unattractive and may hold unrealistic and perfectionist standards. For example, girls with an eating disorder are often high achievers and extremely active in school, yet still feel unworthy.

When there is a possibility of an eating disorder, the parents or caretakers should be encouraged to make arrangements for the youngster to be seen by a physician immediately. An eating disorder may also involve psychological considerations, which might be relevant to an assessment by a qualified mental health practitioner. Contacting other types of professional helpers may also be appropriate. An interdisciplinary approach is often needed, which might include medications prescribed by a physician along with mental health services or some other type of professional help. Severe cases may require inpatient treatment.

Unusual eating practices cannot be ignored, excused, or rationalized as being personal peculiarities on the part of the child or adolescent. They are warning signs that adults who care about the youngster's well-being must heed.

Overweight Kids

According to various public health sources, America's youth are experiencing a high and frightening incidence of being overweight. Research makes it clear that obesity has the potential for devastating physical and mental health effects.

There are some children and adolescents who become overweight for physiological reasons, such as glandular problems. In these instances, medical attention is necessary. However, in many cases of childhood and adolescent obesity, the problem is due to poor eating habits and inactivity.

A good diet does not require eating broccoli and spinach all the time, but it does call for truly nutritious meals. More importantly, young people of all ages need to be protected from the addictive appeal of junk foods. When I was in law school, one of my professors was only half-joking when he said, "Feeding kids junk food should be declared legally to be child abuse!"

Healthy exercise through enjoyable physical activity should be the norm for youths. Research has established exercise as essential for good health – at all ages!

Allowing a child or adolescent to become a couch potato deprives the youth of opportunities to feel physically strong and to enjoy activities with others kids. Sitting clued to the tube watching mindless television programs can start a pattern of isolation, passivity, and overeating that carries over into adolescence and adulthood.

Fortunately, a little exercise goes a long way. There is reason to believe that even a few minutes each day of rigorous exercise will have a noticeable and healthful effect.

Once in my neighborhood, I lived down the street from a family with over a dozen children. It was very common to see one or more of the brood jogging by my house. The age of the joggers ranged from elementary to high school. When I asked one of the teenagers about it, he said that his parents would not allow any child a privilege unless it was earned, and a favorite way to earn a privilege was to jog a lap around the block. Also, any time discipline for misbehavior was deserved, the parents did not impose spankings, they required exercise. Although the advisability of using exercise as a consequence of misbehavior can be debated, it seems better than sending a child to a bedroom that is equipped with television and video games.

Mental health professionals should advocate two principles. First, children of all ages need to eat healthily, and they also need exercise. Second, it is up to parents and other responsible adults to make sure that children follow a healthy path.

All adults (including professional helpers) should also, of course, try themselves to be positive role models. This means that adults, too, should govern their eating and exercise. To really maximize the best outcome, parents and other responsible adults should often join in the activities with the youngsters whom they love and care for.

Who Will Abuse Substances

Among young people, there certainly seems to be a rash of substance abuse. To the shock and dismay of many adults, substance abuse can happen at almost any stage of childhood or adolescence, right down into the elementary school years and continuing on into adulthood. Of course, substance abuse can happen at any time in adulthood.

Most commonly, substance abuse involves smoked or chewed tobacco, drinking of alcohol, smoked or chewed marijuana, sniffed or breathed chemicals (called "huffing" inhalants), smoked or injected hard drugs (crack, cocaine, heroin, etc.), use of medications not prescribed for the user, and swallowing ecstasy or LSD. And there can be other substances, not the least of which could be food.

Certainly adults need to oppose substance abuse. Professional helpers should be a source for information that adults can use in the context of adult–child guidance. The intent would, of course, be for the relevant adults to provide youngsters with the facts and risks of substance abuse that will be critically important for prevention.

As discussed previously, it is known that kids imitate what they observe, and they adopt the values expressed by others. Regrettably, some adults, because of their own substance abuse, essentially plant the seeds for abuse in the minds of children and adolescents. It is hypocritical, of course, for adults to speak against any kind of conduct and then go ahead to do it themselves. Likewise, joking about substance abuse is inappropriate and off the preventive message.

Stated bluntly, preventing substance abuse by children and adolescents starts at home and in their relationships with parents, family members, and other responsible adults. Even then, the youths may abuse substances. The question is, who will be a substance abuser?

A simple answer to that provocative question is impossible (Geiger, O'Neal, Petri, Stanhope, & Whittinghill, 2005). Genetics may create a predisposition for substance abuse in some people. Regardless of heredity, a person can, however, be reinforced to be or not to be an abuser.

In keeping with the discussion of the family–school–community nexus in Chapter 1, an important component of modern education is for the school curriculum to provide health-related information. Although there are numerous topics that the health curriculum should cover in the classroom (e.g., nutrition, physical fitness, responsible sexuality, and so on), the perils of substance abuse merit ongoing, accurate coverage extending throughout the school years.

It is known that children, as they mature, are quite malleable in their beliefs and values (including into young adulthood) and are significantly influenced by their classmates or peers. Research pinpoints that youngsters who think it's cool to use tobacco, alcohol, or drugs, especially if friends also share this belief, may be at increased risk of substance abuse.

In their relationships with children and adolescents, all adults should be tuned in for any attitudes or beliefs that support negative or risky behaviors. In addition, information about health-related issues, such as substance abuse, is an absolute necessity for guiding young people into healthy maturity and social responsible lives. As said several times, adult–child guidance is best accomplished when adults practice what they preach.

Whenever there are signs of substance abuse by a child or adolescents, adults must get past the disbelief or denial response. In many situations, adult oversight and supervision, along with services from professional helpers, may be necessary. This could lead to a referral for interventions by professional helpers in a variety of contexts. If all else fails, the juvenile justice system may help stop the kid's path to inappropriate conduct. Substance abuse must not be tolerated.

Alcohol and Aggression

Most people are aware that violent scenes in television or movies can stimulate some people to become more hostile. In fact, if someone is already angry, seeing some sort of depiction of violence can trigger an aggressive outburst. This principle may potentially lead some persons to feeling more aggressive from being around a weapon. Moreover, alcohol consumption increases the likelihood of aggression. The individual's usual inhibition response is impaired, and he or she can become more easily angered and hostile.

The abuse of alcohol, and of other controlled substances as well, has been clearly documented for its negative effects on behavior. Research reveals a correlation between alcohol intoxication and various types of aggression, including (but certainly not limited to) domestic violence and abuse, assault, rape, and even homicide. It is also known that intoxication impairs decision-making and lessens the ability to control physical actions, such as the thought process and skills needed for driving an automobile safely.

Rather than creating a biochemical stimulus to be more aggressive, alcohol weakens normal personal restraints against aggression. In becoming less restrained, the individual loses the ability to think clearly and judge or evaluate personal thoughts, feelings, and behavior – and effective control of behavior deteriorates.

When intoxicated, the person resorts to automatic or impulsive responses. This is termed *disinhibition,* which results from a decrease in one's ability to process information and respond in a meaningful way. As the situation becomes more difficult or complex, disinhibition becomes more pronounced.

With the foregoing somewhat highfalutin explanation, the message is that reduced self-awareness can lead to behavior that otherwise would not have occurred. For example, a person who is always well behaved may, when intoxicated, become a "mean drunk." When someone says things that he or she regrets later, the excuse may be, "it's the alcohol talking."

For some people, being intoxicated allows them to create a justification (though irrational) for aggressive behavior. In other words, the drunk person may try to concoct a self-excuse for having acted irresponsibly. This is what the Alcoholics Anonymous approach calls "stink thinking," whereas rational thinking is that an aggressive act, such as abusing a family member, is never justifiable. Anyone who acts violently when intoxicated cannot be excused for the wrongful behavior.

As part of educating a child or adolescent to have a realistic understanding of the effects and risks of consuming alcohol, parents and other responsible adults need to convey the message that no one can confidently handle liquor. That is, everyone is potentially susceptible to the adverse effects of alcohol, and certain other mind-altering substances as well.

Teenage Alcohol and Substance Abuse

In some ways, teenage drinking of alcohol is considered a rite of passage, something that all teenagers do. The same can be said for the use of certain other mind-altering substances, such as marijuana. Regrettably, irresponsible drinking and other substance abuse by youths has resulted in countless deaths and ruined many lives.

The notion that "all kids do it" or "I only drink at parties" is no justification for adults to tolerate use of alcohol by youngsters. From the point of view of society, all adults should demonstrate responsibility by preventing underage access to alcohol or other illegal substances. Although a teenager may be able to gain access to alcohol, to do so is against the law.

It is known that parents or other adults often provide alcohol to underage drinkers. No adult should condone abuse of alcohol or other addictive or illegal substances by minors. Not only could the adult who makes alcohol available to youths be potentially charged with a crime, if any destructive effects of intoxication result, the chain of liability could extend to the adult who enabled the teenage drinking.

The reason for preventing alcohol use by children or teenagers goes well beyond the law per se. It is unhealthy for young people to rely on alcohol or other mind-altering substance as a way to deal with life (the same can be said for adults). It is a faulty lesson to teach kids that, instead of analyzing and dealing directly with a problem, the use of a substance can lessen the burden. To restate, abusing a substance in a manner that creates jeopardy for self and others is absolutely indefensible, regardless of the age of the individual.

The foregoing is not to say that consuming alcohol is, in and of itself, something that should not be done – by an adult. The message is that youths of any age are not prepared for mature behavior, and using a legally controlled substance is unacceptable and a legal violation. Responsible adults should guide children and adolescents toward healthy attitudes and behaviors, and teenage consumption of alcohol or other mind-altering substances contradicts this goal. This objective is commonplace in mental health services.

Likewise, although it is legal and acceptable for an adult to drink alcohol, it is well known that overindulgence of alcohol – at any age – leads to all sorts of problems, such as in work productivity, family relationships, and daily events (e.g., driving under the influence and creating jeopardy for the public). Again, other mind-altering substances (including abuse of prescription medications) can have the same adverse effects on an adult.

Responsible adults should monitor their own consumption of alcohol and other mind-altering substances to be sure that they do not impair their health or functioning. By effective self-regulation, the adult will teach youngsters that legal and restrained use of alcohol or other mind-altering substance is the only appropriate way to use the substance. Without exception, use of illegal drugs should not be condoned, whether by adults or young people.

Parents and other responsible adults must be consistent and emphatic with the message that underage use of alcohol, no matter what the occasion or how limited, is wrong and will not be accepted to any degree. In addition, the parents should seek or make opportunities to discuss with their children the information about why underage drinking is unacceptable, the potential for criminal conduct, and a framework for appropriate consumption in adulthood, including a caution about negative effects for health, work, family, and life in general.

(Note: Any mental health professional with a substance abuse problem creates risks to service users, and may well be held or alleged to be an *impaired practitioner* by the licensing agency in the state in which he or she provides services. The mental health professional should be the first to be concerned about his or her possible abuse of substance and seek professional help.)

Use of Illicit Substances

Many societies worldwide suffer a scourge of addiction. Any substance abuse will tend to cause problems at both the micro (individual) and macro (societal) levels. It is incomprehensible that some governments ignore the risks and do little or nothing to stem the availability of harmful substances or to provide treatment and rehabilitation to addicts. The use of alcohol and other mind-altering substances by children and adolescents is, of course, particularly troubling. No responsible adult can let this problem go unattended. Certainly, all professional helpers should assiduously campaign against substance abuse and in favor of more governmental support for treatment and rehabilitation.

Worldwide, substance abuse varies in incidence. At some point in life, about one fourth of the general population in the United States has a substance use disorder. With youngsters, about half have used an illicit drug sometime (Daley & Moss, 2002). Substance abuse takes a heavy toll on kids, their family members and friends, and our society.

There is reason to believe that, because they are still developing, children and adolescents are more vulnerable to the bad effects of drugs than adults. For a youngster who uses harmful substances, there is a distinct possibility of alteration of the brain, which may be permanent. That is, the brain of a child or adolescent may suffer drug-induced developmental delay or arrest. Rosner (2005) warns of drug abuse resulting in a failure of normal cognitive development, even for adolescents who eventually stop using drugs. He gives the caveat: "Whether the teen-aged brain can ever recover from a drug induced developmental delay or arrest is unknown at this time" (p. 20), and points to possible learning problems, poor impulse control, unwise judgment, and impaired comprehension.

Drugs can produce mental and conduct disorders and health problems that lead to flaws in daily decision-making, job performance, and social relationships. Also, there is an elevated risk of criminal conduct.

Use of drugs by children and adolescents creates a bleak outlook. It is, therefore, imperative that, regardless of country, all adults, especially parents and caregivers, become well versed in the effects of illicit drugs, including the side effects of withdrawal. If there is any hint that a child or adolescent is using a mind-altering substance, the adult must take decisive action. For example, despite any resistance by the youth, the adults should obtain a screening test. In keeping with the idea of family–school collaboration, educators can often "grease the skids" to get an appropriate assessment. Help is likewise commonly available from a variety of professional helpers.

Adult and peer attitudes have a powerful effect on a youth's predisposition to use alcohol and other drugs. Permissiveness, such as joking about marijuana usage, may be interpreted as condoning or endorsing substance abuse. Allowing a child or adolescent to associate with kids who are bad influences results in bad role models. A youngster with low self-esteem, a tendency to be nonconforming, a lack of involvement in activities within the school or religious contexts, and tendency toward sensation-seeking is at increased risk of substance abuse.

Warning signs meriting consideration include a child or adolescent with ongoing or recent school problems, health issues, family conflicts, or difficulties with peers. These are sometimes signs of vulnerability to substance abuse.

To counter the negatives, adults should help all youths, regardless of age, develop strong ties with their families and community, and get involved in constructive social groups (e.g., in the school or religious context). In the framework of adult–child guidance, there should be reasonable and appropriate limits on activities, along with caring supervision. Efforts should be made to reinforce optimism, positive activity, self-esteem, and avoiding risks.

In the long run, there is no substitute for a youngster having healthy interactions with others, adults and peers, and having caring guidance from (particularly) relevant adults, such as parents and caregivers. Without these positive influences, the risk of use of, and addiction to, illicit substances can potentially impact any child or adolescent.

In closing this discussion about substance abuse, it should be noted that liberal views do not justify a mental health professional's creating an exception to the law. One mental health professional said, "There is nothing wrong with using marijuana" – however, the statutes of the state in which the mental health professional practiced contradicted this opinion. For licensed mental health professionals, it is mandatory that the laws of the jurisdiction be upheld and reflected in the professional services provided under the auspices of the licensing granted by the jurisdiction. To do otherwise is a contradiction of professionalism. Of course, if the mental health professional believes that any law should be changed, it is, indeed, highly professional to seek to influence legislation or administrative codes by lawful means.

9 Adolescence

Without mental and physical health, a person of any age will be deprived of a full life. In any contacts with young people, adults should guide them toward positive values and practices for healthy behavior. In fact, the same can be said to be a logical principle of any social relationships – that is, an interpersonal experience should reinforce positive values and healthy behavior.

Children need to live in a safe haven, which requires that adults keep a constant vigil for risks. It must be remembered that, due to immaturity, a child or adolescent is not capable of adult-level reasoning and judgment. Therefore, adult monitoring and guidance are essential.

By providing health-promoting information and experiences, adults can instruct and guide kids of all ages toward healthy lifestyles. Perhaps of most importance, the adults in a youth's life need to practice what they preach, and be role models for constructive and healthy behavior.

The adult–child relationship should establish mutual receptivity to new ideas, and the youngster should be an active participant. Health information should be presented in a positive framework, and resistance by the child or adolescent should not thwart strategic efforts to motivate positive changes.

With kids, emotions and moods should be monitored for red flags of impending risky or unhealthy conditions. Throughout childhood and adolescence, adults, especially parents and caregivers, should devote special attention to indications of eating problems, obesity, and any kind of substance abuse.

Adolescence ushers a myriad of unique considerations. VandenBos (2007) states: "During this period major changes occur at varying rates in sexual characteristics, body image, sexual interest, social roles, intellectual development, and self-concept" (pp. 21–22). During the teenage years, social, emotional, and behavioral problems are common, and it is important that adults in the adolescent's life help with resolving these problems.

The Teenage Trajectory

When a teenager is in, or has graduated from, high school, there is an increase in self-determinations. Not having as much parental or adult guidance can lead to decisions that will expose the adolescent to risky situations, such as drinking alcohol or other substance abuse, associating with people who are not positive role models, and going places that adult or mature wisdom would oppose. Said simply, the teenage years potentially pose special pitfalls and challenges. If adverse conditions are experienced, the youngster will be at risk for engaging in faulty judgments and unwise behavior, some of which may have lifelong consequences (e.g., being convicted of a crime).

In earlier years, preadolescent children are more reliant on directions from others. To varying degrees, a child relies on, and usually complies with, the directives and expectations of responsible adults, such as family members and teachers. In other words, a child's life is structured by the adult world.

For many teenagers, structure from the adult world tends to decrease. Along with experiencing powerful peer influence, normal maturation brings an increased need for problem-solving and self-determination. As the teenager graduates from high school and external structure decreases, the youth must initiate steps to embark on a plan or trajectory that will lead to a rewarding life. This challenge may justly lead to reliance on professional helpers.

It would be helpful for every child and adolescent to have the benefits of wise adult guidance to stay on a constructive course of action. Regrettably, not every youngster has protective, wise, and compassionate support from responsible adults, which is why professional help should be an option for dealing with critical issues.

In keeping with effective guidance and helping principles, adults should appraise the trajectory or pathway of development engaged in by a young person. This monitoring should, of course, be consistent and take place throughout the early years of childhood and on through adolescence.

Contrary to popular misconception, teenagers are not locked into a particular trajectory. Change is possible, and the youth can turn in a positive direction or enter into a slip-sliding away toward a negative track.

Although it is up to the teenager to "own" a positive trajectory by choosing healthful goals, a conscientious and responsible adult can help a young person develop a structure for self-management. A logical strategy is to help the adolescent identify factors that require attention (e.g., the resources that are available to pursue certain ideas), the steps that are necessary to achieve a particular goal, the way to shift gears when necessary, and the trigger for concrete actions. For example, if a newly graduated teenager believes that a new automobile is essential, adults should point out the need for a substantial income to pay for the car and the amount of interest that will accrue on any loan needed for its purchase.

Without the foregoing wisdom, the youth may rush into a bad judgment about, among other things, finances. For example, reaching the age of 18 allowed one young man to qualify for US $10,000 from a trust fund established by his grandparents. Although he was not, and did not aspire to be, a professional musician, he spent all of the money on guitars and amplifiers – and drugs! The grandparents had hoped that the money would be used for college tuition.

When offering guidance, a good starting point is for the concerned adult to ask the teenager, "What are the most significant things that you have experienced in life, the good and the bad?" And then, "How are these experiences going to help you decide on what you want out of life, your goals for your life?"

If a youth shares personal goals and aspirations, another technique is to ask, "What do you need to accomplish your goals?" and "Can you get the resources – how and where?" In other words, adolescents will benefit from responsible adults cultivating critical analysis and planning. Again, meeting the challenge often requires professional help.

A mental health professional can provide useful information and suggestions for the teenager's consideration. The psychological principle is, of course, that everyone can improve and expand their alternatives by receiving ideas from others. If the youth is open-minded, additional information may lead to self-directed alterations in the trajectory.

Although older teenagers commonly place high value on self-determination, they can always potentially benefit from ideas and information from others. All relevant adults should remain open to contributing support to the adolescent's efforts to develop logical plans, and to establish and maintain a healthy and constructive pathway in life. When in doubt, these adults should seek support from professional helpers.

Teenage Social Acceptance

It is important for mental health professionals, and other relevant adults as well, to understand how self-esteem and personal identity develop in children and adolescents. By recognizing the social pressure that the youngster is experiencing, which may be real or imagined, the professional helper or responsible adult can decide on how to offer support and guidance.

Although a person's ideas about self-worth occur throughout life, adolescence is particularly crucial for shaping the youth's personal assessment and outlook on his or her potential and opportunities in the stream of life's events. For example, research indicates that teasing and rejection are greatest in middle childhood (say ages 10 to 12). As one psychologist described it, "The pain is deep with middle school kids."

In adolescence, individual differences allow some teenagers to cope well with disappointments, such as when they are not admitted into the "in" crowd, while others may exaggerate or over-react to disappointments. After the ups and downs of teenage turmoil, most young people eventually move toward being resilient or start to grow in personal strength.

The struggle to win approval from fellow students may lead a vulnerable teenager to make impetuous efforts to be accepted. In attempting to be distinguished in a way that will win approval, the youth may begin to act out characteristics, almost like an actor on a stage. Of the actions intended to bring about social acceptance, some can be healthy and constructive, such as seeking good grades or being active in school or community activities, and some will be misguided, such as being negative toward school or adopting weird or antisocial behaviors.

Playing out different roles on life's stage is not necessarily bad. It allows the young person to search for an individual style and purpose. If something does not produce the desired results, another role can be tried. For example, I remember that my efforts in high school sports produced far less social reward than my playing a musical instrument and performing at teen dances. Eventually competencies emerge and become permanent parts of the person's identity. (Yes, I still play my musical instruments daily.)

If the role-played persona is accepted by other teenagers, the kid's social status is elevated. For example, it is not uncommon for athletes, those in musical ensembles and performances, and the like to feel higher self-esteem than those students who retreat into the shadows.

The effort to win acceptance is not without risk. In the event that the other teenagers frown on or ridicule something that a student does, the rejection or shunning can inflict severe mental injury. A sense of rejection by peers has been found to be a characteristic common to youths who have resorted to violence. In their analysis of school shootings, Newman, Fox, Harding, Mehta, and Roth (2004) say:

> When students go to school and shoot randomly at their classmates, they are, more than anything, trying to send a message to everyone about how they want to be seen. . . . By randomly targeting their classmates, they showed that they were less interested in revenge against particular individuals than in broadcasting their message to the peer and community structure that had rejected them. (p. 127)

Mental health professionals should assist responsible adults in developing insights and skills for monitoring constantly how a youth's efforts to win peer acceptance are being received and, in turn, how the young person is dealing with the reactions from peers. Offering a helping hand, such as opening doors to social acceptance in untried ways, may be life-saving. Said simply, all professional helpers and responsible adults should support youngsters in their quest for peer acceptance, and keep their social tactics on a constructive and healthy path.

Teenage Dating

As any mental health professional, parent, or responsible adult will quickly attest, understanding child development and offering guidance to youngsters is always challenging. Adolescence introduces additional perplexing issues, particularly romantic attraction. When adolescence arrives, young people are biologically programmed to feel attraction toward others with interest in close personal relationships, which potentially includes emotional and sexual intimacies.

Social expectations and personal needs lead teenagers to engage in dating and other social activities together and to form couple relationships. It is not unusual for "young love" to enter the picture.

Most commonly, the dating is appropriate and, indeed, healthy to help an adolescent learn how to relate to others and about expectations and rewards of relationships. As is often the case, too little or too much of a good thing can, of course, be detrimental or problematic.

If the youth tends to retreat from social relationships and dating, the isolation can lead to negative emotions and create a threat to self-esteem.

Self-confidence involves a realistic understanding of personal qualities, and the payoff goes well beyond popularity with other teenagers. Young people who believe in and value themselves make the most of opportunities, such as in learning, careers, and relationships with others. Consequently, responsible adults, especially parents and caregivers, should encourage, not discourage, adolescents to engage in diverse teenage activities, including dating numerous others.

On the other end of the continuum, however, a youth who becomes obsessed with social relationships, to the exclusion of other constructive activities, may be penalized. For example, an early dating relationship that blocks shared experiences with a variety of teenagers can detract from essential attitude and behavioral development. Therefore, professional helpers and responsible adults should provide adolescents with guidance for understanding and accepting why having a host of friends is much more healthy for all concerned than becoming locked into a relationship with one person.

It is not unusual for a teenage couple to think that they have found "true love." And adults should not discount the fact that young people do experience intense feelings of love and caring for a partner. However, some societies, such as in the United States, are not structured to support the profound intimate bonding of teenage couples, such as through marriage.

An 11th-grade boy who was a sports hero and a 12th-grade girl who was Miss Popularity in their high school became singularly focused on graduating from high school and getting married. Their mutual obsession resulted in the loss of enriched social relations with others and realistic planning for college and careers. Despite all of their potential talents, their exclusivity and obsession with an early marriage limited their emotional development and minimized their opportunities for the rest of their lives. Soon after her graduation, a blow up occurred and both suffered greatly – but by then there were irreparable adverse effects.

Mental health professionals should educate adults and youngsters alike about how social relationships are potentially invaluable for helping young people discover who they are and what their talents are. In addition, through dating and friendships, teens learn how to have healthy relationships and to judge character – their own and that of others. Professional helpers can assist parents and other adults in encouraging teenagers to enjoy and learn from relationships with other youths.

Adult wisdom, compassion, and supervision are essential for helping young people through the ups and downs of teen friendships and couple relationships. As reflected in mental health services, listening with compassion to an adolescent's experiences is the first step. Next, adults should encourage a teenager to engage in a variety of social activities. Finally, adult supervision and, in some cases, setting limits may be necessary for a youth who is on an extreme course – either of isolation or of an intensely intimate couple relationship. Since some adults find supervision and setting limits difficult or impossible, professional help may be needed.

The Blame Game

It is a fundamental psychological principle that everyone, regardless of age, wants to avoid criticism. No one wants to be at fault. Why? Simply put, the person receives rejection, whereas there was likely some internal expectation of, and preference for, a reward that motivated the person's behavior.

In the early days of psychology, justifying a negative outcome relied upon what was called a *defense mechanism*. Words like *projecting* (attributing one's own motives or weaknesses to another person), *identification* (pretending to be like an admired person), *rationalizing* (making excuses), and *repression* (shutting unpleasantness out of mind) were used in everyday conversation.

Today people still try to deny or avoid acknowledging shortcomings by using alternative explanations. Instead of examining a negative outcome and looking for one's own part in this, some people explain successes and failures by *attributions,* such as pointing an accusatory finger at an alleged cause other than oneself.

At an early age, children attempt to justify failures. Up until about age 5, children have little understanding about causes of behavior or outcomes. Over the next few years, they start recognizing, understanding, and coping with things that lead them to behave in way that will produce chosen or preferred outcomes.

By about age 13, children are able to differentiate between effort and ability. They realize that, no matter how hard they try or how strong their effort, they may not have what it takes to be successful in certain situations. Prior to this, children often freely entertain fantasies about the grandiose achievement that comes to very few people.

When children begin to recognize the realities in their lives, they begin to know personal limitations. This awareness is potentially healthy and can prevent unnecessary disappointing outcomes. In other words, by being realistic, the youngster does not get involved in a situation that is totally beyond his or her capability.

Some children and adolescents may tend to deny that they caused or had a part in a problem behavior. Instead of accepting responsibility, these kids claim that circumstances were imposed on them against their will, such as by an event or the acts of others. In other words, instead of accepting the role of their own choice or action, these youngsters strive to convince others that the cause was due to external factors. Of course some adults do the same thing.

Mental health professionals should inform parents and other adults that when a youngster has a behavior problem, relevant adults should help him or her face the music. They should not browbeat them about the unacceptable conduct; they should provide support and guidance.

Mental health professionals should promote adults helping children and adolescents recognize or own their part in the behavior. The relevant adults should offer guidance and support so that the kids will be able to improve, change, and control their behavior in the future. It is important to help them learn from a situation of misconduct and see the value of accepting responsibility.

A good strategy is for adults to acknowledge that they too have made mistakes in the past, and describe to children and adolescents how they went about attaining better self-understanding and avoiding their problem behaviors later on. Since young people may idealize the adults in their lives, especially parents and caregivers, a healthy reality check may occur when responsible adults admit limitations and talk openly about what was necessary to eliminate the cause of a negative outcome.

The basic psychological principle is, of course, that an important ingredient for all people, regardless of age, is to own responsibility for personal behavior. By accepting that there were internal causes, important and healthy controls can be developed.

Adolescent Regression

When their brood of kids is being rambunctious, many parents find solace by thinking: "One of these days, they will grow up and act maturely." The notion is that, by the teenage years perhaps, maturity will govern, and the youngster will act with more good sense and propriety.

It is true that growing up does lead to more decorum. That is, the child progressively becomes more apt to behave in a manner that reflects the values of the family and society for correctness, politeness, and courtesy.

By the teenage years, there will be glimpses of dignity and modesty. Most strikingly perhaps, it is common for adolescents to harbor a clearcut wish to convey positive qualities to people, especially other teenagers. It becomes highly important to be respected and create a positive impression in those with whom the adolescent has contact.

But even in the teenage years, there will also be incidences when the youth will revert to what seems like childish behavior. Sometimes these forays into immaturity appear to come for no reason; other times, they seem to be due to some uneasiness, uncertainty, or stress being experienced.

Regression is reverting to an earlier stage of development. It is often relied upon as a way of defending against or escaping present-day anxieties. By becoming childlike, the person finds a mental excuse for not having to cope with some problem that is being or needs to be faced. "Excuses" contradict responsibility.

In addition to anxiety reduction, regression can occur because of powerful reinforcements. For example, when my three adult offspring come together at holidays, there is commonly roughhousing and silly comments that belie the professional status and maturity that each has achieved. Although there may well be a degree of anxiety because of the joy of their coming together as a family (they live in different geographical areas and seldom see each other), the togetherness allows the magnetic pull toward recreating a simpler, less demanding atmosphere to be acted out with siblings.

Being around people with whom one grew up leads a person, regardless of age, to think and act to some extent as was done in yesteryear. At high school reunions, it is common for adults, even in their "advanced" years, to respond to each other as they did in high school. For example, at my high school reunions, the same cliques of former students who shared interests in high school still group together (e.g., the cheerleaders, the athletes, the class officers, the "bandies"), even though as adults they might have much more in common with others from the class.

Regressing is not necessarily a bad thing. It can be useful for refueling the energy needed to deal with life's challenges. It becomes a problem only when it is used as an illogical crutch for avoiding responsibilities (e.g., acting in a way that eliminates effectively taking care of a task or problem) or it blocks benefits that might be achieved through adult behavior (e.g., making new friends at a class reunion).

Stupid Acts

There is truth to the old saying "Kids will be kids." The message is that children and adolescents will sometimes do things that are not mature actions. When youngsters do foolish things, responsible adults are left scratching their heads, wondering why such behavior occurred.

Being a child or adolescent is no justification for doing something that is risky, inappropriate, or potentially damaging to property or injurious to people – be it self or others. Youthfulness does, however, offer a reason that certain things happen that responsible adults would consider a stupid act.

Research on child development leaves no doubt that gaining good judgment requires knowledge of social principles (how to deal with others) and society's values (what is or is not acceptable). Schools, of course, shoulder much of the responsibility for helping kids learn about social relationships and develop their ability to make appropriate, constructive decisions. This supports the notion of family–school–community collaboration to assist youngsters of all ages with their development. As I have said many times in this book, it is fundamental that all adults should help children and adolescences cultivate mature thinking and actions, and the net of responsibility is wide.

In addition to knowledge and understanding of acceptable conduct, self-regulation must occur. Children and adolescents may experience unbridled impulses, and must learn to consider the consequences. Adults should guide and teach kids about how to evaluate an impulse to act and choose a wise behavior, not a stupid act.

With all persons, any information received is pigeonholed in their minds. With children, growing up means adding new mental categories for storing information. This process can be accomplished by helping the youth understand the basis for rules and laws.

The term *rebel without a cause* is well known; it reflects foolishness in the adolescent years for no justifiable reason. Although glamorized by the entertainment media, simple rebellion among teenagers is not a positive or inevitable trait. Many adolescents are readily able to conform to social expectations and adopt a commitment to constructive conduct that leads to the most positive way of life.

Among the stupid acts that may occur in childhood and adolescence are drawing graffiti on public property, stealing some unneeded item, doing something that could easily cause serious bodily injury, and the list goes on and on. Whenever there is a stupid act, responsible adults, especially parents and caregivers, should seize the moment and talk in a firm and informative way with the youngster.

The stupid act should not be ignored. Its wrongfulness should be acknowledged and talked about. But condemnation alone does not teach and should be avoided. After letting the child or adolescent know that the conduct was inappropriate or wrong, the talking should include an explanation of why other conduct should be chosen. Hopefully the young person will pledge to act in a more wise and mature fashion in the future.

Night-and-Day Difference

After reading a newspaper account about a youth who has committed a horrendous act, like taking a gun to school, many people wonder why the parents or other responsible adults did not take preventive steps. Often the explanation is that there was no reasonable way that others could have anticipated or detected that the wrongful act would occur.

Mental health professionals should seek to educate all adults that, although much of human behavior can be predicted by past behavior, there are always exceptions. Further, adults need to realize that every child or adolescent has the potential to do something that is out of character.

As I have discussed earlier, adult monitoring of kids, especially by the parents and caretakers, is an important part of effective family–school collaboration and family management. For example, when there is a school shooting, it is justified to question why the parents did not know about a gun and ammunition being in their household or if they did know, why these were accessible to the child or adolescent. It is also reasonable to question whether the parents and teachers were paying attention to the kid's emotional and psychological state. Professional helpers should increase public awareness that it is important for all adults to be watchful for, and sensitive to, conditions that might point toward serious problems with a child or adolescent that could lead to unacceptable behavior.

When a youngster, regardless of age, has had seemingly good adult guidance and yet acts in a way that is totally unexpected, it may reflect a truism about human behavior: Some persons are responsive to the environment or social context in which they are placed or seek. That is, behavior is influenced by context. For example, there may be a night-and-day difference in the kid's behavior at home with family or in the classroom compared with when he or she is in a shopping mall or party situation with friends. As another example, some (but not all) youths who go to a rock concert may get caught up in the moment, and act in an outlandish manner. The rock concert milieu or context is such that the audience responds to the music differently from parishioners sitting in church listening to a choir perform.

To better understand the influence of context, consider the adult who is quiet and subdued at work, but comes home and starts ranting and raving in an aggressive manner. The workplace imposes restraints that are not imposed by the family context.

Mental health professionals should help people, regardless of age, recognize how certain situational or contextual factors can trigger conduct that will be regretted later. The end goal, of course, is for the youngster to be able to avoid responding to stimulation from any context that could lead to negative consequences, and to exercise effective self-regulation and self-management.

Simply attending a rock concert does not mean that everyone will misbehave or that it is an unacceptable place to be. Many in the audience maintain appropriate self-controls for the context and enjoy the music and the experience. These persons have a stable and cohesive sense of self. That is, they have a sense of self-identity and live by their personal values and standards, regardless of what goes on around them.

Impulse control is, to some degree, influenced by biology. However, with proper insight, reinforcement, and motivation, inept and impulsive decisions do not have to occur. By understanding that he or she is responsible for behavior and choices, the youth can build defenses against giving into temptations that are unhealthy, counterproductive, or criminal.

Professional helpers should prepare parents and relevant adults for purposefully introducing the topic of self-regulation and helping the young person explore it, evaluate alternatives, and make decisions about a preferred way of behaving. Then, when powerful environmental cues or peer pressure pushes the child or adolescent toward risky or antisocial behavior, the youth can choose a right course of action – that is, maintain effective self-management.

Extracurricular Activities

Regardless of grade level, a student must decide whether or not to be involved in extracurricular activities. Teachers report that some students are prone to go to extremes. That is, they are involved in either too few or too many activities. Either extreme can bring problems; for example, learning in the classroom may decline, and negative behavior may occur. All adults, including mental health professionals, should be willing and able to assist young people in balancing their activities.

To paraphrase Shakespeare, the threshold question is "to be or not to be" involved in sports, clubs, social events, and so on. There is no single or simple formula. The choice about involvement depends on the personal characteristics of the child or adolescent.

Responsible adults can certainly cast the die by encouraging, disparaging, or adopting a laissez-faire attitude toward nonclassroom activities. For example, parents and caregivers should know that extracurricular activities have the potential to offer new learning, cultivate positive socializing, and promote personal development, including such qualities as self-confidence, cooperation, sensitivity to others, and leadership.

Adults should tune into a youngster's particular activities as well as offer suggestions or options. As children develop, they increasingly become aware of needing to do certain things. To clarify, psychological research reveals that each person has a unique *need system* that strongly influences the types of activities they will enjoy and find rewarding. To accomplish effective adult–child relationships, adults need to be aware of a kid's activities, including the source of motivation (i.e., what needs are being fulfilled).

The underinvolved youth misses out on important experiences. To some degree, a child or adolescent who avoids or withdraws from activities may be doing so appropriately. That is, perhaps there is a limited psychological need for affiliation, achievement, and so on. If the motive, however, is due to extreme shyness or fear of rejection, the youth's avoidance keeps him or her away from potentially enjoyable and rewarding activities that could benefit the youngster. If childhood or adolescence is relatively devoid of diverse activities with others, especially peers, the young person can experience feelings of emptiness and loneliness (e.g., possible precursors of depression).

On the other hand, the overinvolved youth who plunges into many activities may face different problems. By being overinvolved, he or she may find too little time for homework, enjoying friends and family, or just plain living a healthy and relaxed lifestyle. On the last point, remember the old adage "all work and no play" leads to a dull person.

Promotional helpers should guide parents and other responsible adults in monitoring the schedules of youngsters. Adults should encourage kids throughout childhood and adolescence to participate in activities that will likely yield benefits, but they should also caution about overdoing things. The adults should also tune into the reasons a given kid might select a particular activity. For example, some youths are prone to want to do things that will win peer approval, even though the activity may not be particularly enriching (such as hanging out at a mall or on the street). Relevant adults, such as teachers and most definitely parents and caregivers, can help by encouraging the child or adolescent to weigh the seeming benefits and risks of passing up or entering into an extracurricular activity.

Deviancy Training

In accord with the old saw "You are known by the company that you keep," professional helpers should encourage all relevant adults to pay attention to a young person's friends and associates – since they are the ones who offer acceptance and boost the youngster's self-esteem. The question is whether the companions offer encouragement of appropriate, healthful, positive, lawful attitudes, emotions, and behavior.

Youths who create a negative influence rely on deviant talk and behavior. Deviance-prone kids can often attract and seduce unsuspecting people, of all ages, with talk or boasting about antisocial ideas and deeds. Youngsters who are socially deviant do not help companions be healthy and constructive; in fact, they create unhealthy and destructive influences that corrupt others and damage society. Mental health professionals should strengthen relevant adults' abilities for helping children and adolescents be wary of relationships that introduce "deviancy training."

Deviancy refers to being different from the norms that are acceptable to society. For the child or adolescent, being deviant may lead to devaluing learning and achievement, faulty judgments, lack of behavioral controls, poor relationship with friends and family, and running afoul of the law.

Obviously no responsible adult would want any child or adolescent to experience deviancy training. Dishion and Stormshak (2007) state:

"For problem behavior, we find that a youngster's affiliation with anti-social peers is the single best predictor of antisocial behavior from first grade through late adolescence" (pp. 36–37); and they recommend, "One critical component of family management is guiding the selection of peer groups and monitoring peer dynamics" (p. 37).

It is possible for responsible adults, especially parents and caregivers, to promote healthy autonomy and independence in the child along with keeping a watchful eye on the contacts that a child or adolescent has with others. Throughout life, every person will be blessed if there is someone standing by ready to raise a question as to whether a particular relationship is a good idea. Adults should put forth special efforts during the formative childhood and teenage years to recognize when an unhealthy relationship is starting or being maintained.

It does not take much for a youth to change from being on a straight-and-narrow path to wandering into the social wilderness. Dishion and Stormshak (2007) say: "Subtle changes in responding within a relationship can often lead to rather large changes in the emotional experience, the ability to self-regulate, or the probability of unpleasant conflict" (p. 39).

Behavior offers clear signals of a problem relationship. For example, if a child or adolescent changes behavioral patterns and begins acting in a questionable manner, such as in hanging out instead of engaging in some constructive activity (like reading, practicing music, hobbies, sports, etc.), adult concern is justified.

More difficult to recognize are emotional signals. Emotions are used to express personal needs and to control relationships. If a child or adolescent shows signs of depression or irritability, these emotions may be a way to cope with or escape a deeper problem. Emotional distress is known to make matters worse in family and peer relationships, and pave the way for severe mental health problems.

It is not always a good idea to try to force a youngster to terminate a relationship with a person (of any age) who seems to be a bad influence. In psychology, the term *psychological reactance* means a person who faces a demand may strongly resist, essentially saying, "No one is going to dictate to me!"

Instead of a cease-and-desist demand, the best strategy for confronting a youngster's relationship that is promoting deviancy may be for the responsible adults to remain unemotional about the situation, offering information that will promote awareness and try to engage the youth in problem-solving and making his or her own thoughtful decisions. After a period of trying out a new decision, the relevant adults should help the child or adolescent evaluate the results. Of course, these troubling situations may require services from professional helpers.

An adult–child relationship that reflects support and love and opportunities for new rewarding experiences that will involve more desirable companionship can provide positive social reinforcement and new information to help the young person make wiser decisions in the future. In practical terms, this means getting the youth involved in rewarding experiences that do not involve deviancy-oriented companions.

Balancing School and Work

Most families have values that embrace the work ethic. Consequently, everyone in the family hears the message that "you get what you work for" and "work is a virtue." With children and adolescents, however, credence should be given to the adage "All work and no play make for a dull kid." To help children and adolescents, adults should seek healthy balancing of youthful activities.

In no way should the work ethic be disparaged. Being committed to constructive activity, such as performing work-related tasks, is a necessity for social and economic survival and most certainly a virtue. Thus, from the early childhood years, adults should guide youngsters to appreciate the role that work plays in everyone's life and develop a personal commitment to explore and choose employment and career options.

By adolescence, the teenager has commonly begun to think about what would be an appropriate career path. At this stage, however, the ideas are often unrealistic, and few adolescents decide on a definite career. Instead, exploring possible job opportunities may well be a life-long effort, and the actual choices may be due to chance or serendipity. Also, the resources that are or are not available to a particular person may determine a career move. That is, resources are needed for gaining education and training and enjoying certain opportunities. Similarly, personal qualities such as intelligence and attitudes will influence career success.

The adolescent years are important for career development. While still in high school, many teenagers work part-time. This experience can be useful for vocational planning. Seldom, however, does the work experience provide for a career per se; more often, the payoff is that the young person learns to accept responsibility and cooperate with coworkers.

Many teenagers work part-time primarily out of need or desire to earn money, such as for clothes or having a car, both of which can bring acceptance from other teenagers. Adults should help kids keep the part-time employment in a realistic perspective. Until the adolescent has completed his or her education, such as high school or college, employment should remain a supportive, not primary, activity.

Some schools offer a work–study plan whereby the student is supposed to gain important job-related learning. Even with this educational objective, the focus should be on developing the youth's commitment to learning in general. This is a topic that is certainly appropriate for family–school collaboration, and mental health professionals can contribute to the process.

Adolescence is a stage in which there may be little long-term planning. As opposed to many adults, teenagers tend to be focused on the immediate future, that is, what can be done now. This short-term view of life can produce a detriment, especially if acting on the "now" eliminates opportunities for the long-term future. Adults should monitor for signs of instant gratification or impulsivity that could lessen the youth's opportunities in adulthood or throughout life.

Planning a Career

Many, probably most, responsible adults have concerns about the career that a young person will choose later in life. The common hope is that a kid will make the most of educational opportunities and, as an adult, move into a career that will provide economic security and personal satisfaction.

Some parents try to talk with their kids about career aspirations early on, even in the elementary school years. It is understandable that parents may tend to emphasize high-status or well-paying jobs. A more productive approach is to informally chat about what various jobs involve.

What a child or adolescent does well in school, say mathematics, may get discussed as an indicator of growing up to enter a particular kind of employment, say engineering. It is unlikely that doing well in a given class in high school will or should determine a career choice. Adults should be wary of pushing a particular career on a child or pushing an agenda based on their own needs or preferences.

Perhaps wanting to please the adults in their lives or adopt what television portrays as desirable, preteenagers may claim to aspire to become an astronaut, engineer, doctor, attorney, rock star, or whatever. Research reveals, however, that comments about careers made by a child prior to the adolescent years seldom have any basis in reality or in actual interests.

In the teen years, the youth is usually able to crystallize thinking about work, and start to mentally explore career possibilities. However, unforeseen events may lead to major shifts in work-related plans.

For a variety of reasons, I was a lackluster student in high school, chanced to go to college, encountered a nurturing advisor, and became motivated to study. Any predictions based on my high school grades, achievement test scores, or expressed plans for the future would have been markedly wrong.

Entry into a career track is seldom the end solution. More often than not, students often change their career plans. The reason is simple. With more experience, a student might recognize that a certain job is not as satisfying as originally thought.

Of course adults too, once they are into work, may change jobs. Having a change in employment or career is a common aspect of life, and should not be disparaged. Certainly, the evolution of society, such as advances in technology and the economy, creates significant implications for career issues.

Exploring different careers throughout life can be enriching. The search is for a type of work that is interesting and stimulating, accommodates personal needs and preferences, and yields essential rewards. Unfortunately, some people never enjoy their work. Often the dissatisfaction is due to a poor choice in the past, or it could be due to personal limitations.

In my careers in psychology and law, I quickly and have consistently realized the value attached to certain performance issues, such as being efficient with tasks, having good relations with colleagues, communicating well, and continuing to gain new knowledge and skills. Like anyone, I have experienced payoffs in striving for excellence in performance. This is a value that responsible adults should impart to youngsters.

Every student must make choices; these will depend on the resources available within the family, barriers to certain prospects, and opportunities that arise. Ideally, young people can encounter unexpected support and find new opportunities that prove rewarding. Although there are never guarantees, those who are willing to make the commitment will often discover or create the resources needed for success.

Mental health professionals should educate adults to avoid trying to direct or dictate a child's job interests or a teenager's career-related choices. The youngster is ultimately responsible for deciding on a field of study or type of employment. Therefore, adults can offer invaluable encouragement, information, and guidance, but in the end, the choice is only for the particular young person to make. Of course, part of the message from professional helpers should be that the youngster has to be prepared to accept the success or failure that occurs because of career-related decisions, and the parents or other relevant adults should not shoulder the burden, once the youth reaches adulthood, of faulty career choices.

10 Delinquency and Crime

The last chapter opened the door to understanding adolescence, and set forth a number of suggestions of approaches for mental health professionals to use for helping kids through this complex stage of life. The teenage years are fraught with risk, which adults must assess and seek to minimize or eliminate; adults will commonly need assistance from professional helpers. For example, adolescence is a stage that will benefit greatly from effective family–school collaboration, as well as other community resources.

Each youth adopts a unique teenage trajectory or pathway toward maturity, which is defined by his or her personal psychological needs and the resources that are available. There is no simple road map.

A major aspect of adolescence is the emphasis placed on gaining and maintaining social acceptance. The teenage years are turbulent and require that adults maintain considerable patience, support, and understanding and offer adult–child guidance. Blaming and commanding are counterproductive.

In adolescence, it is common for the youngster to seemingly move toward and then away from mature judgments. In other words, a teenager may regress into immature thinking and actions, and then do a turnaround that reflects maturation. Some acts by the kid may seem unexplainable, and the nature of a given context may lead to night-and-day differences in how the adolescent behaves.

It is important for a teenager to establish positive relationships. Extracurricular activities have the potential to foster experiences that benefit development and education. Adults should steadfastly help the children and adolescents avoid contacts with bad influences, be they from a person (youngster or adult) or a context (where unlawful behavior by others may occur).

The teenage years commonly introduce career planning, and school and part-time work should be balanced. Throughout all the vicissitudes of adolescence, there should be a strong commitment by adults, especially parents and caretakers, to family–school collaboration and making other community resources available to the teenager and the responsible adults in his or life. Mental health professionals can be instrumental in fashioning these positive conditions for adult–child relationships and promoting constructive and healthy opportunities for youngsters.

This chapter focuses on adolescents who are potential victims of criminal conduct and those who are alleged to be or are convicted teenage offenders. As will be evident, vigilance by adults is the key to preventing and counteracting delinquency and crime.

Teenage Crime

Having survived my three children being teenagers, I know well how a parent is always concerned that one's offspring might break the law. Been there and done that! Yes, I gave frequent and strict "sermons" to my kids, urging them to drive safely, avoid alcohol and other drugs, and obey every law.

No responsible adult wants any child to be a juvenile delinquent or to grow into an adult criminal. Most adults tend to believe that the teenage years create a special risk of behavior that will violate the law. Actually, research suggests that so-called persistent antisocial behavior starts much earlier than the teens, sometimes appearing in even the preschool years!

What causes delinquency? There is no one cause. In fact, there is no simple explanation.

Some professional helpers believe that the teenage "crime problem" comes from, or is at least promoted by, certain conditions in our society, particularly the glorification of violence on TV and in movies. Adding to the mix is racism, poverty, sexism, and the child's ability to obtain a firearm.

Habitual misbehavior by a person of any age, especially aggression and nonconforming to social values, suggests a potential for delinquent or criminal behavior. For children and adolescents, specific red flags include being untruthful, stealing, setting fires, violation of curfews, underage drinking, running away from home, not wanting to attend school and being truant, purposefully breaking property, and hurting animals and people. For boys or girls, any bullying behavior is a bad sign.

When responsible adults, such as parents or teachers, are unable to deal well with an unruly child, it is probably only a matter of time until the words *ungovernable* and *incorrigible* enter the picture – and this should be the trigger for enlisting professional helpers in dealing with the problems. At this point, regrettably, family–school collaboration is in the forefront, and if collaboration is poor, solutions will not be gained. That is, the parents, caretakers, school personnel, and other relevant adults must unite in trying to help the youth, and if unsuccessful in their efforts, they likely should turn to the juvenile justice system and/or mental health professionals for support and action.

The most common problems referred to the juvenile courts appear to be crimes against property, crimes against persons, and drug offenses. Of interest, girls far outnumber boys for juvenile status offenses such as running away from home, truancy, and underage drinking.

When seeing any potential problem, including (especially?) in early childhood, the responsible adult should recognize that the child is in need of adult–child guidance – and perhaps consideration should be given to seeking mental health services. Certainly, the parents, caretakers, and school personnel have the potential for counteracting many problems, but there are times when the complexity or seriousness makes it obvious that expertise from professional helpers from various disciplines or roles will be essential.

Care should be taken not to overreact to the problem. Rather, a calm and logical effort by responsible adults, which goes beyond the current conduct, will provide the best insurance against an act of delinquency or a criminal violation that will require the entry of law enforcement.

Juvenile Rights

Some adults stereotype teenagers as thinking that they know more than anyone else. To some degree, a know-it-all attitude and a discounting of adult advice or guidance are common to adolescence.

After leaving the teen years, many young adults marvel at how the responsible adults in their lives have become much more intelligent with the passage of time. That is, immaturity leads some teenagers to think that adults do not understand the needs and rights of young people; but after adulthood is achieved, most of those same former-teenagers will recognize that the adults in their life really did have their best interests at heart.

Juveniles who get in trouble with the law do tend to reflect a know-it-all position about life (Bartol & Bartol, 2008). And it is often to their disadvantage.

Although juveniles have Constitutional rights in court proceedings, they may be unaware of these. For example, most teenagers facing an alleged violation claim to know the consequences of not having legal representation, and they go ahead and speak to law enforcement personnel without an attorney being present.

No matter how much they muster bravado, when a youth speaks to a law enforcement officer, it is a stressful situation. For people of all ages, stress can lead to poor judgment, and this is especially true in adolescence.

Research indicates that most juveniles younger than 14 do not understand the meaning of the *Miranda* warning (*Miranda v. Arizona*, 384 US 436, 1966). (Note that there are other cases that have relevance to the same kind of Constitutional rights for minors, such as *Fare v. Michael C.*, 442 US 707, 1979, and *In re Gault*, 387 US 1, 1967.) Nor do juveniles understand the implications of waiving their rights, such as against self-incrimination (Grisso, 1981).

A substantial number of juveniles confess to crimes that they did not actually commit. The younger the child, the more suggestible, and this factor can influence the child – to the point of being willing to confess to a crime not committed.

In juvenile court proceedings, the youth must be able to demonstrate effective participation. This means that the juvenile must be capable of making logical decisions, weighing alternatives, and understanding consequences.

Regrettably, some youngsters are unable to participate effectively. As compared with all teenagers, those who are brought into juvenile courts are more likely to be intellectually limited, have mental disorders, or be emotionally and socially immature.

Juveniles today are more likely to come in contact with the legal system than ever in the past. In the United States, each year, millions of juveniles face actions in the juvenile courts. In dealing with children and adolescents, adults should recognize that any know-it-all stance is inappropriate and do whatever is possible to offer meaningful adult–child guidance.

Reducing Crime

It sure seems like crime is increasing, including with young people (Borum, 2006). Actually, in recent years, there is some indication that the overall incidence of crime has decreased. The news coverage has, however, increased. Consequently, today the average person knows more about what is happening on the crime scene than was true in bygone days.

There are all sorts of opinions about why crime is such a great problem today. One of the most common ideas seems to be that mentally ill people commit most criminal acts. It has been estimated, however, that just 7% of police contacts involve a person who is mentally disordered. And only about 16% of inmates in US prisons and jails have mental disorders (Bartol & Bartol, 2008).

It is true that there are fewer mental health services now than, say, back in the 1970s. Why? The government has changed priorities, and there is less funding for mental health services. In every state, legislatures have coped with budget issues by closing state hospitals and clinics or reduced substantially the mental health services to a mere skeleton of what was offered in the past or what is needed in the present.

The lack of professional helping services means that people with psychiatric problems, regardless of age, are left to struggle on their own without adequate professional support or treatment. As a result, they make bad judgments, and law enforcement agencies must take charge.

When a mentally disordered citizen has a negative encounter with a law enforcement officer, it means potentially being taken into custody, arrested, or channeled (if possible) to a mental health facility. Or the law enforcement officer will make a stopgap resolution of the problem on the spot. Since space in a psychiatric facility is difficult to obtain, an arrest is often the only option available.

Being arrested is most apt to happen if the person is unknown to the police. One of the benefits of rural or less-populated areas is that law enforcement officers become well informed about, with all due respect, neighborhood characters. While this leads to more tolerance than might be true in a large city, it also means that the person may not receive much-needed mental health services – rural areas commonly are quite distant from essential health care services, especially for mental disorders.

Everyone is concerned about improving the conditions of daily life. When it comes to reducing crime, every citizen should encourage government sources to provide more funding for mental health services and other professional helping services. Certainly all professional helpers should advocate this objective.

Imprecise Vigilance

Being dedicated to raising a healthy, happy, and productive child or adolescent requires constant vigilance. As more than one parent has said, "Before my child was born, I never dreamed that I would have to constantly monitor to be sure that all is well." With a laugh, one parent commented, "Not only did I have to develop eyes in the back of my head, I became able see and hear through walls and over great distances – call it 'parental intuition.'"

Responsible adults, especially parents and caretakers, try to get kids to believe that adult monitoring is always present, that the adults are keeping a guardian's watch over them. Raised in a strict home, one mother told me that her father always said, "No matter what you do, I'm going find out about it." This was literally true for one of my college students. The daughter of two police officers, she humorously told how she could be driving from her hometown to a larger nearby town, and all along the route, law enforcement officers would, upon spotting her, send a radio call to her parents, saying something like, "Just asking if your daughter is supposed to be driving south on the freeway now."

Responsible adults, of course, try to keep track of what a child or adolescent is doing, hoping to ward off any unwise decision or potentially harmful dilemma. Research supports the idea, however, that direct parental intervention is far less effective than helping young people themselves to become wise decision-makers.

For example, in this age of increased violence by and toward youths, responsible adults would like to be able to detect signs of whether a child is prone to be violent, so that preventive action can be taken. From research, it is known that there is potential for violence if a child has a conduct disorder, certain types of serious mental illness, or chronic family problems; engages in or is the victim of bullying; has antisocial friends; is influenced by the culture of violence (e.g., video games, hostile music, and the like); or has access to guns for no good reason. However, for every child who acts violently after experiencing one or more of these conditions, there will be many more children who have experienced the same things, but who will not act violently. There are no clear-cut predictors of violent behavior.

Professional helpers should promote the concept that vigilance is an important part of effective parenting and adult supervision, but there are no guarantees. One teenager who killed classmates is known to have had only a couple of hostile rap recordings, but many more recordings of his favorite music: barbershop quartets and gospel songs! Responsible adults must scan the many conditions that might be relevant to the development of problems, and help children and adolescents manage any possible negative influences and find more healthful alternatives.

Realistic Vigilance

The constant vigilance mentioned in the preceding section must be realistic. The view expressed was that parents and other responsible adults should monitor for conditions that might suggest that problems are developing and help the child or adolescent manage any negative influences and find more safe and healthful alternatives. A watchful eye should consistently survey the scene, both the people and the context, for potential difficulties, problems, risks, or dangers.

The word *vigilant,* from the Latin *vigilantia*, requires that the person's senses be in an alert state. Although the youngster will eventually develop sensitivity to negative conditions, being tuned into possible pitfalls comes only with maturity. Until the child or adolescence acquires needed safeguards, there can be no laxity in vigilance by the adults in the youth person's life.

Professional helpers should teach all adults to apply risk appraisal to youngsters' communications and conduct. Relative risk appraisal involves being accurate about what does and does not constitute a risk or danger. Personal attributes and values merit consideration. What is a risk for one child may not be a risk for another child.

There can be a downside to adult vigilance. Being overly cautious can be a detriment to all concerned. Some worry, concern, or fear is normal, healthy, and appropriate. Realistic caution is useful for knowing when and how to act defensively for survival. Undue or extreme fear can signal social phobias, panic disorders, and generalized anxiety disorders.

Prudent adults should, of course, be concerned about realistic risks and threats to children and adolescents, but they should guard against exaggerating the possibility of danger. If not kept in a realistic perspective, vigilance can mushroom into hypervigilance, and detrimental effects may occur.

Hypervigilance can lead to an obsession about danger, and emotional symptoms may develop. Also, both the adult and child may experience overgeneralization. For example, one set of parents would not allow their kids to ride bicycles, swim, or walk around the neighborhood without close adult supervision – there were negative consequences for all concerned. Distortions and disproportionate fear can disrupt mental processes. There may even be paranoid or delusional thinking. The result could be illogical caution, which could deprive the youngster of the richness of diverse experiences. In other words, being vigilant in excess of what is justified under the particular circumstances is potentially constricting and detrimental.

Mental health professionals should help parents, caretakers, and other responsible adults be realistic about risks. Certain low- or controlled-risk activities can actually provide positive gains for personal development and social maturity.

Growing up necessarily means that the child or adolescent will take some risks. There must be some degree of self-determination, which should become more and more present as maturity is achieved. Regrettably, every youngster makes some bad decisions, falters in caution, decides on a foolish action, and so on. Missteps in the process of maturing are unavoidable. In these situations, the parents, caretakers, and other responsible adults can help the child or adolescent learn from the experience – and they should continue to be vigilant to alert the youth to any relevant negatives that might be on the horizon.

When there is excessive or illogical worry or fear about difficulties, problems, risks, or dangers, responsible adults should make an effort to bring both their and the youngster's patterns of thinking and behaving in line with reality. Regrettably, there may be times when professional help will be needed for this effort.

Sexual Assaults

In virtually every society, there are certain topics that are taboo for civil conversation. One that is universally troubling is sexual assault.

The disdain directed at sexual assaults too often leads to denying that young people of all ages are at risk. All adults, especially parents and caretakers, need to recognize the problem. They should discuss the risk of sexual assaults with children and adolescents and do everything possible to safeguard them.

From research, it is known that, although adults are most often the targets of rapists, the large majority of victims of other kinds of sexual assaults are under the age of 18. Contrary to popular misconception, only a small number of sexual assault incidents are committed by strangers. In fact, most victims of rape and other sexual assaults had some sort of prior relationship with the wrongdoer (Bartol & Bartol, 2008). (Note: There may be cultural differences on this matter.)

Another concern is that not all sexual assaults are reported to law enforcement agencies. Attempted rapes and other sexual assaults are less often reported than completed acts. Even if there are physical injuries or medical services are received, a substantial number of the sexual assaults go unreported.

When a family member, friend, or acquaintance commits a sexual assault, there may be a reluctance to report the situation to child protective services or to law enforcement agencies. That is, family sexual abuse may be cloaked in secrecy.

Sexual abuse committed by any person – including a member of the family, a friend, or an acquaintance – absolutely should be reported to law enforcement. To not report it elevates the risk of further physical and psychological abuse and injury. It could be argued that anyone who shields a person who commits sexual abuse or assault is just as guilty as the abuser or offender.

Regrettably, contemporary society poses many threats to the safety and well-being of all citizens, regardless of age. Adults should carefully monitor the everyday comings and goings of children of all ages, and they set well-defined limits to going someplace or with someone who might enable the occurrence of a sexual assault.

With appropriate sensitivity, responsible adults should educate children and adolescents to be mindful of risk and danger, and to adhere to strict guidelines about being out and about. Rather than this sort of caution being paranoid, it can be appropriately considered to be prudent.

For either the youth or the responsible adults, the notion that "a sexual assault will never happen" is foolish, and may indicate immature or illogical thinking. Sexual offenders commit acts that are seemingly unpredictable, random, and horrible. Being realistically defensive and relying on law enforcement are two rules for safe living and effective parenting. (For additional information see the website for the Fox TV program *America's Most Wanted:* http://www.amw.com/)

Child Abductions

It is a parent's worse nightmare. While going about his or her everyday activities, a son or daughter disappears. The national media give great emphasis to these traumatic events. In the United States, Adam Walsh (Florida), Polly Klaas (California), Megan Kanka (New Jersey), Dru Sjodin (North Dakota), Katie Poirier (Minnesota), Dylan Groene (Idaho), Sarah Lunde (Florida), Jessica Lunsford (Florida), Carlie Brucia (Florida), and Kelsey Smith (Kansas) are but a few of the youthful victims of abduction and murder who have become part of our society's ignoble history.

By definition, child abduction is an unlawful taking, enticing, or detaining of a child. The youth may seemingly go along willingly with the abductor, but being a minor, the child cannot consent to or condone the abduction.

Effective parenting and caretaking involves implementing steps to put child abduction into a realistic perspective. For example, parents and other responsible adults must understand the risk and the possible negative effects on the child, and create protective conditions accordingly. Child abduction is a topic appropriate for adult–child guidance.

There is no reason for responsible adults to go to great extremes to ward off a possible abduction by a stranger. It is has been estimated that a child is many times more likely to die in a car accident than to be abducted and murdered by a non-family member.

Most abductions of a child involve a parent, such as one who is embroiled in a custody dispute (Wilson, 2001). Other family members, friends, or acquaintances are also frequently involved in child abductions, and it is common for the primary abductor to have an accomplice.

Even if the abductor is a parent or someone who the child knows, the situation can potentially pose danger for the child. Force and threats are common. One study revealed that the majority of male and about one fourth of female abductors had a history of violent behavior (Greif & Hegar, 1993).Without exception, child abduction merits the immediate attention of law enforcement.

Abductions by persons connected to the family occur most often with young children (younger than 6). About an equal number of boys and girls are abducted. If a stranger does the kidnapping, about two thirds of the victims are female. It has been estimated that 57% are teenagers. When the abductor is a stranger, the large majority of offenders are males (see Finkelhor & Ormrod, 2000).

When juveniles are taken by acquaintances, most victims are females – and about 30% of the time the abductor is a teenager. The motive is often a "romantic obsession," but risk is present because the abductor often seeks revenge or a forced social or romantic relationship (Bartol & Bartol, 2008).

Professional helpers should encourage parents, caretakers, and other responsible adults to talk to youngsters about the risk of abduction and what to do in such a situation, considering alternative scenarios according to whether it is a known or unknown abductor. No adult should ignore or condone abduction, even if it done by, say, a parent in a child custody dispute. In any event, law enforcement should be alerted immediately to the situation. Being a parent, caretaker, or responsible adult carries the legal duty to safeguard all youngsters. (For additional information, see the website for the Polly Klaas Foundation: http://www.pollyklaas.org/)

Threats of Youth Violence

Due to the mass media, children and adolescents today live in a society that conveys violent images and messages, much more than was true in previous generations. As a result, mental health professionals should help all adults be prepared to deal effectively with any indication of possible violence by a youngster (or anyone else, of course).

The risk of a violent act varies according to what the child or adolescent experiences throughout the process of growing up. At a low level of risk, there may be talk about or fascination with negative ideas (e.g., harming others), violence (e.g., on television and the Internet, or in video games), or outlandish fantasies (e.g., supernatural exploits). Risk increases when the youth has personality traits and behaviors that reflect disregard for rules (e.g., within the family or at school) and laws (e.g., delinquency), experiences a chaotic family (e.g., impaired or abusive parents), faces social rejection or academic failure at school, and lives in a violent environment with other youths who resort to antisocial, violent, or extremist beliefs and acts.

Of particular concern, professional helpers need to guide all adults into taking seriously any child or adolescent who states ideas or wishes to harm himself or herself or others. Some adults are prone to deny the significance of a youngster's threat of violence, especially when the kid says something like "I was just joking." Remarks about a threat of harm or violence are never humorous.

When there is a threat, immediate intervention by and supervision from parents, caretakers, and other responsible adults is essential. There should be sincere adult–child conversation about whatever led to the threat, such as having been bullied. There should be no condemning. Rather, there should be support for understanding why violence is not a solution and discovering healthy and lawful alternatives for dealing with the perceived source of the problem. Immediate professional help may be needed.

To prevent violence, parents and caretakers should create safeguards within the home. There should never be any endorsement for the use of harm to oneself or others. Violence should be identified as a despicable action that cannot be part of conflict resolution. If the adult–child guidance goes unheeded, the adults should turn to professional helpers in education, mental health, health care, social service, and law enforcement to get the youth on a positive track. Potential violence is definitely an appropriate topic for family–school collaboration, along with possible involvement by other community resources (perhaps including law enforcement).

Obviously the adults in a kid's life should control their own words and deeds, so as to not expose children to domestic conflicts (e.g., they should avoid angry disputes), substance abuse, or threats. In accord with firearm safety, no minor (not even a teenager) should have unrestricted access to a gun. Regardless of age, adult monitoring of violence on television and the Internet and in electronic games is necessary. Any indication of substance abuse should be countered. Professional helpers should encourage and teach all adults to cultivate relationships with every child and adolescent that will bring about a positive outlook on life and a commitment to constructive problem solving.

The Front Line of Defense Against Youth Violence

Recent years have ushered in increased concern about violence by young people, especially school shootings. Newman, Fox, Harding, Mehta, and Roth (2004) correctly note: "For the country as a whole, school shootings opened up a searching self-examination as only a total shock can" (p. 14) and "Rampage school shootings terrify us because they contradict

our most firmly held beliefs about childhoods, home, and community"
(p. 15).

It is false to believe that extreme violence occurs mainly in urban
areas or within a particular ethnic group. Violence can erupt in places
where people might least expect it and within any sort of family, school,
or community.

By now, most adults have read about school shootings and gang violence, and tried to figure out why a particular teenager acted in a brutal
and murderous way. The tendency is, of course, to grab onto the obvious,
such as believing that the youth had been a bully or (more likely) bullied,
or was socially isolated or enraptured with negative ideas (e.g., death-
oriented music, video games, and the like). None of these stereotypes is
adequate for explaining violence among youngsters.

When a social problem receives widespread coverage in the news
media, research occurs. Despite all of the coverage given to profiling
individual shooters, behavioral scientists have not yet provided a definite
answer to the simple question: why does a kid resort to deadly actions?

A useful statement is provided by Goldberg (2000):

> Violent acts seem unexplainable only to the extent that we fail to recognize
> the vicious influences that bear upon children in contemporary society and
> how children react to these threats. Violence by juveniles is a product of our
> social and domestic conflicts and failures. We live in a society which despite
> lavish attention given to children's entertainment largely ignores their basic
> emotional needs. (p. 208)

The message is clear: The first line of defense is for parents, caretakers,
and other responsible adults to be sensitive to a child's needs and promote overall positive emotional development for the youngster.

Although obviously not a solution, some young people rely on violence to eliminate a problem. Of course, it creates far greater problems.
There are countless reasons a given child or adolescent might embrace
violence as a solution. For example, a child who has experienced abuse
and severe neglect, parental criminality, family conflicts and violence,
and behavioral maladjustments is at risk for becoming prone to violence.
Also, it is known that the mental illness, substance abuse, and anger can
contribute to violence.

For adults, every child and adolescent should be the focus of attention for help with emotional and behavioral problems that suggest the
potential for violence. The range of concerns is broad, such as maintaining adult behavior that is exemplary, eliminating conflicts, and building

strengths for positive thoughts, beliefs, and behaviors. Certainly any sign of a mental problem should lead to an intervention (e.g., from an appropriate professional helper), substance abuse must not be countenanced, and destructive emotions (e.g., anger) must be reversed.

Preventing Violence

Universally, there is great concern about what seems to be an increase in violence among youths. All sorts of ideas have emerged, some of which are provocative ("I think that there is a social contagion for violence among teenagers") and some that are well reasoned ("we need to identify negative influences on our kids"). Instead of waiting until a child or adolescent offends with violence, the primary strategy for adults should be to prevent violence from occurring in the first place.

The problem of chronic violence in adolescents is severe. Dodge (2008) provides a summary of the effects pointing out that the annual financial cost of crime in our contemporary American society exceeds US $1 trillion, and each chronically violent individual costs society US $2 million. He believes that an expenditure of a little as US $1,000 per high-risk youth would produce economic returns.

Although it is known from research that certain factors or conditions may make a youngster a high risk of violence, the factors that reinforce violent characteristics are not understood fully, and the best methods to successfully counteract the negative forces have yet to be determined. In other words, the government has not adequately developed public policies and laws that will potentially prevent (or at least lessen) chronic violence among American youth. Notwithstanding public endorsement for financial allocations to prevent youth violence, even programs that have solid evidence for effectiveness are not funded well.

Studies of kids and guns, moral impoverishment, the epidemic of drugs and substance abuse, and faulty family relationships go largely ignored. The current economic crisis means that it is unlikely that there will be any substantial increases in funds for behavioral and mental health, education, and family strengthening.

Regardless of age, children and adolescents are impressionable. Peer influence is strong. For responsible adults, the challenge is to intervene in a meaningful and supportive way to filter peer influences, blocking out anything that, and anyone (child or adult) who might, reinforce violence and create other adverse characteristics within a child or adolescent.

Research leaves no doubt that associating with deviant peers, even if in a group treatment program, can lead to deviant behaviors. Consequently, a young person who commits a first offense is most likely to benefit from being placed in a program with modest risk peers or non-offenders. It makes sense to keep a violence-prone child or adolescent away from peers who have already engaged in violent activity.

The problem of youth violence merits preventive efforts by all adults, especially those active in the youngster's life. The term *prevention* is, of course, defined as taking steps to, as VandenBos (2007) puts it, "reduce the risk of disorders, diseases, or social problems for both individuals and entire populations" (p. 727). Therefore, the basis for prevention is more than helping the particular at-risk child or adolescent, it is to benefit everyone in society by preventing violent occurrences.

Watching for Childhood Violence

The increased concern about violence in the school adds great support for family–school collaboration to deal with the problem. Of course, others in the community should be involved as well. Too often, potentially dangerous situations are ignored.

Regrettably, some people and communities do not take preventive steps until after a tragic situation has occurred. Only in the aftermath of destruction do some parents, educators, and community leaders express alarm and take steps to ward off other violent acts. The old adage "Closing the barn door after the horse has been stolen" applies to after-the-fact concern. The best approach is for responsible adults to be watching for possible childhood violence.

Certainly school-based shootings (such as those in Littleton, Colorado; West Paducah, Kentucky; Jonesboro, Arkansas; and elsewhere) deserve great attention. However, violence by and between children takes other forms as well, such as bullying.

When there is a bully, the inclination to wait until the problem behavior festers before taking action is ineffective. If the classroom bully picks on others and is only minimally disciplined, something should be done to counteract the bullying possibly advancing to criminal assault. It is ill-advised to wait until a problem child assaults other children or inflicts self-harm, and only then turning to professional helpers.

The preferred approach is for responsible adults, especially parents and educators, to be on the lookout for the signs of potential violence and take preventive measures. No child or adolescent should be exempt from this vigilance.

Professional helpers believe that there are four types of youngsters, which progress from slight (but significant) risk to a high risk of violence:

Type A children have no particular history of emotional or conduct problems, but do something, perhaps an isolated event (e.g., bringing a plastic gun to school), meriting concern.

Type B children demonstrate thoughtless or reckless behavior (e.g., threatening violence as a joke, ridiculing other children).

Type C children may or may not have a problem history, but are revealing distress signals that suggest that they may not be able to handle the pressures or conflicts of life (e.g., reveals foolish thoughts, such as in drawings or essays, that, if acted out, would harm self or others).

Type D children also may or may not have a history of emotional or conduct problems, but give clear evidence of being poor decision-makers or problem-solvers (e.g., having an interest or plan in hurting self or others).

Responsible adults should continually watch for telltale signs that might suggest one of the four risk types. All children and adolescents deserve to have adults watching over them for their well-being, and protecting everyone from any sort of violence.

When there is some indication of possible violence by a child or adolescents, adults should ponder the possible underlying motive, what has actually happened (as opposed to suspicions without a factual basis), the likely targets of any violence, the availability of means or weapons to inflict harm, the youngster's emotional condition and past history of conduct problems, and how quickly a violent act could occur. Mental health professionals should be prepared to help with these analytic efforts.

Upon determining that there is reasonable cause for concern about the young person's engaging in some sort of violent act, the adults should gather resources. For example, in keeping with the notion of family–school collaboration, a teacher should initiate communications to the parents, and vice versa. Pooling ideas and views from several vantage points, such as home versus the classroom, will improve understanding of the kid and possible risk of violence – and pave the way for preventive and remedial strategies.

If the possibility of violence is slight and not apt to happen soon, the follow-up steps can be remedial or preventive. This might involve getting the child or adolescent to talk to a counselor, teacher, or other trusted adult – obviously an understanding parent or caregiver would be the best source of support.

If there is an elevated risk of an act of violence, now or in the future, decisive action by all adults involved is important. At some point, contact should be made with social services for children and families and law enforcement (including the juvenile court). When justified, law enforcement will do its job to protect all concerned, but a punitive approach should be avoided whenever an effective positive intervention is possible. Juvenile courts are, of course, structured to avoid punishment to treat or rehabilitate the youth.

In any event, actions by responsible adults should be calm, reasoned, and directed at helping the young person avoid any violent or destructive behavior. A child or adolescent who is at an elevated risk of violence is in need of help. Typically this will necessitate the youngster meeting with, say, a mental health professional, as well as parents, educators, and other responsible adults and professional helpers working together as a team.

Granted, the news media have elevated awareness of youth violence. While realistic sensitivity to the problem of childhood and adolescent violence is important, an exaggeration of the risk is unwise. In fact, schools still remain one of the safest places for a kid. However, to quote an old advertisement: "An ounce of prevention is worth a pound of cure."

Detecting and Stopping Bullies

Since bullying in the school context is so common and great in its potential for impeding efforts to learn and inflicting negative emotional and behavioral conditions, it deserves further discussion. Regrettably, there is scarcely a classroom anywhere in which some form of bullying does not occur. From surveys, it appears that the large majority of preteens report bullying as a regular occurrence at school and consider bullying at school to be a big problem. A substantial number of kids are directly involved in bullying incidents. Although there is bullying in the elementary grades, it grows worse in high school. Bullying of special education children is much more frequent than what is experienced by non-special education children.

Often the bullying has racial or sexual overtones. Also, it is not unusual for bullying to advance from verbal taunts to actual physical assaults. One teenage girl in special education, who had been the long-term victim of bullying, was stomped to death by other girls in a public place during the day! The deceased girl's mother had warned the school of the bullying, but the school had taken no protective action. Unfortunately, this is but one of many similar incidents.

Beyond the literal threat to life and limb, even low-level bullying is known to take a terrible toll on the emotional well-being and learning of the children who are bullied. It is obvious that bullying is a problem that all responsible adults should address.

Bullying is conscious, willful, purposeful, and deliberate hostility. It is intended to harm or induce fear or terror in the bullied child. It is dehumanizing, and reflects that the bully is following a path toward antisocial behavior. Bullying is a red flag for possible assaultive conduct and other criminal acts.

There are at least three types of youthful bullying, none of which can be tolerated by any adult: verbal bullying; physical bullying, and relational bullying.

Verbal bullying: Name-calling, spreading rumors and lies, taunts, and threats are intended to hurt and terrorize the bullied child. Any notion that one child's calling another child a derogatory name is a sign of "kids will be kids" is naïve and misguided.

Physical bullying: When a child maliciously pinches, incessantly tickles, scratches, shoves, pokes, slaps, punches, kicks, bites, chokes, or spits on another child, it is bullying behavior. The term to remember is *impermissible touching* – that is, the bully has no right whatsoever to invade the physical privacy of another child by touching in any manner. Such physical contact is not cute, fun, typical of kids, or tolerable.

Relational bullying: When a child or group of children, a clique or gang, overtly shun, ignore, isolate, or exclude another child, the act of omission has the potential of bullying. Although no child should be forced to be friends with any other child, every child does need to develop socially acceptable behavior. Relational bullying is unacceptable antisocial behavior.

Each of these three of forms of youthful bullying should be viewed as a risk indicator for the bully's moving into even more assaultive conduct and potentially criminal conduct. Even a single incident of bullying by a child or adolescent requires authoritative attention. When bullying behavior occurs, adults should take immediate and decisive action.

To the credit of teachers, it is known that many, perhaps most, teachers are ready and willing to try to counteract bullying. That is, teachers tend to try to get a bully to cease and desist from harming others. Although the teacher is on the front line for detecting bullying, the teacher can seldom, alone, reduce or counteract bullying.

To be effective in helping the bully reduce his or her inclination to harm others, the teacher needs support from school administrators, parents, and other community leaders. Bullying is another problem for which family–school collaboration is especially important.

Too often, some adults are reluctant to become involved with identifying and dealing with the bully. However, an adult should welcome being told that a child or adolescent needs help to avoid further bullying.

Finally, certain adults deny or pretend to not be aware of bullying behavior. The severity of emotional and physical injury to the victim of bullying makes it imperative that no adult ignore or condone any form of bullying. To fail to stem bullying early on is increasing the likelihood of the bully doing severe harm to others and eventually being dealt with by law enforcement and the criminal justice system. Mental health professionals should convey this message at the micro and macro levels.

Avengers in School

Since the shootings at Columbine High School and other places, society has heightened concern about violence in the school. Many schools have adopted zero tolerance for any semblance of a weapon, and stern disciplinary measures are taken against students who violate school policies.

Even with educators and other responsible adults being on the lookout for signs of potential violence, especially if a weapon is involved, there continue to be inappropriate actions. For example, a 16-year-old boy brought a loaded handgun to school, and was arrested for carrying a concealed weapon, making terroristic threats, using a weapon to commit a felony, possession of a handgun by a minor, and possession of a firearm on school property. In other words, the youth was forcefully subjected to law enforcement. Again, this example is just one of many that occur on a frequent basis in the school context.

The question remains: Is it possible for parents, caretakers, educators, or other responsible adults to predict and prevent a youth's penchant for violence? The answer should acknowledge that there is no 100% assurance of predicting and preventing violence by a youngster, but a good faith attempt should be made. Even if not foolproof, efforts to identify potentially dangerous young people may enable violence to be avoided in school and elsewhere. Moreover, the troubled youth can receive adult guidance, including (if needed) from professional helpers, and avoid a downward spiral into pathological or criminal conduct.

From research on school-based shootings, it is known that often the potential shooter is a child or adolescent who is not particular distinctive. For example, the kid who plans to be violent at school may not be a bully. In fact, the youngster could be the one who was bullied, and the violent act is vengeance against a person or a group of people whom the downtrodden child believes is responsible for his or her being miserable.

Although there are uses of weapons in school by juvenile gangs, these gang members are usually known for potential violence to both educators and law enforcement before the violent act occurs, and preventive actions are taken. The school-based shootings that have justly captured national attention were done by another type of youth.

From studying school-based shootings, researchers have found that the "classroom avenger" often has a history of discipline by parents, educators, and law enforcement authorities and/or rejection by peers or friends. With the motive being vengeance, the youth could be profiled as having an average age of 15, and being White, physically healthy, and from a blue collar to middle-class home. The youth often has a family background and relations that are dysfunctional, such as divorced parents and frequent intense friction between parents (and between the parents and the youth). At home, there is overt and covert anger and hostility. The parents tend to be overly harsh in disciplining the youth. By the way, it seems that parents (and possibly educators) are at greatest risk of violence from the youth.

The physical appearance of classroom avengers is not noticeably different from other students, except perhaps for a preference for military attire. Classroom avengers often have a negative body image, and believe that they were unattractive, and classmates often call them something like "geeks" or "nerds." The classroom avenger tends to be friendless, immature, and a socially inadequate loner.

Although their development in the early years tends to be delayed, classroom avengers do not commonly have major impairments. As they grow up, they start encountering problems with bonding and attachments, and others consider them to be unaffectionate, standoffish, aloof, and overly fearful. They expect rejection, are suspicious and distrustful, and blame others for their disappointments. There are indications of antisocial tendencies, such as deceit and lying, bed-wetting, fire-setting, and animal abuse. Temper tantrums and sibling relationships are often problematic. There is seldom a blatant mental disorder, and intelligence is usually above average.

The availability of firearms is often a target of criticism. There is no reason to condemn a youth's safe use of firearms; however, achieving responsibility requires that the child or adolescent receive proper training and continued supervision from adults. As any responsible person familiar with firearms knows, unattended firearms should not be available to, or accessible by, children and adolescents. Indeed, adults should restrict the availability of firearms to young people.

The foregoing said, it is important to recognize that any generalization of characteristics for violent youngsters is not foolproof. There can always be exceptions.

Moreover, psychological profiling is not infallible. With all psychological profiling, the characteristics of the offenders can be found with some nonoffenders as well. It is important to recognize that, despite the negative signs that seem to be present with classroom avengers, a lot of children and adolescents who would never be violent experience the same conditions (such as in a dysfunctional family) or demonstrate the same problem behaviors.

With the ambiguity present, parents, caretakers, educators, mental health and social service practitioners, health care professionals, law enforcement personnel, and other responsible adults should not attempt to apply a formula to detecting a potentially violent youth. Rather, common sense should prevail. If a child or adolescent demonstrates antisocial (hurtful and hostile) behavior, is victimized by students and other adults, does not have sources of emotional supports (no friends), has parents or caregivers who do not provide love and nurturance, or seems isolated, alone, and depressed (to name but a few of the warning signs), it is obvious that thoughtful intervention is needed. Commonly relying on a mental health professional leads to the intervention of choice.

Referring a troubled youth for professional help is essential. Moreover, given the importance of family life, an attempt should be made to involve the parents and siblings in a family intervention. Family–school collaboration can map out an intervention plan that will be supportive and therapeutic.

When a potential or clear-cut act of violence occurs, such as bringing a weapon to school, law enforcement should be asked to intervene. In many cases, allowing a youth to reach this stage is too late to either prevent harm to others or salvage the youth for a productive and law-abiding life.

Staying Out of Trouble

When a family member is convicted of a crime, it is upsetting to all concerned. Whatever sentence may be imposed, the offender will hopefully gain understanding about the negative aspects of criminal conduct and acquire stronger self-control to avoid committing other crimes in the future.

Unfortunately, society does not presently give much emphasis to rehabilitation. Oftentimes, the offender suffers incarceration and after release, has a parole officer, but little, if anything, else that might cultivate rehabilitation and defenses against going back to the kind of activities that brought on the trouble in the first place.

Sadly, without effective rehabilitation, there will continue to be all too many reoffenders. The term *recidivism* refers to committing another crime. Without getting into a lot of statistics, suffice it to say that research reveals that approximately one third (or more) of offenders released from incarceration are convicted of another crime within the next few years (Bartol & Bartol, 2008).

Offenders of all ages need social support from others. Since immaturity may mean undeveloped coping or problem-solving skills, adolescent offenders especially need family members and other adults to rally to help them avoid further violations of the law.

Just being sympathetic is not helpful; however, sharing understanding and exchanging warmth and love certainly benefits everyone. In other words, helping an offender, regardless of age, avoid more problems should have a backdrop of sincere caring, sharing, and positive acceptance.

For many families, having positive relations with an offender (again, of any age) may be a difficult task. Often antisocial or criminal conduct, especially by youths, reflects the fact that the offender suffered family problems or dysfunction. If the family is unable to provide constructive support, there is a strong need for professional help.

When considering why an offender recidivates, it appears that a major reason is that the person has not truly rejected antisocial values. After paying his or her debt to society by incarceration or other punishment, the released offender needs to adopt prosocial ideas and behavior. Here again, family members and other supportive adults can be extremely helpful, but even then, the offender may benefit from the services of professional helpers. It may well be that a professional helper will be more objective and effective than family members or friends in helping the person gain true self-awareness and adopting positive life values.

People who are persistent in antisocial or criminal conduct through-out life commonly had behavior problems as children, engaged in vio-lence, and were unable to establish healthy and loving relations, such as with a spouse. Obviously this strongly ingrained negative track needs to change, and substantial or lasting change may not happen quickly – just as it took years for the problems to develop, and it may take years to eliminate them.

Helping the offender get and stay on the straight and narrow will not be an easy job, and the offender and family members and other helpful adults alike must make a strong commitment to changing the values that con-tributed to the unacceptable behavior. The slippery slide back to another criminal act can be counteracted by stoic resolution, aided often by help from others, such as family members, friends, and professional helpers.

Effective Adult–Child Guidance

This chapter has emphasized detecting the potential for delinquency and criminal conduct by children and adolescents. Also, to promote pre-vention of problem behaviors, professional helpers should encourage parents, caretakers, educators, and other adults to help troubled young people.

Parents and caregivers are the most important protective source for children of all ages. There is no substitute for effective nurturing for de-veloping constructive and law-abiding children and adolescents. Every youngster needs help from responsible adults in their quest to achieve positive beliefs, morals, and values, and develop maturity with effec-tive abilities for critical analysis, logical reasoning, judgments, problem-solving, and behavioral controls.

Regrettably, all adults in the lives of children and adolescents do not provide positive and nurturing relationships. For example, a lot of youngsters are subjected to detrimental home situations. Due to the lack of caring, inattentiveness, or inability to cope with child-rearing, the child moves toward defiance of authority and, in the process, aggressive and hostile behavior. Rather than these negative behaviors occurring just in school, often the potential for uncontrolled aggression starts and is revealed in the family home and community.

Children do what their parents and caregivers do (i.e., their role mod-els), including unhealthy and unlawful conduct. In other words, children imitate the behavior they witness. The conduct that is observed in the home and daily activities reinforces the child to act out similar behavior.

Keeping relevant adults, such as teachers and other responsible adults, from knowing what is going on in the home is often how some parents and caregivers shield or deny their own inept behavior and poor child-rearing. If uncorrected, the child subjected to poor parenting moves toward unacceptable emotions and conduct. This potential deficit in child-rearing is, of course, another reason for family–school collaboration, as well as obtaining support from other community sources.

Parents and caregivers sometimes purposefully or inadvertently neglect the needs of children. Beyond physical neglect, emotional neglect is harmful to a child. This includes a parent's spurning, rejecting, isolating, abusing, terrorizing, or corrupting a child. The parent or caregiver does not provide the child with the emotional responses necessary for healthy psychological development.

Abuse of a child of any age seems to have a strong connection to the youngster's becoming antisocial and running afoul of the law later in life. It is believed that abused children, when compared with nonabused children, are more likely to be arrested for violent crimes. Neglected children also have an elevated incidence of arrest. Behavioral science research supports the idea that, just as abusive parenting can lead to violent crime, nonabusive parenting is useful for reducing a child's likelihood of engaging in violence.

If the adults in the life of a child engage in alcohol or other mind-altering substance abuse, the child is apt to suffer. Regrettably, some infants are exposed to a mother's prenatal use of drugs, with the possibility of severe consequences, such as brain damage or fetal alcohol syndrome. Stated bluntly, alcohol and drug use by a parent or caregiver constitutes serious child maltreatment.

Educators, mental health and social service practitioners, health care professionals, law enforcement officers, and judges are cautious about inappropriate infringement on the family zone of privacy. However, when the welfare of a child is at risk, there is a legal basis for taking protective steps. The US Supreme Court has made it clear that a family cannot deprive society of healthy children. Under neglectful and abusive circumstances, it is lawful for professional helpers to protect children, even if a parent objects.

Every adult should be committed to preventing children of any age from being prone to violence and other criminal acts. If an adult recognizes a problem within the home, professional help is available, such as from social service and mental health agencies. Presumably, family–school collaboration would be the threshold to obtaining professional help for a troubled kid.

Educators needs to be vigilant for signs that a child or adolescent, regardless of age, is being exposed to ineffective parenting or caretaking, including neglect or abuse. It is proper for educators and other professional helpers to work with the adults in a child's life to remedy the situation or, if there is neglect or abuse, initiate a prompt report to children's protective services. Otherwise, the last resort to protect society will be to rely on law enforcement and the juvenile and criminal justice systems.

References

American Psychological Association. (1996). *Reducing violence: A research agenda.* Washington, DC: Author.

Bartol, C. R., & Bartol, A. M. (2008). *Introduction to forensic psychology: Research and application* (2nd ed.). Los Angeles, CA: Sage.

Borum, R. (2006). Assessing risk of violence among juvenile offenders. In S. N. Sparta & G. P. Koocher (Eds.), *Forensic mental health assessment of children and adolescents* (pp. 190–202). New York, NY: Oxford University Press.

Bowlby, J. (1969). *Attachment and loss: Vol. I. Attachment.* New York, NY: Wiley.

Campbell, L., Vasquez, M., Behnke, S., & Kinscherff, R. (2010). *APA ethics code commentary and case illustrations.* Washington, DC: American Psychological Association.

Carey, K. B., Leontieva, L., Dimmock, J., Maisto, S. A., & Batki, S. L. (2007). Adapting motivational interventions for comorbid schizophrenia and alcohol use disorders. *Clinical Psychology: Science and Practice, 41,* 39–57

Christenson, S. L., & Sheridan, S. M. (2001). *Schools and families: Creating essential connections for learning.* New York, NY: Guilford.

Clinton, H. R. (1996). *It takes a village and other lessons children teach us.* New York, NY: Simon & Schuster.

Corey, M. S., & Corey, G. (2007). *Becoming a helper* (5th ed.). Belmont, CA: Thomson Brooks/Cole.

Daley, D. C., & Moss, H. B. (2002). *Dual disorders: Counseling clients with chemical dependency* (3rd ed.). Center City, MN: Hazelden.

Dishion, T. J., & Bullock, B. (2002). Parenting and adolescent problem behavior: An ecological analysis of the nurturance hypothesis. In J. G. Borkowski, S. Ramey, & M. Bristol-Power (Eds.), *Parenting and the child's world: Influences on intellectual, academic, and social-emotional development* (pp. 231–249). Mahwah, NJ: Erlbaum.

Dishion, T. J., Burraston, B., & Li, F. (2002). Family management practices: Research design and measurement issues. In W. Bukowski & Z. Amsel (Eds.), *Handbook for drug abuse prevention theory, science, and practice* (pp. 587–607). New York, NY: Plenum.

Dishion, T. J., & Stormshak E. A. (2007). *Intervening in children's lives: An ecological, family-centered approach to mental health care.* Washington, DC: American Psychological Association.

Dodge, K. A. (2008). Framing public policy and prevention of chronic violence in American youths. *American Psychologist, 63,* 573–590.

Eaton, D. K., Kann, L., Kinchen, S., Shanklin, S., Ross, J., Hawkins, J., . . . Wechsler, H. (2008). Youth risk behavior surveillance – United States, 2007. *Morbidity & Mortality Weekly Report, 57*(SS-4, June 6), 1–131.

Egan, G. (2007). *The skilled helper: A problem-management and opportunity-development approach to helping.* Belmont, CA: Thomson Brooks/Cole.

Ferguson, C. J. (2010). Introduction to the special issue on video games. *Review of General Psychology, 14,* 66–67.

Finkelhor, D., & Ormrod, R. (2000, June). *Kidnapping of juveniles: Patterns from the NIBRS*. Washington, DC: US Department of Justice, Office of Juvenile Justice and Delinquency Prevention.

Fiske, S. T. (2004). *Social beings: A core motives approach to social psychology*. New York, NY: John Wiley.

Franzoi, S. L. (2009). *Social psychology* (5th ed.). New York, NY: McGraw-Hill.

Fredrickson, B. L., & Losado, M. F. (2005). Positive affect and the complex dynamics of human flourishing. *American Psychologist, 60*, 678–686.

Geiger, B. F., O'Neal, M. R., Petri C. J., Stanhope, K., & Whittinghill, D. (2005). Developing an instrument to measure students' predisposing factors for drug use and violence. *American Journal of Health Studies, 20*(4), 204–211.

Goldberg, C. (2000). *The evil we do: The psychoanalysis of destructive people*. New York, NY: Prometheus Books.

Greif, G. L., & Hegar, R. L. (1993). *When parents kidnap: The families behind the headlines*. New York, NY: Free Press.

Grisso, T. (1981). *Juveniles' waiver of rights: Legal and psychological competence*. New York, NY: Plenum.

Halpern, D. F. (2005). Psychology at the intersection of work and family. *American Psychologist, 60*, 397–408.

Harris, J. R. (1998). *The nature assumption: Why children turn out the way they do*. New York, NY: Free Press.

Hergenhahn, B. R., & Olson, M. (2007). *An introduction to theories of personality* (7th ed.). Upper Saddle River, NJ: Pearson Prentice Hall.

Holcomb-McCoy, C., & Bryan, J. (2010). Advocacy and empowerment in parent consultation: Implications for theory and practice. *Journal of Counseling & Development, 88*, 259–268.

Kern, M. L, & Friedman, H. S. (2008). Do conscientious individuals live longer? A quantitative review. *Health Psychology, 27*, 505–512.

Keyes, C. L. (2007). Promoting and protecting mental health as flourishing. *American Psychologist, 62*, 95–108.

Koocher, G. P., & Keith-Spiegel, P. (2008). *Ethics in psychology and the mental health professions* (3rd ed.). New York, NY: Oxford University Press.

Langens, T. A., & Schüler, J. (2007). Effects of written expression: The role of positive expectancies. *Health Psychology, 26*, 174–182.

Maslow, A. H. (1968). *Toward a psychology of being* (2nd ed.). New York, NY: Van Nostrand.

Maslow, A. H. (1970). *Motivation and personality* (Rev. ed.). New York, NY: Harper & Row.

Mehrabian, A. (1981). *Silent messages: Implicit communication of emotions and attitudes* (2nd ed.). Belmont, CA: Wadsworth.

Milton, N. R. (2010). A new framework for psychology. *Review of General Psychology, 14*, 1–15.

Mills, N. (1997). *The triumph of meanness: America's war against its better self*. Boston, MA: Houghton Mifflin.

Myers, D. G. (2005). *Social psychology* (8th ed.). Boston, MA: McGraw-Hill.

National Association of School Psychologists. (2005). *Position statement on home-school collaboration: Establishing partnerships to enhance educational outcomes*. Retrieved from http://www.nasponline.org/

Newman, K. S., Fox, C., Harding, D. J., Mehta, J., & Roth, W. (2004). *Rampage: The social roots of school shootings*. Cambridge, MA: Basic Books.

Olson, C. K. (2010). Children's motivations for video game play in the context of normal development. *Review of General Psychology, 14*, 180–187.

Patterson, G. R., Reid, J. B., & Dishion, T. J. (1992). *A social learning approach: Vol 4. Antisocial boys*. Eugene, OR: Castalia.

Pinsof, W. M. (1995). *Integrative problem-centered therapy: A synthesis of family, individual, and biological therapies*. New York, NY: Basic Books.

Preves, S. E., & Mortimer, J. T. (2011). *Classic and contemporary perspectives in social psychology*. New York, NY: Oxford University Press.

Rosner, R. (2005). The scourge of addition: What the adolescent psychiatrist needs to know. *Adolescent Psychiatry, 29*, 19–31.

Schoor, J. B. (1992). *The overworked American: The unexpected decline of leisure*. New York, NY: Basic Books.

Shiron, A. (2004). Feeling vigorous at work? The construct of vigor and the study of positive affect in organizations. In D. Ganster & P. L. Perrewe (Eds.), *Research in organizational stress and well being* (Vol. 3, pp. 135–165). Greenwich, CT: JAI.

Shiron, A., Toker, S., Berliner, S., Shapira, I., & Melamed, S. (2008). The effects of physical fitness and feeling vigorous on self-rated health. *Health Psychology, 27*, 567–575.

Urban, W. J., & Wagoner, J. L., Jr. (1996). *American education: A history*. New York, NY: McGraw-Hill.

U.S. Public Health Service (1999). *Mental health: A report of the Surgeon General*. Rockville, MD: Author.

VandenBos, G. R. (Ed.). (2007). *APA dictionary of psychology*. Washington, DC: American Psychological Association.

Wilson, J. J. (2001, January). From the administrator. In J. R. Johnson & L. K. Girdner (Eds.), *Family abductors: Descriptive profiles and preventive interventions*. Washington, DC: US Department of Justice, Office of Juvenile Justice and Delinquency.

Woody, J. D. (2002). *How can we talk about that?* San Francisco: Jossey-Bass.

Woody, R. H. (2000). *Child custody: Practical standards, ethical issues, & legal safeguards for mental health professionals*. Sarasota, FL: Professional Resource Press.

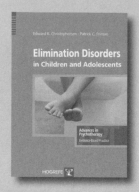
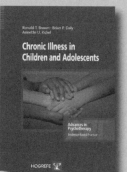